THE TOUCH OF DURRELL

THE TOUCH OF DURRELL
A Passion for Animals

Jeremy Mallinson

Book Guild Publishing
Sussex, England

First published in Great Britain in 2009 by
The Book Guild Ltd
Pavilion View
19 New Road
Brighton, BN1 1UF

Typesetting in Garamond by
Ellipsis Books Limited, Glasgow

Printed in Great Britain by
CPI Antony Rowe

A catalogue record for this book is available from
The British Library.

ISBN 978 1 84624 370 7

For *Gerald Durrell* who provided me with a career which was
'More Fun than Fun'

In fondest memory of *Odette,*
and for our children
Julian and Sophie
and our grandchildren
Jay and Zac and
Claudia and Melanie

CONTENTS

ILLUSTRATIONS

Colour plate section (between pages 82 and 83)

Gerald Durrell, 1983. © Durrell Archives
Infant male Lowland gorilla, Mamfe, born Jersey, October 1963.
© Philip Coffey
The author with six year-old female Lowland gorilla, G-Ann, at Jersey Zoo, 1985.
© Robert Rattner
Gerald Durrell with female two-year-old Lowland gorilla, Bamenda, born Jersey, October 1975. © Philip Coffey
The author with European red fox vixen on board RMS *Warwick Castle*, Gulf of Aden, October 1961. © 'The Lamp Trimmer'
Conservateur Adrian Deschryver communicating with the Silver-back Eastern Lowland gorilla, Kasimir, in the Kahuzi Biega National Park, Kivu, Zaire, October 1975. © Jeremy Mallinson
Two male cheetahs in the Kafue National Park, Zambia, October 2007. © Jeremy Mallinson
Aye-Aye at Jersey Zoo. © Mark Pidgeon
Taken after the author's retirement lunch at Les Augrès Manor, June 2001. © Stuart McAlsiter
Golden Lion tamarin. © Philip Coffey
Black Lion tamarin. © DWCT Archives
Golden-headed Lion tamarins. © Mark Pidgeon
Official opening of Bristol Zoo's Zona Brazil in July 2002. © Bristol Zoo
Gerald and Lee Durrell at their tenth wedding anniversary, 24 May 1989. © Durrell Archives
Sir David and Lady Attenborough with the author at the time of Sir David's official opening of the Jim Scriven Orang-utan Home Habitat, May 1994. © DWCT Archives
The Sumatran Orang-utan Home Habitat at the Durrell Wildlife Conservation Trust. © Gregory Guida
Sir David Attenborough, Lee and Gerald Durrell, Sarah Kennedy and Dr Desmond Morris, 1993. © Durrell Archives
The author with his wife, Odette, after receiving an Honorary Doctor of Science (DSc) degree at the University of Kent, Canterbury, July 2000. © University of Kent

Black and white plate section (between pages 178 and 179)

Durrell family reunion, Les Augrès Manor, Jersey, Christmas 1960.
© Durrell Archives
The author on his Lambretta scooter at King George VI Barracks, Salisbury,
Southern Rhodesia, October 1956. © Jay Duncan
The author with Dingo puppies at Jersey Zoo, 1961. © Michael Armstrong
The author under the discerning eye of Gerald Durrell, the founder and
Honorary Director of the Jersey Wildlife Preservation Trust.
© Rosemary Gilliat
The author and June Kay, with Roger holding a snared Marabou stork,
Okavango Swamps, Bechuanaland Protectorate (Botswana), Easter, 1962.
© Robert Kay
Clio, the author's pet female Chacma baboon, 1963. © E. D. H. Johnson
The author with his favourite female Lowland gorilla, N'Pongo, at Jersey Zoo,
1968. © Philip Coffey
Male Silverback Lowland gorilla, Jambo, under sedation at Jersey Zoo, 1981.
© Philip Coffey
Female cheetah, Paula, taking the author for a morning run at Jersey Zoo,
1969. © JWPT Archives
The author introducing Paula to his Basset hound, Scobie, at Jersey Zoo, 1969.
© Peter le Breton
The author with the 3½-year-old lioness, Chinky, soon after her arrival at
Jersey Zoo, May 1962. © *Jersey Evening Post*
The author with a two-year-old Bornean Orang-utan, Gigit, born Jersey,
November 1990. © *Jersey Evening Post*
Pygmy hog sow with five piglets in one of the three Breeding Pens named
after Gerald Durrell, Richard Magor and Jeremy Mallinson at the Basistha
Centre, near Guawahati, Assam, India, 2006. © Michael Hammett
The wedding of Gerald Durrell and Lee McGeorge in Memphis, Tennessee,
with the pianist Mose, and the best man, the author, 24 May 1979.
© Durrell Archives
The Princess Royal with Gerald Durrell and the author at the time of the
placing of a 'Time Capsule' in the foundations of the Princess Royal Pavilion,
Jersey Wildlife Preservation Trust, December 1988. © *Jersey Evening Post*
The author, soon after his appointment as Zoological Director, Jersey Wildlife
Preservation Trust. © Robert Rattner

ACKNOWLEDGEMENTS

During my 42 years of working at the Jersey Zoological Park and the Jersey Wildlife Preservation Trust (now Durrell Wildlife Conservation Trust), I was grateful for the support given to me by my colleagues and friends who include: John Hartley, 'Shep' Mallet, Simon Hicks, Quentin Bloxam, David Jeggo, Anthony Allchurch, Dr Anna Feistner, Bronwen Garth-Thornton, Tracy Le Couteur, Betty Renouf, Anne Binney, Robin Rumboll, Lord (Jack) Craigton CBE and Catha Weller. Also, during my time serving on various national and international zoo and conservation committees, I benefited greatly from what has represented a stimulating and wonderful long-term collaboration and friendship with Dr Michael Brambell, Geoffrey Greed, Professor Janet Kear OBE, Dr John Knowles OBE, Dr Thomas Lovejoy, Dr Robert Martin, Peter Olney MBE, Dr Ulysses Seal, Professor Ian Swingland OBE and Professor Roger Wheater OBE.

During almost 30 years of involvement with the conservation of lion tamarins (*Leontopithecus* spp.), both in the wild state and in world zoos, it has been my privilege to have shared comradeship and significant friendship with the major contributors to the success of these model conservation programmes. First, with Dr Devra Kleiman, who in the US led the survival programme for the Golden Lion Tamarin in association with her colleagues: Dr Jonathan Ballou, Dr Andrew Baker, Dr James Dietz, Lou Ann Dietz and Dr Russell Mittermeier. And in Brazil, to have been able to follow the outstanding leadership provided by the doyen of the country's primatologists, Dr Adelmar Coimbra-Filho who, in collaboration with Dr Maria Iolita Bampi, Admirante Ibsen de Gusmão Câmara, Dr Cecilia Kierulff, Dr Alcides Pissinatti, and Denise Rambaldi, have contributed so much to the conservation of species and associated habitat of the *Mata Atlantica*. In addition to these scientists it has been my privilege to have shared a similar degree of friendship with those also involved with the 'International Committees for the Conservation and Management' for the other three species of lion tamarin (golden-headed, black lion, black-faced): Dr Bengt Holst, Dr Kristin Leus, Dr Valadares-Cláudio Padua, Suzana Padua, Dr Anthony Rylands, Dr Faiçal Simon and Guadelupe Vivekananda.

During some of my formative years in Southern Rhodesia (Zimbabwe) I would especially like to thank Robin and Pris Falla (Glendale), Harry and Sue Stobart (Arcturus), Christopher Faber (Salisbury/Macheke), Jay Duncan and Michael Hammett (R & N Staff Corps), for their constant support and friendship. Also, within the British Isles, I am particularly grateful to brother Miles and his wife Jane Mallinson, David and Carol Garton, Jurat Colin Jones and his wife Jenny and Sally Mallinson, for having been such wonderful friends and for having been so supportive throughout the majority of my life.

Finally, I am forever indebted to my late wife, Odette, who generously put up with my long working hours, my passion for animals and my love of travelling to little known places. My gratitude to Douglas Botting for allowing me to quote from the text of his biography of Gerald Durrell; to Paul Masterton for authoring the postscript to this publication; to Fiona Fisken and Tony Bremner for their editorial help; and my great indebtedness to Peter Olney for his invaluable editorial input, for fixing inconsistencies and for so successfully managing to curtail my various degrees of untamed verbosity. I have dedicated this book to my Jersey family of *Homo sapiens* and to my mentor, Gerald Durrell, who enabled me to greatly benefit from his vision, unswerving support and deep friendship. Lastly, I am most thankful to Dr Lee Durrell for over thirty years of collaboration and significant friendship; for giving me access to the Durrell archives and granting permission to quote from some of the texts and to reproduce photographs from this source; and particularly for writing such a generous Foreword.

FOREWORD

I have known Jeremy Mallinson for more than thirty years. He was with me from the beginning to the end of my life with Gerald Durrell, first as 'best man' at our wedding. It was by no whim that Jeremy was chosen for this role, as he had been Gerry's right-hand man virtually since Gerry began his wildlife conservation work in Jersey fifty years ago.

Jeremy was 'best' in every sense of the word. His passion for animals, which is so delightfully revealed in this book, made him the perfect acolyte to Gerry's mission to save species from extinction, which was started by the founding of the Jersey Zoo in 1959 and carried on by the charitable Trust set up to run the Zoo. Jeremy's loyalty and tenacity of purpose were greatly treasured by Gerry, especially in the rambunctious early years when the Zoo was teetering on the edge of bankruptcy and the governors of the young Trust were apparently bent on sidelining the Founder.

Some years after Jeremy became the Trust's Zoological Director, we three were much amused by a note from a supporter who had just visited the Zoo, referring to Jeremy as that 'quiet academic gentleman'. Academic indeed, as Jeremy was the prime mover in developing the research and publications programme at the Trust on species rarely seen in captivity or in the wild. *The Dodo*, our in-house journal, was Jeremy's bailiwick, and under his editorship, with his many original contributions, it became a model for other conservation-minded zoos endeavouring to study the species in their care.

The quiet exterior, however, belied an appetite for exploration and adventure. Whetted by his journeys in Africa and South America as a young man, Jeremy's love of travel became a cornerstone of our work. Whether to gather data on the plight of a species in its natural habitat or attend a high-level international conference, Jeremy's travels away from our headquarters in Jersey always resulted in a significant advance in conservation, much to the credit of the Trust.

You will read in this book of Jeremy's many different activities on behalf of all animals, and in particular of his tireless efforts for the largest and the smallest of the primates – the gorillas of Africa and the diminutive lion tamarins of Brazil. The significance of this work is perhaps even greater than Jeremy suggests. Innovative protocols for the rigorous management of gorillas and the other great apes in zoos in Britain and Ireland and of the four species of lion tamarin held in worldwide collections were pioneered by Jeremy and his colleagues. The tamarin work became a model for other such international efforts in species conservation.

When a male gorilla comes of age and assumes leadership of his social group, he becomes the *silverback*, named for the silvery sheen across his back. Jeremy's achievements and interactions with zoo directors and senior conservationists from all over the world established him firmly as a silverback in the world of conservation for the last two decades of the 20th century.

It is fitting that Jeremy tells his story in this year, which marks the 50th anniversary of what his mentor, Gerald Durrell, started in Jersey, and which Jeremy himself played such a large part in shaping.

As I said, he was with me from the beginning to the end of my life with Gerald Durrell. My 'best man' was sitting quietly with me in the hospital room when Gerry died, having provided comfort and strength during those last days, both to me and to his mentor. For this, and for his unswerving devotion to the Trust and the animal kingdom, I am eternally grateful.

Lee Durrell
Honorary Director,
Durrell Wildlife Conservation Trust
Jersey, February 2009

Chapter One

THE ACORNS WERE PLANTED

As long as I can remember, I have been fascinated by anything to do with the animal world and the quality of the natural world around me. I well recall picking up a black kitten in a pet shop; the velvety feel of its fur, the rhythm of its purring made me blush with delight. The enthusiasm for animals that most children have can be seen in their faces when they first encounter a kitten, a puppy, or newly born farm animals. The desire to touch and hold a young animal seems to me to be instinctive, a part of one's natural behaviour.

As far as I know, no previous member of my family demonstrated any particular interest in England's wildlife apart from enjoying the company of their domestic pets, and attending point-to-points and sheep-dog trials at the local agricultural shows in the Yorkshire Dales; they did at least have the countryman's enthusiasm for field sports. Here, it was made quite clear to me that the sportsman's acceptance of a 'closed season' was the only way to maintain sustainable populations of England's native fauna. Before my tenth birthday, I underwent the ritual of being 'blooded' after both hare and fox kills. My paternal grandfather had been the Master of the Hunt of the Airedale beagles, which were tucked away among the moors of Yorkshire's West Riding; and both my father and uncle had 'walked' hounds and had 'whipped-in' for the hunt during the 1920s. By tradition, the family participated in the annual Easter fox hound meet at Howtown, in the Lake District, where hunt followers energetically trailed the artful fox on foot among the steep hills and valleys above Ullswater. This initial exposure to country people and the rural hunting community provided me with my first insight into the understanding and skills of a huntsman with his pack of hounds, the

1

dexterity of the hunted, and the magnificence of the surrounding countryside.

During the bleakest years of the Second World War, when I was almost five, my parents sent me with my elder brother Miles, to a boarding school on the shore of Lake Windermere. Fallbarrow Hall was an imposing building, a country gentleman's residence of the early nineteenth century. It commanded an impressive view of Belle Isle with its famous classical rotunda house, which, with the backdrop of the fells, represented a dramatic panorama of the Lake District's largest lake. The preparatory school had oak-panelled classrooms, spacious dormitories, dingy attic rooms and some ghostly dark cellars. In the grounds a small stone-built, slate-roofed boat house accommodated the headmaster's old motor launch which he had named *Swallow*, after the sailing boat that Arthur Ransome had featured in his much-loved book *Swallows and Amazons*. The Hall was surrounded by well-established woods and undulating parkland, which were a sanctuary to a wealth of animal life. I remember in these idyllic formative years my delight in seeing for the first time a family of Red squirrels frolicking around their moss and stick drey, halfway up the trunk of a large pine, and in another part of the grounds, the horror of witnessing at dusk the agile Pine marten raiding the nest of a pair of Tree creepers, and then leaping on to another branch to devour the chick; this was my first observation of the predator and prey phenomenon.

One day the school was visited by the ornithologist and author Captain Charles Knight, accompanied by his famous pet Golden eagle, 'Mr Ramshaw', about which Captain Knight had just written a book entitled *An All British Eagle*. I was in the sickbay at the time, and when Captain Knight was kind enough to pay the few patients a visit, he perched his enormous eagle on the metal bar at the end of my bed. The massive dark-plumed form of Mr Ramshaw started to flex his yellow talons, no doubt to demonstrate the impressive size of his sharp black claws. He then stretched out his 2 m (7 ft) wingspan, hunched his body, and with his head crooked to one side, stared directly at my pale head; almost as if it was being offered to him on a sacrificial pillow. The enormous bird suddenly emitted high-pitched whistling noises and I resigned myself to thinking that I was about to provide Mr Ramshaw with an early supper.

During these formative school years, I cannot recall learning anything of real academic note, though I was becoming increasingly interested and enthusiastic about animal life. At the time of the Normandy Landings though, in the summer of 1944, I unexpectedly won the Form 1 Prize, *Tales From the Bible* by Enid Blyton, which no doubt was presented to me on the strength of the contents of my nature note books. In later years I realised how fortunate I had been at this time, living in the peaceful Lake District, and not having been born ten or twelve years earlier and having to fight.

With the end of the war in 1945 the school moved to Newton Hall, near Hadrian's Wall in Northumberland, a building situated in an even more spacious setting than we had had on the shores of Lake Windermere, surrounded by hundreds of acres of mature park and woodlands. Four drives, the longest over a mile long, snaked their way up to the mansion. At the bottom of the 'Home Park' was a sizeable lake, with a small island and a boathouse. It was within the grounds of this exciting new place that I found ready access to a treasure-chest of the animal kingdom to observe and study. Whenever the opportunity arose I would escape from the academic curriculum and explore every nook and cranny of this varied country estate.

Many years later I was told by the headmaster, Frank Marchbank, that if I was ever absent from the school buildings I could be found mucking-out, or grooming the school's ponies in the nearby stables; for it was the stable-yard that had become my second home. This was where, as an eleven-year-old, I shouldered my first real responsibility in life: helping the attractive teenage riding mistress, three mornings a week, to bring in the ponies from the Home Park, before Miss Rosemary Hopper gave her afternoon riding lessons.

After 60 years, it often astounds me how the subconscious can store so much, and then so clearly bring it back again. Here it is evident that the stable-yard represented for me the most memorable environment of my preparatory school days; for it provided the type of sanctuary that gave me the direct contact with animals that I cared about so much. The stable-yard stood by itself some quarter of a mile from Newton Hall; it was a quadrangle, built in the same attractive local sandstone as the Hall itself. Its ornate wrought-iron gates provided an air of opulence, and as I passed through them I felt that I was entering a special world of contentment.

3

Standing almost in the centre of the flag-stoned yard was an attractive fountain, whose waters tumbled quietly into a stone drinking trough, where horses had refreshed themselves for generations, and to where flocks of white fan-tailed pigeons had fluttered down from their lofts above the main coach house. What particularly impressed me was the almost palatial, spacious, wood-panelled loose-boxes and stalls, surmounted by metal bars which enabled the horses to have direct contact with each other. There was room for well over 20 horses. The two mahogany-panelled harness rooms, with their glass-fronted sliding doors, had no doubt once boasted some of the best saddlery in the North of England.

During this period of my school days I started to recognise how much I seemed to thrive in an atmosphere of uncertainty and at the same time I experienced a feeling of excitement when potential adventure presented itself. Although I knew only too well that an offender, if caught, would be 'in for the high jump', which in those days meant a caning. Some 17 years later I dined with the by-then-retired headmaster Frank Marchbank, and found myself reminiscing about one of my first adventures at his school – a midnight ride I had had with a co-conspirator in the Home Park. The two of us, in our dressing gowns and slippers, crept out of our dormitory and descended the 'out of bounds' main staircase. I recall being startled by the big grandfather clock in an alcove halfway down striking midnight. The occupants of the gilt-framed family portraits appeared to be frowning disapprovingly upon us as we quietly made our way into the gloom of the marble-floored hallway and out of a side door into the driveway.

By the time we reached the iron railings of the Home Park we knew that our adventure was about to begin. The ponies knew both of us well and it was easy to coax them to us and to put the rope halters over their necks. In the moonlight, we led the ponies away from the Hall, jumped onto their backs and, with our dressing gowns flowing behind us highwayman-fashion, galloped across the lower slopes of the Home Park. Perhaps our greatest deed that particular night was to canter up one of the steep slopes with our backs to the pony's head, and to slide off their rears onto the ground. The headmaster listened to this tale, which I related as dramatically as I could, and told me that he found it almost impossible to believe that such nocturnal adventures had ever taken place at his most respected seat of learning.

However, after some further sips of the excellent claret we were enjoying, he charitably reflected that as his preparatory school, Mowden Hall, had always boasted of providing a broad spectrum of educational activities that perhaps, in my case, such an exploit had sowed well the seeds of adventure. For Frank Marchbank was aware that within a week of our dinner together I was due to fly to La Paz, in search of a legendary animal that Colonel Fawcett had described in the early part of the twentieth century during his travels in northern Bolivia.

Apart from nocturnal adventures, there was an abundance of bird and mammal life within the school grounds, and many different species of waterfowl on the Home Lake to study. I recall, in particular, seeing an adult pair of badgers, with their three six-to-eight-week-old exuberant cubs, interacting around the entrance to their sett. I watched the parental play and discipline, and noted how the mother meticulously groomed her young, one at a time, while her cubs made high-pitched squeaks of fun. And how such familial bliss was interrupted when the nearby presence of our natural history class was detected, and the alarmed badgers disappeared into their sett.

In September 1946, the headmaster's daughter Judy had the great misfortune to be struck by polio and the school was closed for the rest of the term. That autumn my parents borrowed a friend's flat in Walton Street behind Harrods in London. As an inquisitive nine-and-a-half-year-old, it did not take me long to find Harrods' pet department on the fourth floor, where I started to spend most of my free time. Here I soon got to know the staff, as well as a delightful assortment of puppies, kittens, rabbits, guinea pigs, hamsters, white mice and pale-coloured rats. I also had my first encounter with exotic species like African Grey parrots, Scarlet macaws and Amazon parrots from South America, and a pair of young Red-backed squirrel monkeys from Costa Rica; all for sale as pets. Due to the evident degree of enthusiasm that I had showed for the animals, the amount of spare time I had at my disposal, and my willingness to help in any aspects of their care and maintenance, the manager of the pet department allowed me to arrive at the staff entrance at 8 a.m. Mondays to Saturdays, and help before the store opened. I had a wonderful time for over five weeks and I made some memorable animal friends, but more often than not I was sorry to see some of them being carried away by what I thought were unsuitable purchasers.

5

During the following year, 1947, the glorious sunshine and high temper-atures of the summer contrasted dramatically with the arctic conditions of the ensuing winter. During the heaviest of the snowfalls Newton Hall was snowbound, which gave us boys the fun and adventure of having to collect food and stores on sledges from the nearby village, hauling them through the snowdrifts up the mile-long south drive to the Hall. Memories such as these make me appreciative of my good fortune as a child; that early exposure to an ideal environment of unspoiled landscapes and animal diversity. Such a blissful childhood nurtured the passion for animals that has never left me.

The final part of my twelve years at a boarding school was spent within the precincts of one of England's greatest cathedrals, which had as its centre-piece the magnificent 1498 Bell Harry tower, whose 75 m (248 ft) dwarfed the rest of the precinct's ancient buildings. In compar-ison to school in a country mansion surrounded by spacious wooded parkland, my freedom was much curtailed by the harness of some of the traditions and history of England's oldest seat of learning. It was while I was at Canterbury that I developed my unquenchable thirst for natural history and travel books. Charles Darwin's *On the Origin of Species*, Gilbert White's *The Natural History of Selborne* and a number of Richard Lydekker's natural history volumes, were all added to my personal library.

My fascination with the travel and adventures of such great African explorers as David Livingstone, Samuel Baker, Richard Burton, John Speke and Henry Morton Stanley, gave me a great desire to go to Africa and to visit some of the places that they had explored in the nineteenth century. Henry Bates's *The Naturalist on the River Amazons*, and Charles Waterton's accounts of his wanderings in South America, made me determined to travel one day to the New World and see some of the magical forests that they had both so enthusiastically written about. Fortunately my future did eventually allow me to realise the majority of these embryonic ambitions.

The King's School, Canterbury, was founded in 597 as part of Canterbury's sixth century Benedictine monastery. The school has always been associated with the cathedral and is blessed with an unusually civilised environment, and some of the finest architecture in England. The precincts of the cathedral, with its Christchurch and Mint Yard gateways, its ancient cloisters, chapter house, undercroft and areas of grass and trees, provided the students with a degree of solace difficult to find elsewhere. The headmaster during my time at King's was the scholarly and charismatic Canon F.J. Shirley, fondly known by the boys as Fred. His personal drive and enthusiasm to see the school prosper, and his ability to inspire both staff and boys, were qualities seldom surpassed by other headmasters.

At the start of my first term I was delegated to act as a personal study 'fag' (servant) to an upper-sixth prefect, Patrick Walker (who later in life became the head of MI5 and was later knighted). My responsibilities were to polish his shoes daily, make his bed, and produce coffee and tea as required. For these duties I was paid the princely sum of 10 shillings (50 pence) for each of the three terms that I fagged for him.

During my first year at King's I felt rather like a high-spirited horse during the process of being broken-in, for I had to conform to the early 1950's discipline of an English public school. I had failed my Latin Common Entrance examination, and I knew how important it was for me to catch up academically and to benefit as much as possible from the teaching. I knew that in all probability I had only got in to King's, after my short interview with Canon Shirley, on the strength of my brother Miles's prowess in representing the school in cricket, hockey, rugby, squash and fencing.

When I did eventually settle down to the cloistered regime and started to feel that I was being kept on too tight a rein, I made a few early morning forays to the 'out of bounds' parts of the precincts. These jaunts ranged from descending into drainage tunnels located within the Cathedral's precincts, to raising a chamber-pot to the top of the flag-pole on the tower of the Deanery roof, at that time the home of the 'Red Dean', Dr Hewlett Johnson. This latter prank did result in a photograph appearing in the East Kent Gazette of the pot-festooned flag post, with a note that the miscreant had achieved his aim without disturbing the Red Dean's bodyguard. Fortunately, I had not been aware of the existence of such a person, for no doubt if I had known about him, I might well have had second thoughts about such an escapade.

Some 30 years later I learnt from an esteemed zoological colleague that, at much the same time (the autumn of 1953), he had also exercised his spirit of adventure. After successfully being selected for officer training at the nearby Buffs Barracks, he celebrated by letting off a smoke bomb from Canterbury's Stevenson's Rocket and in doing so enveloped a part of the city in smoke. Perhaps the Red Dean's body-guard had been distracted by this event, if it had indeed coincided with the evening of my chamber-pot.

Fortunately I was never caught in these nocturnal adventures although, with what could be considered a degree of poetic justice, I was picked out by a school prefect for talking while the prefects and masters were entering the Cathedral's ancient Chapter House for the morning school assembly. In those days I could easily be identified by a mop of unruly blond hair, which had given me the school nickname of 'Prof'. It made it conveniently easy for the prefects to select me out of a group, and thereby to suffer punishment because of the misdeed of another. Initially I was happy to recognise that none of my illicit escapades had to date caught up with me, and that perhaps I did deserve some type of retribution. However, I had not bargained for what was then known as a 'school beating'; a rite that was eventually abolished at the end of the 1950s.

By tradition, such a beating took place in the school library, which was situated at the top of the sandstone Normandy staircase. Two wooden high-backed armchairs were placed back-to-back, and the ill-fated felon had to kneel on one, then stretch over the backs of the two chairs and grasp the arms of the second one in an ungainly fashion. The cane was passed down the line of seven prefects, adorned in their purple gowns, starched wing collars, black jackets and pin-striped trousers. And, varying with the prefect's particular degree of strength, each inflicted a stripe on my buttocks.

Once the archaic ordeal was over, the tradition was for the victim to go up to the head boy, shake his hand and say thank you. After which you left the library with as much dignity as you could manage, then tried to walk down the outside Normandy staircase as if nothing had happened. You attempted such nonchalant behaviour because you knew that there would be a group of fellow pupils nearby, to see just how well you had taken the role of scapegoat on behalf of some of them for breaching the code of silence of the Chapter House. Once I gained the privacy of a nearby cloakroom, with moisture gathering in my eyes, I remember soaking my handkerchief in cold water and soothing the stripes that had been registered so effectively on my bottom. My housemaster, Sam Prior, a Second World War RAF pilot and a winner of the DFC, held the opinion that all such experiences and traditions moulded the students well to cope with future challenges and responsibilities, and thereby they would be better equipped to deal with whatever life had to throw at them.

I left King's in the summer of 1954 and wondered how much my twelve years at two of England's leading boarding schools would be of benefit in my search for a meaningful future career; particularly as I was not going on to university. I was aware how attitudes in the world were changing, and that as a result of the recent years of socialism, egalitarianism and the welfare state, public school education was starting to come under sporadic, sometimes heavy, fire. Among other things, Great Britain no longer required the previous numbers of Colonial administrators that had, more often than not, been recruited from the public schools for the furtherance of *Pax Britannica* worldwide. So my first foray into employment, which could be considered by some to be the easy way out, was to join my father's wine and spirit business in Jersey as an apprentice vintner.

Chapter Two

A TASTE OF AFRICA

The impressive sign of H. Crosby Mallinson's, Vintners – At Your Service (A Votre Service), stood proudly outside the offices and warehouse of my father's wine and spirit business in Caledonia Place, St Helier, Jersey. My father Hal had sent my brother Miles to train in the wine business with a wine export firm in Bordeaux. Regrettably, such an interesting introduction to the wine trade was not offered to me. Miles had returned from France wearing a navy beret, a polo-necked sweater and a short scarf, insisting that every dish he ate be well garnished with garlic and washed down by numerous glasses of Médoc, though he soon decided on architecture as a career. As a consequence, my father made it clear to me that I would have to earn my spurs before any outside investment on his part.

The business supplied wholesale wines and spirits to hotels and shops, as well as to a few private customers on Jersey. The firm had a number of wine, liquor and beer sole agencies, as well as stocking most of the well-known brands. Just after the Second World War my father twice visited South Africa and was granted the sole UK agency for the Château Alphen vineyards in Constantia. Since that time his vintners had bottled their excellent red and white table wines, as well as their dry sherry. By the mid-1950s it was acknowledged that Alphen's estate-bottled 1944 claret, of which the firm held more than 100 cases, could easily deceive the most discerning connoisseur as a fine French claret.

Although I acquired enough knowledge to deal with a superior *sommelier* in a restaurant, I realised that perhaps the most important thing in life was to recognise what one was bad at, as opposed to what you were adequately good at. I recall how much I used to dread having to take the place of one of the firm's travellers and collect the weekly orders from some of the larger hotels. On some occasions I would be confronted by an aggressive staff member who demanded some personal cash benefit for an order, or a 10% discount on a case. It was sometimes difficult to refrain from saying 'Don't shake it man, we have only three cases left, and you are fortunate in having a special vintage being offered to you in the first place!' It did not take me too long to recognise that this essential part of sales in the wine trade was not my forte, and after about a year I started to seek opportunities further afield.

During this time, my love for animals was partly sustained by my mother Kay, who had started to breed Samoyeds from her founder female, Foam. In 1954 Foam presented us with seven delightful puppies. Samoyeds have an excellent temperament and are undoubtedly one of the most handsome dogs, with their long thick white coats and their tails curled smartly over their backs (although when running, the tails unfurl to help streamline their bodies). Their breed is said to have originated from the Arctic Circle, and takes its name from the Samoyed people of Siberia. Early travellers recorded that you could always tell Samoyed tribesmen by the packs of white dogs pulling their sledges. It was interesting to watch the dogs dig their huge holes in the ground in preparation for the winter, and then lie in them with only their black noses showing.

I was delighted to be able to help wean Foam's seven puppies, to teach them to go on a collar and lead, and later to exercise them over the nearby cliff lands of Noirmont. Calling them to heel was almost impossible. They kept together and hunted rabbits as a pack, appearing to rely mainly on their mother for leadership; she, regrettably, seldom wanted to do what humans expected of her. Fortunately, when the sad time arrived for the puppies to be sent away to new homes, it was decided to keep the most striking of the pups; a male that we named Storm.

It was in the summer of 1954 that a chance meeting and remark made a major change in my life. My father was at that time the Organising Match Secretary of the Jersey Island Cricket Club, and both he and brother Miles played cricket for the island. A member of the visiting Incogs cricket team, Michael Hammett, had mentioned at the after-match party that he had just left Shrewsbury School and was considering joining the Rhodesia and Nyasaland Staff Corps. According to the recruiting leaflet, the Corps was 'A small body of highly trained men' and part of the Federation of Rhodesia and Nyasaland's regular forces. You had to sign up for three years. Recruits would sail free to Cape Town and then make the three-and-a-half day train journey northwards to Salisbury (now Harare), the Capital of Southern Rhodesia (now Zimbabwe).

Having read much about the nineteenth century explorers, big-game hunters and naturalists of darkest Africa, I thereafter found it increasingly difficult to think of anything else. I set my sights on southern Central Africa, to see some of the continent's spectacular wildlife and to have some adventures of my own.

Within four months of my hearing about this, I was interviewed at Rhodesia House in London and signed immigration forms to go to the Federation of Rhodesia and Nyasaland and serve for three years in the Federation's peace-time regular army. The voyage out to Cape Town on the 22,000 ton *Arundel Castle*, with a party of South African university students who had just 'done' Europe, was as memorable for a teenager as any such journey could possibly have been. My first sight of Africa with the dawn just breaking, and the sun starting to melt the cloth of mist that covered the summit of Table Mountain, was as dramatic and as exciting as any arrival on a continent could have been.

During the Scramble for Africa period of 1880–1905, the Cape to Cairo railway was the unfinished dream of Cecil Rhodes. Our train wove its way northwards through arid hills and scrub country over the Orange River and through the Karoo to Kimberley, the richest diamond field in the world and source of South Africa's wealth. Rhodes had sent his Pioneer Column from here in 1890 to cross the Limpopo River and raise the Union Jack over Fort Salisbury, which he named after the British Prime Minister.

The day-time temperature hovered in around 28°C (low 80s F) as our 35-year-old steam engine, fronted by an impressive cowcatcher, laboured heavily through the Kalahari desert, past African villages of mud huts; their straw roofs drawn up into a plumed tuft that contrasted most favourably with the mundane corrugated iron roofs of the European buildings. An hour's stop at Mafeking, of Baden-Powell's Boer War fame; through the border customs post to Southern Rhodesia and on to Bulawayo. In the 1890s, Bulawayo was known as The Place of Slaughter, for it was here that Lobengula, warrior King of the Matabele, was deceived by Cecil Rhodes and began the Matabele Rebellion. At Bulawayo we changed trains for the overnight journey to Salisbury, where we arrived early on a Sunday morning, only 65 years after Rhodes' 'Pioneer Column'. We were received by a remarkably military and stern-looking Afrikaner Warrant Officer and it was only then that it started to dawn on me that I had signed on to spend three years in a colonial army, which might not turn out to be quite my cup of tea.

The Warrant Officer and his African driver took me and a fellow new recruit called Jock Whitton to King George VI Barracks on the outskirts of Salisbury. Here we were dumped outside an almost deserted barrack room and told that this would represent our billet until it was time for us to undergo training. For some reason I had expected to be given a room to myself, but the lack of such a provision was slightly compensated when two civilian Africans were appointed to be our batmen. In about six weeks' time we would be off on a four-and-a-half-month basic training and subsequent Staff Corps Assessment course. The WO told us that we could have the rest of the Sunday off and to report to a Lieutenant Salmon at Defence HQ at 0830 hrs the following morning. He concluded his welcome to the Staff Corps by barking the order: 'And on no account be late'.

So after this initial shock we were left with our batmen, Moses and Persil, to show us the general layout of the barracks and in particular the location of the Mess. Here we met the ebullient Jay Duncan, who had recently left Sherborne School, and like ourselves had decided to seek adventure in Central Africa. Jay provided us with the first real insight as to the role of the Rhodesia and Nyasaland Staff Corps (RNSC), the 'small body of highly trained men' that I had first heard about in Jersey. KGVI Barracks was mainly concerned with the staffing of the Defence Headquarters of Central Africa Command (DHQ CAC), but received the few RNSC recruits on a weekly basis, prior to sending a cadre of them down to Llewellin Barracks at Heany, some 40 km (25 miles) to the east of Bulawayo. Here we would undergo the Staff Corps assessment course that was carried out in association with the Federation's four-and-a-half-month National Service, which was compulsory for the European population.

It had been only three years before, in 1953, that a British Conservative

14

Government had brought about the Federation of the three African States – Southern Rhodesia (Zimbabwe), Northern Rhodesia (Zambia) and Nyasaland (Malawi) – as the Government had been convinced that such a Federation was the only practicable means by which the Central Africa territories could achieve security for the future and ensure the well-being of all their peoples. The regular military forces of the three territories were represented by four African battalions – the Rhodesia African Rifles, RAR (Southern Rhodesia), the Northern Rhodesia Regiment, NRR, and the First and Second battalions of the King's African Rifles, KARs, (Nyasaland), which were all staffed by European officers and NCOs. After the establishment of the Central African Federation, the Staff Corps had been formed to take over these duties from the British Army.

The swearing-in ceremony at DHQ involved placing a hand on the Bible and pledging allegiance to the Federation's representative of the Queen, who was the Governor-General, Lord Llewellin. Then we were taken by the orderly sergeant to the Quartermaster's Stores to be kitted-out. A peaked hat, a white starched belt, a red lanyard with a whistle attached to the end of it, and an assortment of khaki clothing that included bush-jackets, starched shorts, stockings, red garter flashes, socks, jungle boots, brown shoes, puttees, long trousers, blankets, a jungle hat, a waterproof cape, mosquito net, a canvas kit-bag, a brass button-stick, and what I was told would be my 'housewife'. This turned out to be a sewing kit with khaki cotton, needles and thread, and a metal thimble; all items totally alien to me.

As we left the QM stores, Jock was told to report at 0800 hrs on the next day to an Officer in Signals at DHQ; I was told to report to Q Branch and to make sure to be suitably attired in the RNSC uniform. The rest of the day was spent getting our newly acquired military kit properly sorted out, and I trusted that our respective batmen would take on the task of cleaning the gear, and would guide us on the correct Staff Corps uniform to wear during our time at KGVI Barracks – it all seemed so strange. The next morning, making my way up to DHQ in my starched shorts and shirt, and feeling very much like a fish out of water, my attention was distracted by a pair of the attractive black and white African Pied crows, squabbling over a small rodent that one of them had just caught. Unfortunately, this interesting ornithological

15

observation soon came to an end when I heard someone shouting 'Soldier, don't you salute an Officer, there?' When I realised that it was me that the officer was shouting at, I was quick to reply 'Certainly Sir, as soon as I see one.' Whereupon the Adjutant blasted: 'Well keep your bloody eyes open then'. I was quick to respond to such an authoritative command by executing the first salute I had given since my school army cadet days.

At DHQ a Captain Baxter told me that I would be attached to Q Branch, until it was time for me to undertake basic training and the Staff Corps Assessment Course at Llewellin Barracks. Providing I passed this I would be automatically promoted to the rank of a full corporal. It was customary to remain as an NCO for at least two years before being given the chance to do an Officer's Selection Course. This information seemed completely new to me, although I realised that I probably had not paid enough attention at my interview in London. Perhaps I had been too preoccupied by the thought of Africa's wildlife and my future adventures.

My time at KGVI Barracks went quite quickly, although within four days most of my civilian clothes were stolen. During the first weekend I was placed on Orderly Duty, much to my surprise. If any problems had arisen I would not have known what to do; but perhaps there was some hidden military strategy in placing a novice soldier in such a potentially vulnerable position, and in the line of fire. I was stationed in the guardroom at the barracks' entrance for 14 hours, wearing a broad red sash over the right shoulder. Just before 1800 hrs, and in the company of a RAR bugler, I marched to the nearby drill square to meet the orderly officer. While I slowly lowered the Union Jack, the bugler provided a rather stuttered rendering of the Last Post, and the officer saluted. Once the flag reached the bottom of the pole I had to untie it from the rope, fold it neatly before tucking it under my left arm, and then execute a smart about-turn and march with the bugler back to the Orderly Room.

A similar performance was carried out at 0600 hrs the following day, with the bugler disturbing the tranquillity of an African dawn by his exuberant playing of the Reveille, while I slowly hoisted the flag. It had to reach the top of the pole to coincide with the bugler's last note.

Two new Staff Corps recruits arrived at the barracks on the Sunday morning, and I was delighted to see that one of them was Michael Hammett, the young man who had told me about the RNSC last summer in Jersey. It was unfortunate for Mike that the RSM, Willie de Beer, happened to be passing the guardroom as Mike was unloading his cricket bag, golf clubs and tennis rackets. The RSM shouted: 'What the hell do you think you are joining, some type of poncy country sports club?' Mike conjured up a degree of diplomatic submission by saying he hoped he would have the opportunity to represent the Corps in some of the sports concerned. The RSM retorted: 'The only sport you will be doing for the next three years will be army games, so get that kit hidden before I have it taken away from you.' Such an initial welcome to Staff Corps recruits was the norm; the Warrant Officers wanted to establish from the start exactly who was boss. Mike Hammett served in the Federal army until 1959 when he joined the Hong Kong Police. Mike retired from this colonial police force in 1984 as one of its Assistant Commissioners.

My first physical contact with an animal in Central Africa was with a young Alsatian called Kara. The NCO who had adopted her from the Salisbury Animal Shelter had not looked after her properly, so when I first came across her she was scavenging for food, was extremely thin and walked with a limp because of her overgrown claws. People had complained to the NCO about her condition, and he had decided to have her destroyed. When I heard this I was determined to save her life and to adopt her for myself. Some nearby kennels agreed to board Kara for the period of five to six months I would be away on the training courses. The boarding fee was the equivalent to £2.50 and five of us agreed to establish an *ad hoc* Kara Syndicate to share the costs. When I lifted her into the back of the kennel proprietor's van Kara wagged her tail and licked my face, as if in appreciation of our eleventh-hour intervention on her behalf.

The time arrived for us new Staff Corps recruits to be sent down for training. The Adjutant gave me a large brown envelope, inscribed: **CONFIDENTIAL DOCUMENTS – *Property of the Federal Government of Rhodesia and Nyasaland*,** which was to be handed over to the Orderly Officer at Llewellin Barracks. He then put me in charge of the six other ex-public school boys, and we took the overnight train from Salisbury to Heany Junction near Bulawayo. The expected welcome

17

at the barracks, just before 0800 hrs the following morning, was an anti-climax. As soon as we got down from the truck we were shouted at by a drill instructor and taken to the office of Camp's Adjutant. The Captain could not have appeared more uninterested in our arrival if he had tried. I hoped to stress the solemnity of the occasion by the manner in which I handed over the brown envelope. He barely glanced at it. The drill sergeant executed an immaculate salute and we were ushered out of the office with the urgency of an oncoming bush fire. We were then marched at the double to Barrack Room No. 151, at this desolate old Second World War RAF training camp.

After we bundled our heavy kit bags into the barrack room an ex-British Army Korean War veteran, Colour Sergeant Danes, introduced himself. His welcome comprised the following curt utterances: 'My name is Sergeant Danes, you will call me Staff. When I enter the barrack room the first person to see me will open his bloody mouth and call the room to attention. You will then all go to the end of your beds and stand-at-ease. When I address any of you, you will immediately come to attention with your shoulders back and your bloody heads up. I will not stand any nonsense at all. If anyone is to come off best it will be me, so let us get that straight from the start. In the morning you will get out of your pits of iniquity and place your dirty smelly feet on the floor at 0645 hrs. If I catch anybody in bed after the bugle goes, I'll tip him out of his pit and place him on a charge. When I command you to do something, I expect you to do it immediately. If I tell you to go out and crap on the square, I expect you to immediately march out of the barrack room, pull down your pants and strain.' I found it difficult not to laugh at such a tirade, but by the nature of the Sergeant's tone, I recognised that compliance would be sensible.

The-four-and-a-half month basic training course and the subsequent Staff Corps Assessment process was as exacting in discipline as any such British Army training course could have been in the 1950s. However, in the Federation, perhaps the National Service people who found it the most difficult to deal with were some of the young high-earners from the Northern Rhodesia Copper Belt. As soon as they arrived at the barracks in their expensive American cars, they were descended upon by the Staff Corp training NCOs and officers like a ton of bricks. These recruits, who in the Copper Belt had had servants to polish their shoes, make their beds and clean up for them were for their first six weeks given no time to reflect on the delights of their previous privileged existence. Perhaps those of us who had experienced the privations of an English public school were better equipped to adapt to the discipline.

After the rigours of Llewellin Barracks I was posted back to KGVI in Salisbury and assigned to Q Branch at Defence HQ CAC, for it was quite apparent to my superiors that I was not NCO drill-training material. Soon after my return I contacted the dog kennels to reclaim Kara, only to be told that some two months after the Alsatian had been placed in their care a Staff Corps NCO had arrived and told them that he had my authority to remove Kara from the kennels, as I would not be returning to Salisbury. (I would still pay the fees, of course.) I found that the NCO in question had then resigned from the Staff Corps and moved back to a family farm in his native South Africa. We were left with an unwanted debt, but at least with the knowledge that our small syndicate had saved Kara's life.

The only military-type venture that I experienced was in October 1956, at the time of the Suez Crisis, when I could sense a spirit of excitement through the corridors of DHQ; no doubt some of the officers hoped that the Rhodesia and Nyasaland Federal Army would be requested to help the British forces in their risky Egyptian venture. Fortunately this was not to be the case, and my only exposure to any political hiccup was during some riots among African miners on the Copper Belt. This disturbance threatened to bring the country's main export and economy to a standstill, and caused Northern Rhodesia's Parliament to declare a State of Emergency.

As most of the Northern Rhodesia Regiment were currently serving in the Far East with the Malayan Emergency, DHQ decided to organise a small cadre of Staff Corps personnel and to send them on the 515 km (320 mile) road journey to Lusaka; they would be billeted at the Northern Rhodesia Regiment's Barracks, to act as liaison between the Federation's regular armed forces. I was informed that 18 of us would travel in convoy with four jeeps, two Bedford trucks of equipment, and with three 'Staghounds'. At first I was at a loss to understand why some hounds had been attached to our military deployment but fortunately, just before our small convoy was due to leave, and before I had mentioned my puzzlement to anyone else, the three

'Staghounds' staged their noisy appearance on the barracks' square in their designated status of 'Car armoured T17E3'. Their bulky bodies, powered by twin GMC 270 CID 6 cyl. engines, had three 37 mm M6 guns protruding menacingly from their electrically operated turrets. They had been manufactured in the US in 1943 to act as close support vehicles in theatres of unrest.

For some reason or another I was delegated to travel in the first jeep which was to be driven by Rhodesian-born Captain Baxter. As we drove through the night on single tarmac and strip-roads, past Sinoia, Karoi and down through the Zambezi escarpment, I experienced the excitement of hearing for the first time the roaring of two lions establishing their respective territories, as well as seeing the ghost-like silhouettes of the baobab trees. We arrived at the small border post of Chirundu on the banks of the Zambezi, and before we crossed over the bridge to Northern Rhodesia, our leader called the convoy to a halt and told us that as we were about to enter a country undergoing a State of Emergency, we should now load our pistols and rifles and be vigilant. It was only then I reflected that perhaps the reason I had been selected to sit up front in the most vulnerable seat in the convoy was that I was perhaps considered the convoy's most dispensable member.

The Northern Rhodesia Regiment's barracks (now the base of the Zambian Army) were situated immediately opposite Government House (now the President of Zambia's Residence), at the far end of The Ridgeway (now Independence Avenue). The first thing that I noticed in the barracks was a pair of Crowned cranes confined in quite a spacious paddock behind the Adjutant's office. It turned out that Crowned cranes were the regimental mascots. The cranes' two-syllable 'ma-hern' trumpeting proved to be a welcoming regular sound heard throughout the camp, in particular after being prompted by the NRR trumpeter's morning and evening renditions. The Colonel, Keith Coster, who knew about my enthusiasm for the animal kingdom, asked me whether I had heard any birds singing, and apparently I replied: 'I don't think that there is much for birds to sing about here, sir.'

Two days after our arrival in Lusaka (and certainly nothing to do with our Staff Corps presence), the State of Emergency was lifted and our small DHQ representation were asked to a number of social gatherings in Lusaka, which were open to both officers and NCOs. It was at one of these that I met Addie Vaughan-Jones and was subsequently introduced to her father, Tom, who had recently retired from being the first Director of the Northern Rhodesia Game, Fisheries and Tsetse Control Department. During my three weeks in Lusaka, I had little to do but be shown around Lusaka and its environs by Addie, including being taken to her childhood home at the old boma (fenced enclosure) of Chilanga, the original residence of the Game Department's Director.

Tom Vaughan-Jones proved to be a delightfully warm person and a born naturalist. He had started his colonial service as a District Officer in Lusaka, before becoming the department's first director just after the war. At Chilanga he stocked the small dam with various species of fish that he studied, and he and his wife developed a well-landscaped garden with uninterrupted views of the hills to the south. We picnicked just below the old thatched cottage on the hilltop on a number of occasions, and it was here that I started to be fascinated by the diversity of Rhodesia and Nyasaland's wildlife.

It had been only a few years before this, my first visit to Northern Rhodesia, that the Administration had recognised the advantage of nurturing non-hunting tourism that would not interfere with the activities of local hunting. Vaughan-Jones had had the considerable foresight to instruct ranger Norman Carr to take over one of the department's camps and convert it for tourist use, with all revenue going to the local Native Authority. He recognised that without the development of partnerships, where the local tribal people could benefit materially from tourism, there could never be a long-term solution to the conservation of both animals and habitats. In 1952 the Wildlife Authority established a game guard training camp which led to the opening up of the west bank of the Luangwa Game Reserve (Chilongozi) to tourism, and soon afterwards Norman Carr was appointed warden of the Kafue Game Reserve, which with the help of two rangers was soon opened for tourism.

The mid-1950s were early days in the establishment and development of facilities to let tourists see a raw slice of African wilderness with excellent game viewing, bird watching and fishing opportunities. The Kafue National Park was the country's largest protected area, spread over 22,400 square kilometres, about the size of Wales, and is still among the largest national parks in the world. The more Tom Vaughan-Jones talked about his experiences and the diversity of the wildlife in his country, the more enthusiastic I became about joining the Game Department. Regrettably, my hopes were soon dashed when he told me that my chances of employment was almost nil, for the Department usually recruited only locally born Europeans with a background of professional hunting and game control. Also, that the Federal Government took a dim view of immigrants breaking their initial terms of contracts. So it was at this time that I decided to take every opportunity to see as much of southern central Africa's wildlife as possible, as well as to visit some of the best scenic sites in the three territories concerned.

During the next couple of years of my time living in the Federation, I put such a strategy into practice. My first real exposure to the wildlife was on a hitch-hiking trip I did with my Staff Corps friend Jay Duncan, through Southern Rhodesia and Northern Rhodesia to the Belgian Congo (Democratic Republic of Congo). We visited the Wankie (Hwange) National Park north-west of Bulawayo; here I saw for the first time great herds of elephant, buffalo and sable and smaller groups of giraffe, zebra and kudu. I saw family groups of the slender, agile impalas effortlessly skipping through the air; I saw the more solitary diminutive steenbok; all of such sightings filled me with awe and wonderment. And I shall never forget the magical spectacle of seeing in the late afternoon a small pride of lions strolling down to a water hole near to Robins Camp; the large maned male certainly merited his title King of Beasts.

After leaving the National Park we hitched our way to one of Africa's masterpieces; the dramatic splendour of Victoria Falls, which have to be seen to be believed. The missionary explorer Dr David Livingstone, when he first saw the sight in 1855 exclaimed: '... scenes so lovely must have been gazed upon by angels in their flight'. In the flood season some 550,000 cubic metres of water a minute crash down the 100 m (325 ft) height of the Falls along their 1,700 m (5,206 ft) width. Together, the Falls' five main sections are twice as tall as those at Niagara and one and a half times as wide.

Jay and I pitched our tent in a campsite on the Northern Rhodesia side of that great engineering feat the Victoria Falls Bridge, which was completed in 1905 and spans the Second Gorge just after the area known as the Boiling Pot beneath the main fall. Rainforest runs parallel to the falls along the top of the First Gorge for three quarters of the

Falls' length. A network of paths led to vantage points at the edge of the gorge, some without any safety barriers, and incredibly close to the roaring abyss beneath. Small family groups of warthog, Vervet monkey, Chacma baboon, and various species of butterflies were all enjoying the coolness of the fine spray in this tropical paradise.

From the Victoria Falls Hotel (The Gleneagles of Africa) an open carriage on a single track conveys hotel guests down to the Devil's Cataract. We viewed the bronze statue of Dr Livingstone, who gazes serenely out over the savage splendour of the cataract to the main falls, and then four muscular Africans gallantly hauled the carriage back to the tranquil grounds of the hotel, where English tea was served on the broad veranda overlooking clouds of misty spray from one of the world's natural wonders.

From the small town of Livingstone we got a number of lifts in an assortment of cars and lorries by way of Lusaka, Ndola, through the Copper Belt to Mufalira and Bancroft, and then to the small border post of Tshinsenda. From the border we went on to Elizabethville (Lubumbashi), the capital of Katanga Province (Shaba Province) in the Belgian Congo. The only real problem that we encountered was dehydration, for we had foolishly forgotten to bring any water with us. After crossing the border on to an earthen road we spent over six hours of walking, in temperatures in the low 30s C (high 80s F) without a sight of even one vehicle. When a car did eventually come up the track containing a family of Indians, we greeted it as if it were our salvation on our pilgrimage to Mecca. They kindly gave us a lift, and we were so thirsty that we almost completely emptied the canvas water bag that hung in front of the radiator. Since this experience of suffering such thirst, I have never in my later travels been without an adequate supply of water.

In Elizabethville we learned that Tshinsenda was not an official entry crossing into the Congo, and was seldom used because of the state of the earthen roads. The city was a total contrast to Lusaka; we had exchanged a traditionally British colonial landscape for an almost Parisian scene. Pavement cafés with tables shaded by umbrellas proclaiming *Dubonnet* or *Ricard*, and the odours of garlic and French tobacco, evoked an ambience of La Belle France or the restaurant area of Antwerp. But I found the conditions in the local zoo depressing, in particular the

Victorian cages with their constantly pacing lions; bears tossing their heads and walking round in circles; monkeys with parts of their tails missing, and a small moated area of frustrated, balding and excitable chimpanzees.

On our return to the Rhodesias, I took advantage of a contact that I had been given by my father. Lt Colonel Little was a recently retired British Army officer, who had just taken up his post in charge of the Kariba Transport depot at Lions Den, to the west of Karoi. This was the Rhodesia Railways railhead where supplies for the construction of the Kariba dam were off-loaded and conveyed by truck to the dam site. The Kariba Canyon is some three hundred miles downstream from Victoria Falls, and it was here that the Rhodesia and Nyasaland government had decided to check the flow of the mighty Zambezi to provide almost unlimited electrical power.

The concrete for the main dam wall had been poured only a year before our visit in November 1957. Over 16,000 men, Africans and Europeans in equal numbers, were working twelve hour shifts on the site, in temperatures up to 40°C (over 100°F), and the coffer dam was currently under construction. As I looked down at them, the labour force resembled an army of ants responding to the wishes of a demanding queen. About a year later, in December 1958, the Zambezi was finally blocked and Lake Kariba was born. It was then, as the waters of the dam started to spread over the Zambezi valley, that the plight of the marooned animals began to make headlines, and Operation Noah and Animal Dunkirk had to be initiated by a small band of white rangers and African scouts. How I had wished that I had been in a position to volunteer to join teams and to help with what was then the greatest animal rescue operation ever recorded, but my duty was still to the army.

During my last year in the Federation, my Lambretta scooter and I several times made the 515 km (320 mile) journey up to Lusaka to visit the Vaughan-Jones family. During these visits I had the opportunity to see such new species of antelope as the Red lechwe, Puku and the Defassa waterbuck. My first sightings of cheetah, also known locally as the Hunting Leopard, filled me with the greatest desire to get to know the species, for they had a Queen of Sheba quality that could only be admired. I thrilled to the cheetah's speed over a short distance, its aston-ishing ability to swerve as it pursued its prey. I was fascinated by the camouflage of a cheetah's ochraceous yellow short fur, with its small black spots, and the way its coat blended so beautifully with the rust-tinged yellow grasslands of its habitat. In future years this species came to be one of my favourite of all animals.

My farewell to Africa almost ended in disaster, for on my planned journey home from Southern Rhodesia to Durban and down the Garden Route to Cape Town, I fell asleep on my Lambretta. Fortunately, an African passer-by found me lying unconscious under my scooter in a culvert about 18 miles south of the (then small) township of Potgietersrus in the northern Transvaal. The accident was probably caused by my driving all day from Bulawayo, and then through the night with little rest until I breakfasted at Potgietersrus. After this break I was exposed to the monotony of great stretches of tarmacadam road in front of me; in the midday matter took over from mind.

I remained unconscious for about ten days. My father received a telegram from the matron of the Portgietersrus Voortrekkers' Hospital regretfully informing him that his son was on the critical list, and adding the perhaps comforting news that the local padre had performed the last rites. During the twilight days of my recovery I recalled the solace that I had felt at school within the serene environment of Canterbury Cathedral, and I was aware of the presence of something very special, giving a helpful hand. So apart from suffering a permanent concavity in my skull, a damaged left eye and ear, and a multitude of bruises, and experiencing for some time a bad stutter, I was fortunate to pull through from an almost fatal accident relatively unscathed. On reflection, perhaps for those of us who have had such a near death confrontation and such a traumatic experience during our formative years, the period of convalescence does present the time to weigh up the pros and cons of what is really important to you. In particular, to examine the values you have attached to life up to that date, to decide what is important, what not. It was at this time that I started to recognise the importance of what appeared to be stored in the subconscious, resulting from my various life-experiences to date. The subsequent value of a 'gut-feeling' about someone or something, leads me to suspect that perhaps emotional responses are more important to a person than IQ.

In the spring of 1958 I was pronounced well enough to board the Lloyd Triestino liner *MV Europa*, and to set sail from Cape Town on a three-and-a-half-week voyage of recuperation up the east coast of Africa to Europe. The homeward journey took me via East London, Durban, Beira, Dar es Salaam, Mombasa, Aden, Port Said and Brindisi to Venice. A train took me to Paris and I flew back to Jersey. During this time I had decided that as I had been so stimulated by my travels, meeting so many different people, and seeing such a variety of wildlife and habitats, I should do as much as possible to guide my future career to provide me with the opportunity to continue to see some of the jewels of the world's shrinking biodiversity.

Chapter Three

SEEKING A CAREER WITH ANIMALS

On my return home to Jersey I rejoined my father's wine and spirit business in order to give me time to assemble my thoughts on a future career. A timber company in West Africa, the Hong Kong Police and tea planting in Assam, with the latter providing an annual polo pony allowance, were all possibilities, offering adventure combined with a degree of financial security. But as none of these promised direct contact with animals I had to look elsewhere.

After my discussions with the game departments in both Northern and Southern Rhodesia I recognised that the chance of a career with wildlife was now almost impossible. Gone were the pre-war days when it was comparatively easy to get a job with a game or wildlife department in colonial Africa. At my preparatory school, I recalled, just about all of the pony fraternity had set their sights on becoming veterinary surgeons, as this was apparently the only job open to people who wanted to work with animals. Perhaps they cherished the popular image of a country vet sitting on a shooting stick with a black Labrador at his side, viewing a paddock of pedigree cows, and talking wisely to the farmer about the herd's chances of pulling off some top prizes at the next County Agricultural Show. What they had certainly not bargained for were the extremely high academic qualifications required, even before starting a university veterinary degree. However, as far as I was concerned such qualifications were now no longer within either my reach or my ambition.

During the end of my time in Africa I heard that a person with some agriculture training could secure a loan from The Land Bank of Rhodesia to buy, for £1 an acre, land in the region of the Zambezi Escarpment. The more I thought about the potential of owning a farm in an area abundant with wildlife the more excited I became. And it was not long before I amassed a good collection of literature from the Agricultural Training Board in Beckenham, about careers in agriculture with special reference to livestock farming. At this time, to take a diploma course at an agricultural college, candidates were required to do a year's practical farm work prior to admission. So in October 1958 I enrolled at an agricultural college in Kent, found a dairy farm near Maiden Newton in Dorset that was willing to take me on, and began my practical work experience as a trainee dairyman.

I quickly discovered that a job in agriculture demands a great deal of hard work and relies on people who can adapt themselves to a diversity of jobs and be willing to work all hours of the day, and sometimes the night, for most days of the week. My day started at 5 a.m. I cycled to the dairy in the dark, and there donned heavy oilskins and wellingtons, so that in spite of the winter rain I could keep reasonably dry as I ventured into a hilly meadow in search of 76 Shorthorn cattle. Carrying a torch, and before the first light of a winter's grey morning, I would slip and stumble over tussocks of the drenched terrain which was, no doubt, a good initiation into the life of a dairyman and an insight into the individual characteristics of the cows themselves. It was always the case that once I had located and mobilised Thelma the rest of the herd would be well on their way down the muddy track towards the dairy. But Thelma, whom I came to admire for her independent style, always moved in her own time – nothing on earth could persuade her to do otherwise. She would plod her way down towards her morning feed, her muddy tail swinging nonchalantly, and allow herself to be relieved of her sizeable udder-full of milk.

By the time I had managed to close the four-barred farmyard gate behind the herd, the dairyman and his wife had the cowshed in full operation. The first 20 cows were already in their stalls; like regular churchgoers returning to the same pews, each cow would locate her particular milking-bay twice daily. Two cows to each stall gave the dairyman and his wife time to clean the second cow down in readiness for milking, whilst the first occupant was already being milked. At the end, while each cow was enjoying a cubed feed concentrate, a quantity of hay and as much water as required, I would be busy hosing and sweeping out the cow stalls, and then helping to clean and sterilise the milking machine equipment.

Most mornings it was my responsibility to guide the cattle up into a field of kale to graze. I had to move an electric fence 9m (c.30 ft) forward to allow for the strip-grazing of the kale, and I soon found that it was almost impossible to do this without getting a series of electric shocks from the wet wires. In the early afternoon I had to return the herd of Shorthorns from the kale field to the milking parlour, Thelma always taking up her customary place plodding along at the rear of the herd, and the morning's milking procedure would be repeated. As soon as the last cow was released from its stall, I guided the cattle back to their hilly meadow for the night.

During these morning and afternoon activities I was usually accompanied by the dairyman's hyperactive Border collie Susie, of whom I became extremely fond. Susie loved to retrieve sticks or balls thrown for her, although her real dedication was herding cattle. With her piercing eyes and intense concentration, she would chivvy them up by speedily running to and fro, snapping at the odd unruly individual, directing the herd to the required destination. Moreover, Susie and Thelma appeared to have acquired a mutual respect; Thelma remained unperturbed by any attempts on Susie's part to make her hurry.

Such an exacting routine was followed day-in and day-out, with trainees like me getting only two half-days off a week. But at least during my time as a trainee dairyman I was fortunate to experience some of the joys that arise from working with farm animals. I learned the way pedigree herds were developed by the meticulously-kept studbooks that guided the appropriate pairings and matings; I loved helping with the delivery of calves and the rearing of heifers; I learned about animal hygiene, nutrition and welfare. All these things were aimed at increasing the milk yield, so that each animal could make a good contribution to the economics of the dairy farm. Regrettably, after working on the farm for a little over three months, in my first winter back from Africa (which had turned out to be such an extremely wet one), I realised that enthusiasm for the demanding work of a dairy farmer was not mine. Perhaps the last straw came when Thelma's milk-yield plummeted to such an extent that she was no longer considered a viable member of the herd, and although she was still a healthy animal, the farmer decided to have her humanely destroyed – so I had lost a friend.

Due to the close relationship that I had had with a number of domestic dogs and cats, I decided that my next venture into seeking a career with animals was to look at the potential of opening a prestigious boarding kennels for both canines and felines. To achieve this I had found a small farmhouse with outbuildings and an adjoining field near the cliffs on the north coast of Jersey. I had been lucky enough to find a businessman who was prepared to back the venture financially. So at the beginning of 1959 I embarked on a kennel management course at the Basil Kennedy's Boarding Kennels near Woking in Surrey.

In all I spent three months at the kennels and by the end of my first week had acquired many friends among the 120 boarders. I learnt how to sum up a dog on introduction, how their temperaments clashed, and how to disarm bullying individuals without their losing face. An excellent training, I thought, for any young embassy official in the Diplomatic Corps. There were characters like Scamp, a mongrel sheepdog originally from the Battersea Dogs Home, whose charming ways had won the hearts of a wealthy couple from Chislehurst; they had sent him to the kennels whilst they were holidaying on the Cote d'Azur. He wagged his tail when angry and growled when pleased – a truly mixed-up dog. A borzoi belonging to the kennels would race across the exercising paddock as effortlessly as an Arab filly, frequently pursued by a prick-eared and breathless yapping little Yorkshire terrier. A basset hound, with his long drooping ears and bloodshot eyes, would shamble pessimistically on a seemingly fruitless course, eventually stumbling to a standstill and drooling in ecstasy at finding a treasure-chest of smells that the other dogs had overlooked. A miniature English bulldog with a passion for gulping up the muddiest of puddles was one of the many dogs I grew to love. As a consequence, when it was time for a boarder to return to its owner, I was frequently as heartbroken as if some love affair had come to an end. During my early twenties I had not mastered the art of avoiding an over-sentimental attachment to the animals under my charge.

A typical day's work began at 8 a.m. with a preliminary check round the vociferous boarders to see that all was well. Providing the weather was fine, and taking approximately six units at a time, the dogs were shut into their individual outside runs, while the inside accommodation was cleaned. Beds or baskets and blankets were removed to be shaken and aired. The kennels were mopped over with a non-toxic detergent, water dishes cleaned out and refilled, and food dishes removed. By the time the sixth kennel had been serviced, the floor of the first one was dry, so that the bed and bedding could be replaced and the dog could be let inside again. Once the hygiene of the kennels had been completed, both kennel man and kennel maid would share the combing and brushing duties for each boarder. It was at this time, while talking consistently to them, that you gained the best insight into a dog's individual character; and I always sensed a feeling of elation when the dogs responded to my overtures by wagging their tails, even those who did not particularly enjoy being groomed.

The main meal of the day was taken around at midday, and for the majority this comprised raw meat and gravy, mixed with dog biscuits. Some dogs arrived with an accompanying note explaining their food-fussiness, but after a few days of seeing how keenly the other boarders were wolfing up their dishes, these animals abandoned any such fastidiousness.

The early part of the afternoon was taken up by exercising the boarders that had proved to be compatible in a large fenced-in paddock. The excitement of the dogs racing around the paddock, barking their enthusiasms and burning off surplus energy, making new friends, was a joy to witness. Other more introvert and less sociable inmates were taken for a circuit walk on their leads. By 6 p.m. each dog was confined to its indoor kennel and most of them were given additional biscuits and the odd titbit, such as chocolate drops, and water dishes were checked to ensure they were full of clean water for the night. I followed this by giving each dog additional reassurance with a goodnight pat.

A day before each boarder was collected by its owner it was given a shampoo. This usually resulted in the struggling animal making sure that the bath-giver became more drenched than the dog. Rubbing down with a coarse towel was usually all right, but its reaction to a hair-dryer being turned on created protestation and alarm, until it eventually succumbed to the bewitching currents of warm air filtering through its coat. A returning owner would often cross-examine us with the same intensity as a parent quizzing a housemaster after a child's first term at boarding school. They usually wanted a blow-by-blow account as to how their dog had behaved; whom it had mixed with, what human friends it had made; whether it had always eaten its meals, taken its health pill; and what the kennel's vet had said about it. During the farewell I was often flattered by the way the kennel leavers wagged their tails furiously as they jumped up to plant an atrociously wet tongue on my cheek. Such partings always represented a sad farewell to an animal that I would probably never meet again.

Just before Easter 1959, when I had returned to Jersey, I was asked by my advocate (legal adviser) to come to his office. He gave me the devastating news that the financial backer to my kennel project was withdrawing his offer to underwrite the purchase of the Jersey property because of cash-flow problems. This was dreadful; I now had little idea of what future course to pursue. As the fog of disappointment began to fade I read Gerald Durrell's *My Family and Other Animals* which my brother Miles had given me the previous Christmas. He had attached a note saying that Gerald Durrell was about to open a zoo in Jersey, and he thought that he would be just the type of person I would be sure to get on well with.

I became fascinated as I read of Gerald Durrell's idyllic childhood years in Corfu, and I went on to read a number of his animal-collecting books in both Africa and South America. What particularly pleased me about his writing was the remarkably descriptive and humorous way he described the animals that he had met in the various countries he had visited, as well as the characters of every nationality that he had encountered. So mainly because of the charm and inspiration of Gerald Durrell's writings, I visited the embryonic Jersey Zoo at the time of its opening its gates, in the grounds of the rented Les Augrès Manor, during the Easter weekend of March 1959.

Gerald Durrell had been a student keeper at the Zoological Society of London's Whipsnade Park in the early 1940s. After he started his travels, catching wild animals for other people's zoos, he had found it quite heartbreaking to have to part with the wards he had spent six months or so looking after. During 1957, with five animal-collecting expeditions under his belt, he had the visionary idea of establishing a Wild Animal Preservation Trust in the grounds of Upton House, Poole, Dorset. The Trust's chief objective was to save those animals in danger

of extinction by conducting collecting expeditions to obtain rare creatures, and to promote interest in the preservation of wildlife all over
the world. The establishment of such a sanctuary had never before
been attempted and as such would represent a unique conservation
organisation.

Subsequently, suffocated by local government bureaucracy and fright-
ened-off by endless regulations, Gerald Durrell started to look elsewhere
to find a suitable place for his zoo. In the summer of 1958, on his
publisher's advice, he travelled to Jersey to meet one of Rupert Hart-
Davis's old army friends, Major Hugh Fraser, who happened to own
the historic property of Les Augrès Manor. As a result of a casual
remark made by Gerald Durrell to his wife, Jacquie, which was overheard by the Major – 'Wouldn't it make a wonderful place for a zoo?'
the seed was sown which soon germinated into the lease of Les Augrès
Manor being signed on 7ᵗʰ November 1958 for the establishment of a
zoo. Poole Council's considerable loss soon proved to be Jersey's colossal
gain.

Unlike Gerald Durrell, who was reputed to have been smitten with
what he called 'zoo mania' at the early age of two (according to his
mother, the first word that he was able to pronounce properly was zoo),
I was a late convert to the merits of having exotic animals in captivity.
Perhaps this had been because of my first exposure to zoos during the
1940s and early 1950s, when they often resembled Victorian menageries
with stamp collections of animals held in cramped accommodation.
Recently seeing the plight of many of the animals at the zoo in
Elizabethville had done little to alter my opinion. But I had been impressed
by my initial visit to the Jersey Zoo and decided to apply for a summer
job. In the hope that it would help my chances, I highlighted in the
letter of application that I had quite recently been with Mr Tom Vaughan-
Jones, the Founder Director of the Northern Rhodesia Department of
Game, Fisheries and Tsetse Control, and had thereby seen many of
Africa's animals.

Fortunately for me it turned out that as one of the bird keepers had
broken his ankle, a vacancy had just arisen, and a temporary job for the
summer of 1959 was offered to me by the zoo's Superintendent, Kenneth
Smith, providing I could start work in the bird section almost immediately. So on 1ˢᵗ May that year I became involved with a colourful

collection of exotic birds. This delicate cocktail of tropical birds, which I knew absolutely nothing about, included, to mention only a few – Scarlet tanagers, Gouldian finches, Splendid sunbirds, Lanceolated jays, Speckled mousebirds, and a dramatic and remarkably tame Toco toucan. My duties included feeding and cleaning out. The intricate work involved in looking after such a variety of bird species was a complete contrast to my previous experiences as a dairyman in Dorset, or having to cope with 100 noisy dogs in Surrey.

When I started at the zoo, Gerald Durrell was on one of his animal expeditions, collecting and filming for the BBC in Patagonia during the winter of 1958/1959, and he did not return to Jersey with his South American collection until July. The arrival of what was termed by the press 'The Zoo Ship' was a particularly memorable occasion for me. Not only was it my first meeting with the zoo's founder and my favourite animal author, but also I had my first introduction to a diversity of New World species that I had not previously even heard of, let alone considered that I would ever have the opportunity to meet first hand and get to know. The animals included Claudius, the male South American tapir; Juan and Juanita, the White-collared peccaries; Mathias and Martha, the coatimundis; Luna, the puma; Blanco, the Tucuman Amazon parrot; and such other species as a Hairy armadillo named Henrietta, a giant anteater called Amos; agoutis, Burrowing owls, Black-necked swans and Coscoroba swans; all of which were subsequently so eloquently described in Gerald Durrell's book *The Whispering Land*.

Ken Smith was fully responsible for the day-to-day running of the Zoological Park and the employment of its staff; he had come with his wife Trudy from Paignton Zoo in Devon, where he had been their General Curator for more than ten years. In the 1940s, Ken had accompanied Gerald Durrell on one of his animal-collecting expeditions to the British Cameroons and Durrell had dedicated his book *The Bafut Beagles* to him: – 'In memory of Fons, False Teeth and Flying Mice'. Although extremely knowledgeable about the animal kingdom, particularly about reptiles, Ken Smith's method of staff management was somewhat Victorian and quite explosive. Perhaps his most quoted statement was, 'You are not paid to think, you are paid to do what you are told!' His temperament could be as placid as a pink sunset on a breathless summer evening, only to change as dramatically as forked lightning in a tropical thunderstorm. But in spite of such outbursts at various underlings, I always found him a most interesting and pleasant person to talk to, and was able to glean much from his great experience. Trudy, who was quite a lot younger than Ken, had been in charge of the small mammal section of Paignton Zoo and was a delight to be with, always telling those who had received a tirade from her husband never to take it to heart. It was Trudy who was responsible for the running of the zoo's mammal section.

Les Augrès Manor is built of the most attractive pink Mont Maddow granite, as are its outbuildings, lime kiln, and fine stone arches, two of which give entry to the forecourt. The double arch to the east comprises one section for horse and carriage and one for pedestrians; all such characteristics add to the architectural glory of the property. The Manor's undulating grounds cover an area of 12.8 ha (32 acres) and have at their centre a lush water-meadow through which a gently flowing stream meanders. The front drive passes through an avenue of lime trees, and before entering the Manor forecourt under the double arch, runs beside an 18 m (60 ft) granite wall which, during the summer months, is festooned with an abundance of colourful rock and alpine plants.

The work on the zoo's bird section was equally as time-consuming as my previous two work experiences with animals had been and, although not on the whole as physically demanding, the duties involved in looking after exotic species proved to be more exacting. I worked an average 48–hour week with two afternoons off, for which I was paid the princely sum of seven pounds. However, with ever-increasing enthusiasm I found the whole experience enchanting, and my temporary summer job of 1959 soon slid into the winter months, when I decided to remain at my home in Jersey for another year. At my request, although it was made clear to me that I still remained employed only on a temporary basis, I was transferred to the zoo's mammal section, and placed under the supervision of the amicable Trudy. And it was in this section that I realised that the mammal kingdom embraced the types of species that I most wanted to be involved with in the future.

Among these mammals, and not counting the animals that Gerald Durrell had just brought back with him from the Argentine, the zoo had a sizeable and varied collection of the monkey kingdom: Rhesus macaques from India, Java monkeys from the Far East, Mona monkeys and White-nosed monkeys from the Cameroons, White-collared and Sooty Mangabey monkeys from West Africa, Grivet monkey and Patas monkey from East Africa. The baboon family were represented by a rainbow-coloured mandrill named Frisky and his companion, the closely related drill, which had both been previously collected by Gerald Durrell in West Africa. Smaller primates included the nocturnal Senegal and Demidoff's bushbabies, the rare Needle-clawed lemur, Bosman's potto, slender and slow lorises and a common marmoset. Indian Fruit bats, cacomistle – sometimes known as Mexico's Cunning Cat squirrel, African civets, raccoons, Black-footed mongooses, an American marten, Malabar squirrels from India, a Fox squirrel from Mexico, and a pair of Black squirrels from Thailand; all constituted a galaxy of the animal kingdom that I became increasingly fascinated and intrigued by.

As Claudius the South American tapir had not at this stage of the zoo's development got a pool to wallow in, he was scrubbed down like a thoroughbred stallion once a week, an attention he adored. If you scratched his neck he would angle his head to one side, gradually sink to his knees and then roll over on to his side in ecstasy. Similarly, the adult female Collared peccary Juanita enjoyed being picked up and having her shaving-brush chin bristles rubbed, which caused the curvature of her mouth to produce an even more genial smile of contentment than the norm, while she emitted a medley of soft grunts. On the other hand Amos the Giant anteater, who perhaps represents structurally the most perfect design of any terrestrial mammal, seemed to be permanently bad tempered, as if constantly complaining about the weather of the Northern Hemisphere, the lack of a supply of ants and the standard of her artificial rations. Henrietta, the Hairy armadillo, was a much happier animal. When her cage was cleaned she used to scuttle enthusiastically, like a mechanical toy tank, up and down the whole length of the wooden floor of the small mammal house. And when it was time for Henrietta to retire to her accommodation, she would lie on her back to have her stomach tickled.

Gerald Durrell had always championed what he called 'the small and ugly ones' that few zoos seemed to take much interest in. In those days most zoos concentrated on spectacular crowd-pullers like elephants, giraffes, sea lion displays and the chimpanzees' tea party. What Durrell considered to be the forgotten animals were those that he wished most to concentrate upon; although after constant badgering by his Superintendent he did recognise that the odd popular animal species like a lion would help the gate receipts. So in October 1959 a 20–month-old male lion (the unimaginatively named Leo) arrived from Dublin Zoo. Being zoo-bred, Leo was comparatively tame, and greatly enjoyed his back and chin being scratched through the wire of his cage; he would respond with growls of contentment, like a quiet railway engine.

Although I had been won over by the mammals, perhaps the zoo's greatest character was the bird Trumpy, a Grey-winged trumpeter from British Guiana (Guyana). During the daytime he had the freedom of the grounds to run around in and, as far as he was concerned, to patrol. Trumpy would often follow me during my routine work, charging along with his long neck thrust forward and wings partly outstretched, before coming to an abrupt stop. Then he would tip his small head on one side to be gently stroked. His dark eyes would flicker and he would coo in blissful contentment. On such enjoyable personal contact with my wards, it was all too easy to become totally distracted from other duties.

I started to teach myself about the classification of animals. I bought a number of small ring-files, and after borrowing an inventory of the animals in the zoo collection, I made separate files for mammals, birds and reptiles, and placed each animal according to its Order, Family, Genus, Species and Sub-species. I started off with the mammal collection, recording on individual pages the English name, scientific name, its distribution, reproduction and behaviour. Also, the place it had come from, date of arrival at the zoo, its daily diet and particular requirements. I typed up all this information during my off-hours at home, and although Ken Smith willingly gave me access to his private and extensive collection of natural history books, he was overheard one day saying to Trudy: 'The boy's mad; he keeps asking questions about where the animal came from, its required diet, whether it will breed in a captive environment and many other queries. And he writes down everything that I tell him.'

My love affair with gorillas began on 22nd November 1959. Gerald Durrell had secured a loan of £1,200 from his bank manager, and N'Pongo, a female 12– to 14–month old Western Lowland gorilla from the French Cameroons arrived at the zoo, having been purchased from Tyseley's Pet Shop in Birmingham. As N'Pongo's accommodation wasn't quite ready for her when she arrived, she spent the first week living with Gerald and Jacquie Durrell in their flat at Les Augrès Manor. Her favourite toy was a big coloured ball that she would chase around their sitting room and lie on top of, giggling like a schoolgirl enjoying her first prank. The Durrells also gave her a brightly coloured shawl, which she would put over her head and frolic around the room, bumping into chairs and the sofa. Sometimes she would lie on the carpet with the shawl completely covering her and pretend to be asleep. This was one of her favourite games, both in the flat and in her zoo accommodation; for if one peeped under the shawl she would jump up and dash around the place, having played a great joke on us all.

N'Pongo was soon featured on BBC television and in the national newspapers. In December the ornithologist James Fisher, presenter of the BBC television series *News From the Zoos*, came over to Jersey to include the seldom-seen animal species that Gerald Durrell had collected in Africa and South America in one of his programmes. In those days it took a six-man team five days, three miles of film, and 200 man-hours, to make a 30–minute programme. In the same month the zoo also had a visit from two of Gerald Durrell's fans, the Swedish film actress Mai Zetterling and her husband David Hughes, and she was photographed holding N'Pongo in her arms.

Advertisements encouraged people to visit the zoo over the Christmas and New Year holidays to see: 'Gerald Durrell's Tropical Animal Collections and N'Pongo the Gorilla of TV fame'. A supporting article in the newspaper told the public they would be able to see the young gorilla being fed twice a day, and view her fruit and vegetables. The article explained that the glass screen that had been erected in front of the cage was to prevent N'Pongo from catching any human infections from the visitors. As Jersey had received so much good publicity through N'Pongo's appearances in the national papers and on television, I rather boldly took it upon myself to write a letter to the *Jersey Evening Post*. I pointed out that, as the zoo's major new attraction had provided such a significant amount of publicity for Jersey's tourism, the States of Jersey should be duty bound to make a generous contribution to N'Pongo's purchase. Unfortunately, my suggestion fell on deaf ears among the Island's politicians.

Soon after N'Pongo's arrival at the zoo, Durrell was reunited with his pet chimpanzee Chumley (full name Cholmondeley St John). He had collected Chumley as an infant on one of his trips to West Africa, and the animal had lived with him for a while at his sister Margo's home in Bournemouth. Chumley could be frequently seen seated in the sidecar of Gerald Durrell's motorbike while they motored around town. The fun was curtailed because of Chumley's habit of grabbing at passing cyclists as they sped by. While the Durrells had been away in Argentina, Chumley had been billeted at Paignton Zoo so he had had some previous experience of not always being a pampered house guest. Although he started his life in Jersey living in the guest room of the Durrells' flat, he apparently decided that he was not getting enough attention and becoming bored, he would scream like a spoilt child. When he started to pull over furniture, and broke one of the Durrells' favourite pottery animals, the now sub-adult chimpanzee was moved to more secure accommodation in the zoo's mammal house.

It was not long after Chumley's move to the zoo accommodation that Lulu, an ex-London Zoo tea-party female chimpanzee, was found as a companion for him, in the hope that she would calm down his increasingly boisterous and extrovert behaviour. For Lulu, by contrast, was always good-natured, with a sweet temperament, and remarkably tame and loving. She was also pragmatic in recognising that total submission to her new companion's excitable whims was the most sensible behaviour for her to adopt. Because of the deterioration of Chumley's trustworthiness with the general public, he could no longer be taken out for walks or play with the staff on the front lawn of the Manor.

In 1960 Gerald Durrell agreed to take over to the BBC's Bristol-based Natural History Unit eleven different species of primates, including N'Pongo and Lulu, and to record a programme to be called *Zoo Packet* or *A Load of Monkeys*. I was delighted to be asked to drive this select collection of animals to the BBC in Gerald Durrell's expedition Land Rover. In those days, there was an air link for vehicles between Jersey and the UK, and in order to minimise the time that the animals would be confined to their travelling crates, it was decided to take advantage of this flight to Hurn Airport, and then to drive them on to Bristol.

Gerald Durrell issued a Press Release to the local media which stated:

For the first time, live on television, I am able to show the great British public a splendid array of creatures ranging from the tiny, large-eyed bushbabies, through the lorises, the Old and New World monkeys, to the gorilla and chimpanzee, with myself thrown in as an example of *Homo sapiens*.

After a somewhat stressful journey, it was not until just after 9 p.m. that I drove the Land Rover into the precincts of BBC Bristol. The relief of delivering my wards in a safe condition reminded me of the time four years ago, when I had arrived safely in Lusaka during the State of Emergency in Northern Rhodesia.

At the studios two dressing rooms had been put at our disposal for the animals, and it was decided that I should sleep in the Stars' dressing room to keep the VIPs of the programme, N'Pongo and Lulu, company. Before turning off the lights for the night I took both animals out of their crates, which I had positioned either side of my camp bed, held them in my arms to give them their last mug of warm milk for the day, and told them that they could now consider themselves stars. After a last reassuring hug, I returned them to their straw-bedded crates. I had quite a sleepless night; the heaters in the dressing room appeared to have been set to maximum, and Lulu constantly shifted about in her straw nest, snoring. Whereas N'Pongo, being a gorilla, had taken all the disruptions of the day totally in her stride, and had settled down for the night in style without even a whimper.

In the morning, Christopher Parsons, the director, and Eileen Moloney, the producer, gave the Durrells and me a tour of the studio where the programme was to be filmed. A series of benches with side-screens would enable Gerald Durrell to go from one primate to another during the filming. The bushbabies and marmosets were to be confined to glass-fronted cases; the lorises and pottos were to be placed on upright branches that they could cling to and perhaps sleep while the bright studio lights were on them; whereas the collection of tamer sub-adult monkeys were to be fitted with collars around their waists and leather leads that could be tethered to the rear of each viewing bench. The stars of the programme N'Pongo and Lulu would be handed by me, out of camera-shot, to Gerald Durrell when the time came.

Regrettably, at the rehearsal things did not go the way that the producer expected; a scene that was subsequently so expertly described by Gerald Durrell in his *Menagerie Manor*:

> The monkeys, hitherto always tame, placid and well-behaved, took one look at the cow stall (platforms) and had what appeared to be a collective nervous breakdown. They screamed, they bit, they struggled; one (Tarquin, a Cherry-crowned mangabey) broke his leash and disappeared behind some piled scenery, from which he was extracted – yelling loudly and covered with cobwebs – after about half an hour's concentrated effort.

Due to this major disruption in the studio, the Props Department made some imaginative amendments to the security of the larger primates on their show stands, as well as safeguarding the rest of the set. Fortunately when the time came for the programme to be filmed and relayed directly to London, the diverse collection of animals behaved as impeccably as if they had been acting in a church nativity play.

In the *Zoo Packet* programme, Gerald Durrell, by reference to some of his own drawings, explained how various members of the primate family have adapted themselves to their environment, and how in the process the different shapes of their fingers, toes and tails have evolved. The finale saw him holding both N'Pongo and Lulu lovingly in his arms, which provided the type of sensational conclusion that would have brought the house down had the programme been performed in front of a live audience.

During 1960 Jersey Zoo received more and more television and radio exposure, very much due to the increasing popularity of Durrell's books, his own television and radio appearances, and his highlighting of the conservation objectives of his new zoo. A television programme was made from the filming that he had done on his Argentine expedition, and screened at peak time on Good Friday as a part of Peter Scott's popular BBC *Look* series. So as well as the zoo's founder, N'Pongo and Lulu had now achieved considerable notoriety, and I have to confess that I found myself starting to enjoy a degree of reflected glory.

Particularly when visitors watched me as I fed the anthropoids, or played with both of them on the lawn in front of the manor house.

During that summer, while I was trying to make up my mind whether or not to continue working at the zoo, Gerald Durrell asked to see me. And very much to my surprise and delight he told me that he was planning an animal-collecting trip to Malaya in 1961, in association with the BBC film-maker/naturalist Tony Soper, and asked whether I would like to accompany them to help look after the animals that he planned to collect. I was over the moon with joy; I had already read about one of Tony Soper's expeditions to Gough Island in the Antarctic, and I knew that he had co-founded the BBC's Natural History Unit and become its first producer. So this marvellous invitation to join two internationally known naturalists on an expedition to Malaya was beyond my wildest dreams. Any thoughts of leaving the zoo went out the window. In spite of this invitation, Ken Smith made it crystal clear to me that I was still only a temporary employee at the zoo, and it was he who was in charge of the employment of the zoo's staff.

Chapter Four

A COCKTAIL OF EXOTIC SPECIES

During the course of 1960 the zoo continued to receive some fascinating additions. Claudius, the South American tapir, received a young companion, a female from British Guiana (Guyana) who was immediately named Claudette. Claudette was the gift of two of the pioneers of natural history television, Armand and Michaela Denis, whose *On Safari* programmes introduced viewers to the wonders of East Africa's wildlife. Harry Watt, the director responsible for such spectacular blockbusters as *The Overlanders* and *Where No Vultures Fly*, presented his pet two-year-old male cheetah, Peter, to the zoo. Peter and I soon became firm friends; he loved me to kick a ball around his new enclosure. Occasionally, when Peter was asleep in the long grass of his paddock and could not be seen by the visitors, Ken Smith would put out a call to Trudy: 'Tell Jeremy to drop whatever he is doing and get up to the cheetah paddock and kick the ball about so that the animal can be seen.' As the Superintendent often said, 'It's no use having animals occupying an exhibit if they can't be seen by the paying public.'

A fund-raising campaign for a companion for N'Pongo was launched by Gerald Durrell when he gave a talk and signed autographs at one of Jersey's schools. A reporter from the *Jersey Evening Post* recorded:

Nearly 400 school children, who stood on their seats and roared their delight, left Jersey Zoo's famed gorilla, N'Pongo, completely unperturbed when 'it' made a star appearance at the St Helier Girls School ... However, Lulu the chimpanzee displayed the utmost disapproval [of such a reception].

43

A couple of months later, N'Pongo was featured as a 'special attraction' at the matinee and second house performances of the new Cinemascope *Lords of the Forest* film, billed by the local West's cinema as: 'The Most Amazing Jungle Picture Ever Made!' Trudy and I would drive N'Pongo down to St Helier to coincide with the end of each of the two performances, so we could catch the film-goers as they came out. We took turns to hold N'Pongo in our arms (her favourite coloured shawl wrapped around her shoulders to keep her warm), and rattled our collection tins under a big sign that said 'Please Help Buy Me A Mate'. The film-goers responded generously, though the plea for a mate also attracted a selection of ribald remarks.

In November 1960 Nandi, the intended mate for N'Pongo, arrived at Jersey Zoo. Gerald Durrell had had to arrange another bank overdraft to secure this Lowland gorilla (as yet unsexed, though the vendor considered it to be a male), and Durrell's publisher had once again acted as guarantor. The total sum owing was £1,200, and a collection box was attached to the barrier in front of the gorillas' cage, in the hope that once the public had watched the animals at play they would give generously. Nandi was thought to be about six months younger than N'Pongo and was a far more nervous Lowland gorilla than she; Nandi would never dream of climbing into my arms, and was far too wary of humans to allow an examination to confirm its gender.

The gorilla's suspicious behaviour was no doubt due to the type of capture that so many young gorillas underwent in those days; the mother shot by poachers and the young removed. In Nandi's case, a prominent panga wound had left a scar on the right side of the head, and the young gorilla had been confiscated by the local Game Department in the Cameroons. The more I learnt about the manner of their capture, and the illicit trade with the greater anthropoid apes, involving gorillas, orang-utans and chimpanzees, the more I believed that there should be a complete ban on all commercial dealings involving these close relatives of man. At least this sub-adult gorilla had not fallen victim to the burgeoning trade in 'bush meat', and now had a safe environment and a companion to bond with.

When I gave the two gorillas their morning milk, I had always to be careful not to turn my back on Nandi, who would take any chance to grab and pull me over. Such behaviour was well demonstrated on one occasion when the interior walls of the gorilla enclosure were painted.

As the walls had to be given time to dry, the gorillas would sleep on their straw mattresses in the open, with me to keep them company. Nandi lay on one side of the bed, N'Pongo lay in the middle, with me on the far side of her. But just after N'Pongo and I had fallen asleep, Nandi must have wondered 'Whatever am I doing sleeping on the same bed as a human?' Whereupon, she reached over N'Pongo's slumbering body and made a grab at my arm. Pandemonium broke out, as N'Pongo immediately came to my defence and I found myself squashed under a tussling pair of Lowland gorillas. The rest of the primates in the Mammal House joined the two gorillas with high-pitched shrieks and noisy vocalisations. The deafening chorus of excited grunts and screams must have been heard throughout the north-east corner of the island. It took me almost an hour to restore order and to initiate a degree of tranquillity among the occupants of the Mammal House. After the gorillas returned to their positions on the straw bed, I gave them both some more warm milk and a generous bunch of grapes. Also, to help settle down the rest of the occupants of the Mammal House, I liber-ally scattered handfuls of mixed seeds, raisins and grapes into their various night quarters. As a degree of self-preservation was now required, I took the precaution of providing myself with a separate straw mattress for the night, well out of reach of the seemingly jealous Nandi; and I thought of how fortunate I had been that a friendly gorilla had been sufficiently possessive of me to protect me from one of her kind.

Although N'Pongo had undoubtedly become my favourite animal at the zoo, I was pleased to welcome to the mammal collection a pair of Australian dingos, born at Whipsnade, which were quite tame. With my previous kennel management experience, it was not long before I recog-nised that the bitch was pregnant, and once she started to dig a mater-nity den in the earthen floor of her cage, I helped her with its excavation. I knew the importance of providing her with the maximum security throughout her final stages of pregnancy and birthing, and erected a tarpaulin screen over the front of the cage, which gave the dogs privacy but totally blocked the visitors' view. Trudy later told me that when Ken Smith saw what I had done, he stormed into his office and gave his secretary a dose of re-directed aggression, with the comment: 'The boy's mad. If he is allowed to carry on like this following his own devices unfettered, there will be nothing left for the paying public to see.' But

for London, for discussions about his re-writing of the script for the block-buster *Cleopatra*, he mentioned to his brother that he would try and include Peter in the script. Such a film contract could considerably benefit the zoo, which was still desperately short of money.

Before Lawrence Durrell's departure he kindly autographed my copies of the *Alexandria Quartet*, which represented the start of my 38 years of devotedly collecting the written works of the Durrell family. Very much thanks to the kindness and generosity of both the Durrell brothers, the collection currently comprises over 300 items and must be one of the world's largest collections of 'Durrelliania'. One particular remark concerning the degree of poetic licence that is sometimes employed by authors was well demonstrated when I mentioned to Louisa Durrell that I had just read an article about her eldest son being born under the shadow of Mount Everest. Her reply was: 'He may have been there dear, but I was hundreds of miles away from Nepal on that particular occasion!'

In the New Year of 1961 the sun appeared to be smiling upon my good fortunes. I was rejoicing in the happiness of working with so many interesting animal characters. Ken Smith had mentioned that, should Lawrence Durrell successfully manage to include the cheetah in his script of *Cleopatra*, as I was the only keeper who could properly manage Peter, I would have to accompany him to wherever 20th Century Fox planned to film the epic. This combined with Gerald Durrell's invitation to me to accompany him and Tony Soper to Malaya in the autumn for a BBC documentary, offered me the travel and adventure that I had always dreamt of.

New arrivals at the zoo occurred almost weekly. Among the mammals, an infant male Emperor tamarin from Peru, with its great Kaiser Wilhelm white moustache, was immediately named Whiskers, and cost the vast sum of £70. A local resident, Mrs Hope-Platt, presented the zoo with a pair of one of the most dramatically coloured species of primates, the Golden Lion tamarin, increasingly endangered in their homelands of the coastal forest of Brazil. A lone Black Saki monkey arrived from Colombia; a pair of Barbary apes had been presented by the Governor of Gibraltar; a pair of Sykes' monkeys came from East Africa; and a tamandua, with its elongated tapered snout and prehensile tail, arrived from British Guiana.

New to the bird collection were a pair of Black-footed penguins from South Africa, via the Brighton Aquarium, named Dilly and Dolly; both appeared to demand a daily ration of fish far above their body weight. A pair of the attractive Rosy Pastor birds from India, and a pair of Crested cranes from Kenya, which reminded me of the two that had been in the pen behind the Orderly Room at the regimental barracks in Lusaka. Reptile arrivals included two Mangrove snakes from Malaya, whose striking yellow stripes contrasted magnificently with their sleek black-scaled bodies. A pair of Gila monsters from Central America, most handsomely marked in salmon-pink and black were one of the only two species of venomous lizards known. The reptile section was under the supervision of another ex-Paignton Zoo staff member, Bill Timmis.

A number of successful zoo births started to be recorded. The pair of Collared peccaries, Juan and Juanita, produced four delightful piglets. A couple of weeks before their birth, the temperament of the parents changed quite dramatically; Juanita no longer allowed me to pick her up to give her a daily chin-scratching, and Juan had become quite aggressively protective. Because of this change of behaviour they both had to be shut into their inside den while their paddock was being serviced. Three raccoon cubs were successfully reared, though they did not emerge from their den for six weeks. A pair of Common marmosets gave birth to twins, which is usual for members of the marmoset and tamarin family (Callitrichidae), and I was intrigued to see the way the father shared the post-natal handling of the offspring. The latter births represented the first of many successful reproductions of this Neotropical primate genus, for which the Jersey Zoo was soon to become well known. The marmoset births spawned my long-term interest in, and study of, this intriguing family of primates, and I started to add copious notes to my files about their behaviour and nutritional requirements.

A few clutches of eggs were hatched from both the Carolina Wood ducks and Mandarin ducks, and chicks from two species of pheasants, the Golden and the Elliot's, were successfully reared. The Congo Speckled mousebirds managed to reproduce in their small cage in the Tropical Bird House. The pair of Fernandes skinks that Gerald Durrell had collected in the Cameroons, and had described in his book *The Bafut*

Beagles, successfully hatched three young, which were immediately removed by Bill Timmis to an incubator and carefully reared to maturity.

Gerald Durrell had now reached his mid-thirties, and had become a best-selling author of international acclaim, with his seven previously published books translated into many different languages. He had founded his own zoo and between 1960 and 1962 had published four more books: *A Zoo in My Luggage*; *The Whispering Land* with its charming drawings by Ralph Thompson; two children's books: *A Look at Zoos* and *Island Zoo*, which was lavishly illustrated with spectacular photographs by W. Suschitzky, and dedicated to the Smiths' recently born daughter, Caroline. A series of articles about his Argentine/Patagonia expedition was published in *The Observer*. In addition to his many radio and television appearances, the filming that he did in South America was made into one programme, and included in Peter Scott's most popular nature series, *Look*. In 1961, a Hollywood director approached him about making a Broadway stage musical on *My Family and Other Animals* with the possibility of a future movie version.

Although the zoo's founder and director was now a household name, he had the nous to acknowledge the opinion of those who considered it cruel to keep creatures in captivity. When this matter came up during an interview, he would often say that he shared the position of Florence Nightingale in that, while she criticised the hospitals at the time of the Crimean war, she was by no means opposed to all hospitals. Gerald Durrell's aim was to develop a zoo where conservation breeding programmes, public education and research would be of benefit to the animal species in the wild.

A zoological park with such objectives attracted, apart from those who paid an entrance fee, a number of celebrity visitors. In February 1961 the actor John Slater, who had recently appeared in the film *Passport to Pimlico*, visited the zoo, and was photographed with Lulu, who held her hand firmly over his mouth. And in July the distinguished soldier Viscount Alanbrooke, who as Field Marshall Lord Alanbrooke had been Chief of the Imperial General Staff from soon after Dunkirk until the end of the war, came with his wife in the company of Jersey's Lieutenant Governor Sir George Erskine. Lord Alanbrooke said that he had long wished to visit the zoo, for he was a great fan of Gerald Durrell's books. Although Lord Alanbrooke's main interest in natural history was ornithology, the man who had been one of the prime architects of the Allied victory was keen to be introduced to N'Pongo and gladly agreed to be photographed with her in his arms.

As Gerald Durrell's celebrity grew, he and Jacquie Durrell were invited by the Prime Minister Harold Macmillan to a reception at 10 Downing Street during a State Visit by the President of Peru. Here he again met Peter Scott, whom he had first met in 1947 at Slimbridge, soon after Scott had founded the Severn Wildfowl Trust. They spoke briefly about the conservation aims of the Jersey Zoo, and Lord Alanbrooke's recent visit, with Peter Scott mentioning that the great man had been the first President of his Wildfowl Trust at Slimbridge. Soon after their visit to Downing Street the Durrells were invited by the Queen to attend a State Banquet at Buckingham Palace, to mark the official visit of the President of the Cameroons. Years later Jacquie Durrell told me that the Queen had shown some of the diners the fine wooden sculpture that she had been presented with by the Cameroon President. Whereupon Jacquie, who collected such artefacts during their international travels, mentioned to Her Majesty that they had one almost exactly the same at their home in Jersey.

By midsummer, just when I thought that the sun of good fortune was still smiling upon me, I was most apologetically told by Gerald Durrell that the animal-collecting trip to Malaya with Tony Soper had had to be cancelled. He was considering organising a trip to New Zealand and Australia, but was unable to say when this would be, although it would definitely not take place during 1961. Soon after this disastrous bombshell, news filtered through to Jersey that Lawrence Durrell's 10th revision of the *Cleopatra* script had not been adopted. Therefore taking Peter the cheetah to a film set in some exotic location was not to be. Once more the time had arrived for me to try to map out a viable future for my recently found enjoyment of working with a diversity of exotic species.

As the animal collection had increased considerably since the zoo's opening just over two years previously, so had the staff. John (Shep) Mallet, who had done his two-year National Service as a dog handler in Malaya, arrived at the zoo with a menagerie of his own: two dogs, a rough collie and a miniature schnauzer; an African Grey parrot, a Jay, a jackdaw, some waterfowl and a pair of Golden pheasants. He had spent some time as a probationary RSPCA inspector, before working for a private waterfowl collection in Hampshire. Soon after Shep's employment, I collected the lanky 17–year-old John Hartley from the mail boat. John, who had just left school, was particularly interested in reptiles. Shep was put on the bird section to look after the waterfowl, pheasants and other paddock birds, and John became second to Bill Timmis in the Reptile House.

However, in spite of the good reputation of the Jersey Zoo, and the general goodwill of the islanders, the zoo's running costs by far outweighed the income from gate admissions and from the small café. Realising that the zoo could be financially on a slippery slope to disaster, Gerald Durrell held a staff meeting at which he warned us of the probability of staff redundancies and the possibility of closure. On the other hand, with everybody's help, it might survive. Anyone who wished to leave should do so and there would be no hard feelings against them. We heard him out in solemn silence. Instead of resigning, we rallied round, all determined to help him maintain a zoo with a difference. So this event was probably the embryo of what came to be referred to as the cadre of 'Durrell's Disciples'.

With perhaps everybody who has spent some time in Africa, the magic of the Dark Continent works an obsessive magnetism. Africa was now starting to pull me back, and at least my departure from the pay roll would help the zoo to economise. I decided to embark on an animal-collecting expedition of my own. I knew that I could return to Southern Rhodesia where various farming friends that I had stayed with during my time in the Staff Corps would be willing to help me in one way or another. So in September 1961 I set about planning and looking into the logistics of such an expedition, and this fortunately coincided with a small legacy from my Yorkshire grandmother. It was by no means a fortune, but I considered that it was enough to fund my return to Africa and to undertake an animal study and collecting trip of my own. I was single, twenty-four years old, without any particular ties, so there was little to hold me back.

When Gerald Durrell heard about my plans he asked to see me, and told me that he had just been asked by the publishing house Hutchinson's to write an introduction to a book entitled *Okavango* by June Kay. The author and her husband Robert had an amphibious DUKW and lived with two lions in the Okavango swamp region of Ngamiland, in the Bechuanaland Protectorate (Botswana). He told me that if I wanted him to write directly to the Kays to see whether I could visit them after my trip to Southern Rhodesia, he would be happy to do so. This was a wonderful offer that I was quick to accept. Gerald Durrell, probably recalling his early days as an animal collector in West Africa in his twenties, also wrote a most generous 'To Whom It May Concern' letter of introduction, to present to any person or official that I thought could help with my intended animal-collecting. Ken Smith, in a genuine gesture of benevolence granted me leave of absence (unpaid), with an assurance that when I did return to Jersey (and if the zoo was still in operation), a keeper's job on the mammal section would be open for me.

Just before I left for Africa, Gerald Durrell received a letter from Noël Coward in Sydney, who wrote that he had just read *My Family and Other Animals*, and had enjoyed it so much that he had sent his companion Coley (Cole Lesley) out to buy any other Durrell books he could find. By a coincidence I had recently bought, to add to my Lawrence Durrell collection, a copy of Noël Coward's *Middle East Diary* in which he recorded, for 22nd August 1943, while in Cairo:

> The day broke fair and excessively warm but I didn't notice it as
> I slept until 12 o'clock when, with my breakfast tray on my knees,
> I gave an interview to Larry Durrell who lived in Corfu and writes poems.

Although I was not in the habit of writing to well known people on the world stage, I decide to write to Noël Coward to ask him whether he realised that my mentor Gerald Durrell was the younger brother of the Durrell that he had referred to on page 57 of his *Middle East Diary*? I also mentioned that I was great fan of his and had bought a copy of *The Noël Coward Song Book* when I lived in Africa during the late 1950s; and how, during a hitch-hiking trip up to the Belgian Congo in 1957, our theme-tune had been his 1928 song 'World Weary', from his musical *The Year of Grace*. Much to my surprise and almost by return of post I received a letter from 'The Master', from his home in Jamaica. He wrote:

Dear Jeremy Mallinson

What a very nice letter. Having just finished reading 'Menagerie Manor' I really feel that I know you quite well. If this letter looks slightly erratic it is because I am using a new electronic typewriter which I have never used before and it is frightening me to death. That 'M' for instance got up there all by itself.

Of course I will write a little something on a separate piece of paper for your collection, any ordinary humdrum calligraphy will be a comfort after this curious machine. I at once looked up 'Middle East Diary' and now I remember meeting Larry Durrell and finding him most intelligent and attractive. It's the 'Little did I know then' department isn't it? I was dining last night with an old friend of his, Morris Cargill, who is my lawyer here. He let me read some of his early poems which I thought extremely good. Have they been reprinted? Of course my real pin-up boy is your Boss. We have corresponded but not yet met. I intend to remedy this by coming to Jersey next summer. If this comes to pass will you send me some instructions as to where to stay etc? Also please give him enthusiastic messages from me. I shall be here, pounding away at this machine, until mid-April. I am delighted and flattered that you are a fan of mine and I love to think of you striding through the Congo singing 'World Weary'.

Write and tell me how all the Jersey Wildlife is or are behaving. I so long to meet them and all of you.

Noël Coward

Noël Coward enclosed with his typed letter three handwritten verses of the theme song that Jay Duncan and I had adopted for our Congo trip, and under his theatrical signature had written 'World Weary' 1928.

The stormy weather of the autumn had started to arrive, the clocks had been put back for the winter months, and I had gathered together an array of expedition equipment. This included: nylon mesh bird nets from Gundry's net makers in Bridport; two sizes of wire 'live' animal traps from Young's at Peterborough; a tape-recorder; water bottles, and a medical kit with some snake-bite serum. I had also assembled an assortment of tropical clothing: bush shirts, khaki trousers, leather boots, a jungle hat and a waterproof cape. Gerald Durrell presented me with his copy of Austin Roberts' *The Birds of South Africa*, and I managed to get hold of a copy of C.T. Astley Maberly's *Animals of Rhodesia*.

Before my departure from Great Britain, Gerald Durrell had given me an introduction to Dr W.C. Osman Hill, who at that time was the Medical Prosector at The Zoological Society of London, and who had just published the fourth volume of his monograph *Primates: Comparative Anatomy and Taxonomy*. On the strength of Durrell's letter, Dr Hill kindly invited me, with his wife Yvonne who had drawn the anatomical illustrations in the four volumes, to lunch at the London Zoo Fellows' Restaurant, where they could not of been kinder or more encouraging. He told me that he was currently interested in African primates, as these were to be covered by the next two volumes of his primate monograph. When they dropped me off in their car at Camden Town tube station, he said: 'Jeremy, do keep in touch, for I am always interested to hear about any primate observations or material that you may make or collect during your forthcoming African adventures. And good hunting.'

Although I had been working with a diversity of exotic species for almost two and a half years, I still felt very much a novice as far as my overall knowledge about the animal kingdom was concerned. Reflecting on my work experience since leaving school seven years before, I asked myself how different my life would have been had I gone to university and gained a degree in zoology. Perhaps in an attempt to compensate for such academic inadequacy, I wondered whether on leaving I would have had the many stimulating and diverse experiences that my somewhat hybrid career had given me to date? But whatever the pros and cons of this may have been, I was now about to embark on a further chapter in my life; whether it would be a success of a failure I could not tell.

Chapter Five

RED FOXES TO STAIRS' MONKEYS

On a rainy and cold October afternoon in 1961 I sailed from Tilbury docks on board the Union Castle liner, the RMS *Warwick Castle*. As the liner moved off down the Thames estuary into the Channel, bound for the east coast of Africa, I felt all the exhilaration and excitement that I had felt five and a half years previously, when leaving Southampton on the RMS *Arundel Castle,* bound for Cape Town via Africa's west coast.

Before leaving Jersey I had been in correspondence with the Director of Pretoria Zoo to see whether he would be interested in receiving any of Jersey Zoo's surplus animals. Much to my surprise they expressed interest in a pair of European Red foxes. As our zoo had a young dog fox named Reynard, I had placed an advertisement in the *Farmers Weekly* for a young vixen, and was able to obtain one from a farmer in Pembrokeshire. I collected her from Euston Station, just four hours before my ship's departure time. I named the animal Pufelli; I could tell by her collar, and the lead attached to her travelling crate, that she had been a pet.

Apart from the two kennels I had for the pair of foxes, I had an awful lot of baggage with me. There were collapsible wire cages, traps and nets; a Red Cross box for emergencies and two well-weathered trunks for the hold. Suitcases, ancient but cherished, a portable typewriter and a tape-recorder were stored in my cabin. The two foxes were kept on the aft upper deck, where the eventual foxy smell had the satisfactory effect of keeping inquisitive passengers well away.

While the liner was butting its way through a very rough Bay of Biscay, I established that I would have to look after the foxes myself. In theory a member of the crew – curiously called the lamp-trimmer – was supposed to feed all the livestock on board, which apart from my foxes included kennels accommodating five dogs and two cats. As the lamp trimmer appeared to be too timid to clean the foxes' kennels out properly, his solution was to deep-litter them so lavishly that the animals could hardly stand up. Fortunately, I had few problems with my new friends, for although Reynard was rather reserved, Pufelli was very tame and wagged her tail whenever I approached. It was not long before I started to take her out of her kennel and to exercise her on her collar and leash around the aft decks.

Our first port of call was Gibraltar, where I took the opportunity to visit Prince Ferdinand's Battery on the rock to see the birthplace of Charles and Charlotte, the pair of Barbary apes that the Governor of Gibraltar had given to Jersey. This species (apart from *Homo sapiens*) is the only primate native to Europe. They were an entertaining sight, as they peered about from under the heavy prominent brows that protected their eyes from the fierce winds of the Rock; they reminded me of ancient mariners, scanning nautical horizons from under their peaked hats. The greyish-brown adults pestered the visitors for food, whilst the black-furred infants developed their arts of mischief to a high degree of perfection.

In the town I surprised various shopkeepers with a request seldom, if ever, made of them by the usual souvenir-hunting tourist. I needed a quantity of wood-wool as extra bedding for the foxes. They had suffered from the turbulence of the Bay of Biscay, and I thought a bundle of wood-wool placed on top of the wood shavings would make them more comfortable. When I returned to the ship with a couple of sacks of wood-wool thrown over my shoulders, it appeared to some fellow passengers that I had been buying as many tax-free luxury goods as I could carry.

As we cruised through the Mediterranean, I persuaded the ship's First Officer to let me exercise Pufelli along the passenger deck. He had been intrigued to have the opportunity to stroke her head, and remarked, 'First time that I've seen one of these damn animals so close. Usually they have been torn to shreds by the time I catch up with the hounds.' Pufelli appeared to know exactly what had been said about her kind, for she flattened her ears and curled her lips in a snarl, as if recognising an enemy. 'Beautiful animals, really, when you can meet them like this,' the First Officer continued, then added rather defensively, 'People should recognise that if they were not preserved for hunting, and the farming community did not adhere to a closed season, there would be very few foxes left in the countryside, for they'd all be either shot or poisoned by the farmers.' Pufelli was plainly in no mood to accept this familiar argument and uttered a muted growl which, as soon as the First Officer had left on his tour of inspection, was quickly replaced by the constant wagging of her tail.

At Port Said I was able to vary the foxes' rather monotonous diet of minced horsemeat and dog biscuits. There, in the ship's lounge, a magnificent conjuring show was staged by one of the famous 'gully-gully' men; and it was astonishing to see how the magician could produce day-old chicks out of an old man's beard, out of a pack of cards, and even out of a young lady's blouse. The cabaret was excellent, but the chicks looked exhausted as they hung limply from the conjurer's hands at the finale. So immediately after the show I approached the magician and offered to buy his chicks. He assured me that there was no meat on them – 'absolutely none at all', and then, 'You buy postcards of naked ladies?' He ferreted in a leather bag and produced some cards depicting some most un-ladylike poses. I made it clear to him that I only wanted to buy the now almost dead chicks, and in exasperation he named a price for the half dozen stringy, breathless birds. In view of the foxes' supper that night, they no doubt saw in Port Said a real gourmet's paradise.

After the Suez Canal, the orange glow of the dawn would appear slowly on the horizon over the Red Sea. I would clean out the foxes and exercise Pufelli along the passenger decks, much to the envy of the poor dogs who were always confined to their kennels. In the evenings, flying fish would appear, dancing tirelessly in the ship's wake. The temperature rose rapidly and became almost unendurable, although the top aft deck – cooled by the wind of the ship's movement – became the most comfortable and relaxing place for me. I frequently took refuge among the animals, getting to know the dogs and filling up their water dishes as required. As the liner ploughed through the Gulf of Aden and southwards past the arid coast of the Somali Republic, the blinding whiteness of the sandy shore contrasted splendidly with the sapphire blue of the Indian Ocean.

At Mombasa I left the ship as I wanted to see something of the East

African game reserves before going south to start my animal-collecting. I had meant the foxes to stay on board until the ship docked at Durban, where the Pretoria Zoo would have collected them, but as they were both feeling the heat rather badly, I got permission from the local veterinary authorities to take them ashore, and arranged for them to be flown to South Africa. This was a sad farewell, particularly to Pufelli, and I felt personally responsible for their future. I also arranged for the greater part of my baggage to remain on the ship to be off-loaded at Beira in Portuguese East Africa (Mozambique), thence to be railed up to Salisbury where I would arrange for it to be collected.

Before my arrival in Kenya it had been raining almost continuously for weeks, and the air was full of the intoxicating warm earthy smell of the start of the African wet season. The heavy rains had caused the Tana River to overflow, isolating a number of tribes, extensively destroying crops, and cutting communications by road and rail. A State of Emergency had been declared in parts of Kenya, though the possible effect of this on my plans did not occur to me as I breakfasted on the veranda of the small Moorings Hotel. There were African Pied crows, a dazzle of black and white as they quarrelled over worms and the remnants of my breakfast; there were countless smartly marked lizards, one moment utterly motionless, the next dashing like lightning across the polished floor of the veranda, whenever the hotel's Jack Russell terrier appeared. On my second evening a Cream-faced Tropical African hedgehog found its way into my bedroom and under my mosquito net, digging its quills in as though seeking the intimacy of my company and wanting to be the first member of my animal collection.

Before I took the night train up to Nairobi I spent a few days walking under the palm trees, the wet red soil dyeing my shoes. Smiling barefooted Africans passed by with their friendly 'Jambo' greeting, while the warm rain continued to leak from the storm-filled clouds and frogs chorused from the overflowing gutters. Africa had drawn me back, the continent where I felt I belonged. The colour and history of the place were all about me. Fort Jesus, built by the Portuguese, the scene of bloody battles in the past, later used as a prison by the British, now a museum, its ancient cannons still commanding the old harbour; picturesque dhows bringing in their cargoes of dates, salt, spices; the streets crowded and jostling with Indians, Africans and Europeans. The Mombasa

Club still stood there, a monument to colonialism, with its highly polished floors, its servants moving like silent cats and its selection of English sporting and country life periodicals neatly set out on a long refectory table, all pleasantly cooled by a big revolving fan. If only the walls of this part of Colonial history could talk of the many people, from so many different worlds who had met here over so many lifetimes.

When I got to Nairobi they told me that the heavy rains had necessitated the closing of Nairobi National Park. While I decided on my best route to Southern Rhodesia, I accepted the kind hospitality of the Williams family, who had a coffee farm in the Ruiru district east of Nairobi. Even here conditions were wet and difficult. The nearby river was in spate, and its muddy waters rampaged freely through the vegetation. A colony of Weaver birds finding their beautifully woven nests destroyed and their eggs lost, flew about in agitation. Close to the farmhouse, I saw a tubular roll of bark hanging from the lower branches of a blue gum tree, and I curiously prodded it with a stick. Such a rash action caused the emergence of squadrons of very angry bees, which zoomed after me in the best traditions of Fighter Command. I fled to a nearby coffee bean warehouse. Later I discovered that tubular beehives of this kind were an invention of the Wakambo tribe. Seasoned bark would be rolled up, rather like a brandy snap, packed with leaves of a kind that bees found alluring, then hung under the branch of a tree to attract useful tenants. In this way, some of the farm labourers could rely on cropping the bee's combs of succulent honey as an important nutritional resource.

The barred windows and security fence of the spacious farmhouse that stood among hundreds of acres of coffee, gave it an atmosphere of siege, a hangover from Mau Mau days. A locked armoury was built into a wall, and the dogs had been trained not to allow any African on to the premises unless they were permanent household staff, and even these had to be away before the nightly ritual of locking and double checking the doors took place. But during the daytime the atmosphere was much more relaxed and, when the weather allowed, I saw the coffee beans spread out along strips of matting, line after line of them, drying in the sun, while groups of Africans worked industriously, grading and packing them. So far this productive area had not been affected by the increased activities of the land-freedom army.

I pondered over all the troubles that men constantly create for each other, as well as for the animal kingdom in general. Nature may be raw in tooth and claw, but at least she is spared racial, religious and political hatreds. While in Nairobi I visited an exhibition by the East Africa Wildlife Society. They had taken over a sizeable shop window to display a collection of confiscated animal snares, types of snare that had been banned by the government's humane game laws. The idea behind the exhibition was to educate the local population and to make them see how cruel and barbaric the snares were. Most regrettably, the displays were soon found to be having the opposite effect, for many Africans came to view the various traps in order to update and improve their own snaring techniques; the exhibition had to be hastily brought to a close.

The rains continued and the road south to Arusha was still impassable. I decided to take the night train from Nairobi over the mountains of the Rift Valley, to Kisumu on the north-east corner of Lake Victoria. From Kisumu I booked a passage on the MV *Victoria* to take me around the north of the lake by Entebbe, southwards on the Uganda side via Bukoba to Mwanza in Tanganyika (Tanzania). It was here, just over a hundred years before on an early morning in 1858, that John Henning Speke became the first white man to set eyes on this immense stretch of inland water, the world's second largest lake, and later to name it after his sovereign. At Mwanza I visited the Game Department and met the Department's Director, Peter Achard who, on hearing that I was connected in some way or another with Gerald Durrell, kindly invited me to his home for a 'sundowner'.

Over dinner, Peter Achard told me how he had recently trapped an adult leopard on the shores of Lake Victoria, where it had been a nuisance, killing a number of domestic dogs that had been with their human masters as they picnicked at the lakeside. Because the baboon population had increased considerably in the nearby Serengeti National Park to the north-east of Mwanza, Peter had decided to put the trapped leopard on the back of his pick-up vehicle and release it in the National Park to reduce the number of baboons. However, when released, the leopard, instead of it fleeing from the rear of the truck, rushed round to the front of the vehicle and sprang on to the bonnet trying to attack the man who had made it suffer such an indignity. One can only admire the self-assurance of such an animal, when confronted by what it might consider insurmountable odds.

During my voyage on the MV *Victoria* I met an RSPCA inspector who was travelling with his Volkswagen Combo, which was filled with RSPCA educational material and film projector equipment. When we arrived at Mwanza, he invited me to come with him the following evening to an African Teachers' Training College south of the township. After he had presented his excellent talk on the avoidance of animal suffering, he showed an RSPCA film entitled *The Wildlife of Scotland*. The audience appeared spellbound in viewing animals that they had never seen before, but the silence was broken by exuberant chattering as soon as they saw the wholesome body of a highland Red deer appearing so close on the screen in front of them. The hunting instinct was quick to manifest itself, and the male students appeared to reach for their bows or spears to kill the stag for its bounty of fresh meat. Perhaps this was not the most useful film to show the students, and something featuring East Africa's wildlife would have been more appropriate.

From Mwanza, I travelled south by overcrowded African trains, buses and lorries by way of Tabora, Itigi and Mbeya, then over the border to Northern Rhodesia and by way of Ndola to Lusaka. While spending a night at a hotel in Ndola, and re-acquainting myself with a pint of Rhodesia Breweries Castle lager, I got into conversation with one of the locals. When he heard that I had once been in the Federal regular army of Rhodesia and Nyasaland he was quick to introduce me to another man who, after he had bought me several more drinks, sought to recruit me for a very large sum as a mercenary to fight in the nearby civil war in the Congo. The Belgian Government had given Independence to the Congo on 30th June 1960, and the forces of President Tshombe of Katanga (Shaba) Province were currently in fierce conflict with Patrice Lumumba's *Force Publique*. The Kasai Liberation Army, with the help of the warlike Baluba tribesmen, was fighting the Lumumbists, who had committed many atrocities in the Kasai region, and it was hoped that with the help of additional mercenaries that Tshombe's forces would win the day.

I listened politely to all this, with its 'Call to Arms' propaganda, but it did not take long for the purchaser of my beers to realise that the last thing I wanted to be was a 'Soldier of Fortune'. To lay down my life in some tribal dispute, no doubt funded from outside the country, in a conflict over the mineral rights of the Congo, was definitely not the type of adventure I was seeking. If I was going to fight for anything, it would be for the survival of the various endangered species that I had already met in the animal kingdom.

Fourteen months later, in March 1963 in Jersey, I was introduced to John Roberts the author of *My Congo Adventure*. John had been an acting commandant in the Kasai Liberation Army, at much the same time as my visit to Ndola, and had been responsible for some 2,500 Baluba tribesmen, surviving many bloody skirmishes with Lumumba's army, before his capture by the United Nations forces and imprisonment in the Congo. Commissioned during his National Service in the British Army, serving in the Northern Rhodesia Colonial Police, and always smitten by the spirit of adventure, John Roberts appeared to me to personify the typical 'Soldier of Fortune' who had at least been fortunate to have escaped such enthusiasms with his life.

In Lusaka, I met up again with the Vaughan-Jones family, as well as revisiting the Northern Rhodesia Regiment barracks opposite Government House. A pair of Crested cranes was still 'present and correct' in the paddock behind the Adjutant's office, although nobody was able to tell me whether they were the same pair that were there in October 1956. I saw the Adjutant in the hope that the regiment had a vehicle travelling south to Salisbury. My luck was in. A seven-ton Bedford truck was leaving that very evening and, as I was an ex-regular, the NRR Captain gave me permission to travel in it.

A light evening breeze cooled the Bedford's cab as we descended to Chirundu where the one-span suspension bridge crosses the Zambezi River between Northern and Southern Rhodesia (Zambia and Zimbabwe). A chorus of amphibians seemed to pipe us on to the bridge and night-jars flew up as though from under the earth. With the vehicle's windows closed we were shielded from the multitude of mosquitoes that Chirundu was so well known for. As we motored on the single-strip road through the Zambezi escarpment, past the ghost-like silhouettes of the massive baobab trees, I remembered with nostalgia my carefree Lambretta scooter journeys along the same route, to and from Lusaka, four and five years previously.

As we drove through the night south to Karoi and Sinoia, the Staff Sergeant gave me a first-hand account of the sad story regarding the future of the Central African Federation, and the apparently gloomy prospects for the people of all races in the three territories concerned. I was dropped in the heart of Salisbury at the old Meikles Hotel, where I took a room, shaved and breakfasted, and then hired a vehicle to take me out to the Mazoe/Glendale area of Southern Rhodesia, where I had been invited by some former farming friends to establish my base. Major Robin Falla and his delightful wife Pris lived in a sprawling farmhouse at the top of a small kopje, with commanding views over the surrounding countryside, which included land for both cattle-ranching and tobacco farming.

In 1956, Jay Duncan, my great Staff Corps friend and I had been godfathers to the Fallas' daughter Roselle. Robin had served in the Jersey Militia before the Second World War, and then went with the Royal Hampshires to India, where he spent most of the war. With the last assignment cut short by the granting of India's Independence in 1947, Robin returned to Jersey to a family farm. I first met Robin and his new wife Pris in early 1956, just before they had decided to emigrate to Southern Rhodesia to buy a tobacco farm. Before I was allowed to enter the farmhouse, Robin enthusiastically led me down to his tobacco barns. It turned out that one of the four barns was not being used, and he told me I could take this over as my headquarters. He was happy for me to house any animals, providing I did not let any of them escape and frighten his workers. The other three red-brick barns were in full tobacco-curing operation. From the outside these tall buildings looked faintly ecclesiastical, but inside, a mass of horizontal blue gum poles were festooned with pallid yellow tobacco leaves, extending upwards layer above layer to the cathedral height of the barns, resembling the jaundice-coloured thatch of a Cotswold cottage. An exterior coal-fired furnace provided the heat for the flues in each barn and, as the curing process progressed, the humid tobacco odour that filled the inside of the barns became quite suffocating, especially to a non-smoker.

Soon after my arrival at Douet Farm, I contacted the Director of the National Zoological Gardens of South Africa, Dr Frank Brand, who informed me that Pufelli and her mate Reynard had arrived at the Pretoria Zoo in good condition, their integration had been a success, and that they had now settled down well into their new enclosure. I was relieved to learn this, for having to part with any animal wards in the way I had done in Mombasa always represented a degree of emotional wrench. Also, it was good to hear from Robin that my luggage, including the tape-recorder, live-traps and mist nets had arrived safely, and were now waiting to be collected from the Customs & Excise warehouse in Salisbury.

Robin was a tall hefty man with deep-set eyes and a jovial tanned face. As he strode around the farmhouse's *stoep* or veranda he reminded me of a silver-back gorilla, at any moment about to beat his chest in a fine display of anthropoid superiority. As the sundowners of whisky were produced, and the evening breeze leaked through the insect screens that protected us from the countless insects, a kitten ran out from under the sofa, leapt into the air, pounced upon a disembowelled slipper that was lying beside me, and started to savage it murderously. Ordinary kittenish behaviour, you might think; but this was no ordinary kitten. It was a young Serval cat that had been found orphaned and alone on the farm a month or so earlier. Soon she dropped the slipper to study me: her long ears flicked with curiosity as she watched every movement I made with the utmost suspicion. I held out my clenched hand invitingly, but she ignored it and returned to finish off the lacerated slipper. Her attractive yellow-golden coat, marked with irregular brown to black spots, her short tail swishing with enthusiasm as she concluded her slipper-kill, so well portrayed the predator-prey relationship.

'Well, what's going to be your first animal-collecting venture?' asked Robin, in the smart regimental manner of a senior officer addressing a subaltern. I took another gulp of whisky to gain a few seconds to come up with some type of respectable response as to a proposed strategy. I could hardly answer truthfully and say I would take any animal that came the way of my live-traps or a mist-net. Robin came to my rescue with a list of suggestions, which he fired off with the rapidity of a machine-gun: 'Serval cat, caracal, jackal, Hunting dog, civet, genet, mongoose, porcupine, Wild pig, baboon, even leopard – there's lots of that type of stuff around the farm and hiding in nearby kopjes. You should be able to pick them up pretty easily.' As my whisky glass was refuelled and we clinked them together to toast my future success, I conjured up increased confidence by reflecting that if these animals were so numerous locally, I was not after all going to be embarrassed by being the keeper of an empty tobacco barn.

Just when I was about to say goodnight and retire unsteadily to my room, Robin stood in front of the log fire and, with the smile of a stage director about to introduce the final act of a murder mystery, asked the African house boy to let in the farm's mascot. I cringed with apprehension: my head was swimming, and my legs were smarting from their previous exposures to the Serval kitten. What type of animal was I going to have to defend myself against now? I looked around for an escape route; but at that moment the door crashed open and 77 kg (170 lb) of African Bush pig rocketed into the room. This was Porky, a formidable mascot indeed: bulky, covered with coarse wiry red-brown bristles, with long white hairs on his face and tufted ears. He stood downwind of me; backed a little, as though to break cover before charging; then trotted forward in all gentleness to sniff my hand, his eyes bright and friendly. His upturned mouth reminded me of Juanita back at Jersey, and he exuded a similar degree of charisma. I was able to relax and breathe again.

So Robin and I drank some more whisky, naming countless animals that were sure to fall prey to my traps and nets, and thereby become valuable members of my forthcoming collection. We left Porky snoring under the table that he had previously almost upturned by using its central support as a scratching block, and with the aid of a paraffin lamp – there was no electricity – Robin guided me down a white-washed corridor to my room. The Serval kitten followed me, to fight my shoe-laces at every step I made; only giving up such a jolly game when she became terrified by the hissing of a just-extinguished lamp. I collapsed on to the bed as if the curtain had just come down on an African pantomime. My sleep that night was interlaced by a series of night-marish dreams, each one involving the escape of an animal and ending with my disappearance over the horizon in pursuit.

Among the mail waiting for me at the Fallas was a most welcome letter from the Kays, from their base camp on the banks of the Thamalakane River, in the Okavango Delta near Maun, in the British Protectorate of Bechuanaland (Botswana). The letter invited me to accompany them and their two pet lions, Chinky and Timmy, with their amphibious DUKW to the northern region of the Okavango Swamps.

And, if I so wished, they would be happy to help me organise a collection of the smaller mammal, bird and reptile species that were so prolific in this isolated region. June Kay also mentioned that with her first book *Okavango* having just been published with Gerald Durrell's foreword, she had written to him to see whether the Jersey Zoo would be willing to accept the Kays' three-and-a-half-year-old pet lioness Chinky. The removal of Chinky from the Okavango was now necessary as the local tribal authorities, the Batawana, had refused to allow the Kays to release the lioness back into the wild as Joy Adamson had recently done with Elsa in Kenya.

The letter went on to say that, if Gerald Durrell agreed, I could take Chinky back with me to Jersey, with any other animals that I managed to collect during my stay with them. Although a sub-adult lioness had certainly not been on the list as a potential member of my collection, I was excited about the potential of undertaking a second collection in the Okavango. I was anxious to respond to the Kays' letter as soon as possible, so Robin drove me in his old Land Rover to the Glendale post office, where I sent them a telegram accepting their invitation. I said how very much I looked forward to joining them, and their two lions, and particularly the opportunity of an animal-collecting trip in such a remote region of Southern Africa. I added that I should be in a position to join them at their base camp near Maun by mid-December.

With such a change of plan, I started to consider the best way to spend the next six weeks of my time in Southern Rhodesia. Robin had told me that quite a number of farmers were custodians of a variety of bush orphans, so we decided to make it known that I would be interested to hear about any wildlife orphans that they might have. I could also test my live-traps and mist-nets in the immediate area and see what they might catch. But before this, I decided to satisfy my increasing interest in monkeys and to take my collecting equipment to the Vumba Mountains, in the south-eastern corner of the country. This region of Southern Rhodesia is the home of the attractive Stairs' or Mozambique monkey, a close relative of the Sykes' monkey, a pair of which we had received in Jersey just before I left for Africa.

In Salisbury I purchased a second-hand ¾-ton Vanguard pick-up vehicle; cleared my traps and other equipment from the Customs & Excise, and took the opportunity to visit the Game and Veterinary

Departments, in order to get their approval for the type of animal-collecting that I was about to embark upon. My letter of introduction from Gerald Durrell seemed to work like magic, for both Departments provided me with an immediate *carte blanche*. When passing through the south-eastern town of Umtali (Matare), I took the opportunity to visit its small museum, which I had been told possessed a single live Stairs' monkey. When I saw this species for the first time I was immediately attracted to it, and hoped that I could acquire a pair for my Rhodesian collection. The dense hairs of its black coat were flecked with yellow, the hairs on its head and shoulders being slightly darker; its large rufous-tinged tail measured approximately half its body length. Perhaps its most attractive features were its pronounced pale brow, whitish chin, and the long hair of its cheeks that formed impressive side-whiskers.

Unfortunately, the monkey was the personal pet of the museum's Curator, a Captain Boathby, who could not be persuaded to sell it. He did tell me that as he was a fan of Gerald Durrell and if he hadn't been so attached to the monkey, he would have been delighted to have presented it to the Jersey Zoo. I thanked him for such a sentiment, and became increasingly determined to secure some individuals of this most impressive member of the guenon family.

The route through the attractive township of Umtali took me along avenues lined with blazing flamboyant blossoms, resplendent with the pinks and yellows of the aloes. The tarmac road soon gave way to 32 km (c.20 miles) or so of an impacted earthen track which wound its way up into the Vumba Mountains. As the vehicle climbed higher a thick mist or guti came rolling down, reducing visibility to ten metres (c. ten yards) or so; thick vegetation flanked the road, sometimes meeting overhead to form a tunnel, and then clearing suddenly to reveal precipitous valleys eastward to the dramatic range of the Chimanimani mountains in Portuguese East Africa. At intervals, crystalline streams tumbled down the mountainside, flanked by abundant forest ferns and lush tangles of vegetation. Laughing doves and touracos were the dominant representatives of a profusion of bird life, swooping to and fro through the spray.

I was heading for the famous Leopard's Rock Hotel, which had been built by Italian prisoners of war in the early 1940s, but as I had been preoccupied with an over-heated engine, I missed two turnings and found myself at the end of a cul-de-sac. Here a notice on a gate that told me I had arrived at the residence of Lt-Col H.G. Seward. Leaving the engine to cool off I knocked at the front door, which was opened by the Colonel himself. After asking for directions to the hotel, I mentioned that I was keen to catch some live Stairs' monkeys. Whereupon he exclaimed, 'Damn things – I shot a couple raiding my orchard a few months back.' He disappeared and returned with two monkey skins, which had not been properly cured and emitted an unpleasant pungent smell. The Colonel's wife then joined him, and he went on to say, 'I wanted to use them as rugs or to spread them over the backs of chairs, but my good wife won't have it and she has relegated them to the attic. I remembered Dr Osman Hill's interest in this type of primate material and mentioned this to the Sewards. Before the Colonel could protest, his wife offered me the larger of the two skins and told her husband that he could keep the smaller in the attic. I thanked them for the gift, hastily took my leave before any change of mind could take place, and continued on to the Leopard's Rock Hotel.

The turreted hotel stood at the base of a steep, misty mountainside. The atmosphere was as dramatic as a castle in the Scottish Highlands. The building appeared empty, for November was out of the Rhodesian tourist season, and I ate alone in the vast dining room, watched by numerous smartly dressed African staff, while I tossed around in my mind the best way to catch some Stairs' monkeys. Back at Glendale, I had managed to secure from a veterinary surgeon a number of Nembutal sleeping pills. The vet told me that, if one estimated the weight of an adult male monkey at 14–17 kg (30–38 lb), all I would have to do would be to poke a capsule into a few bananas and disperse these among other bananas (to avoid an individual monkey taking more than one and having an overdose). The vet said that once a monkey swallowed a capsule it would become immobilised and therefore, providing I could locate one of the monkeys' feeding places, it should be easy to catch some.

I couldn't wait to get started, and the following morning I rose at dawn and ventured out into the mist, prompting some African Pied crows to squawk their astonishment at seeing a human being at this particular time of day. The path wound its way upward through the thick damp vegetation of the mountainside. I disturbed a number of

Swynnerton's Red squirrel, which dashed nervously around in the upper branches of the trees, their bushy tails flicking, uttering their 'chuck-chuck-chuck' calls of alarm. As I climbed higher, and the sunrise started to melt the early mist that had capped the nearby mountain tops, a troop of Black-faced Vervet monkeys crashed through the thin twigs of the vegetation, scattering showers of water from the leaves. Birds were everywhere, singing their matins like cathedral choristers in the warming rays of the rising sun. But there was no sign of the Stairs' monkey; only the chattering of the ubiquitous vervets.

After some three hours of climbing and becoming quite soaked, I wearily retraced my tracks down to the hotel. When I told one of the hotel directors of my disappointment and failure, he informed me that if I wanted to see these thieving monkeys, all I had to do was visit the dustbin area behind the hotel in mid-morning. Each day a family group of Stairs' monkey came down the mountain to scavenge here, and all I had to do was to set my two larger live-traps and scatter about a few drugged bananas.

Over the next five days I did everything that I could think of to outwit my quarry, but it was I who ended up outwitted. It was almost as if the family troop of Stairs' monkeys had been told of my kidnap plan, for they started to avoid me. Through my binoculars I would see a monkey pick up a drugged banana, but as soon as it came across the capsule it would spit it out; and if one of the wire traps had been prematurely sprung as a monkey jumped on top of it, the incident so startled the rest of the troop that the traps were thereafter viewed with suspicion and given the widest of berths.

During my stay at the Leopard's Rock Hotel I washed the monkey skin that the Sewards had given me several times. I also dusted it liberally with talcum powder and added a sprinkling of after-shave lotion, in the hope that the post office in Umtali would not smell anything too distasteful and refuse to accept the package for airmail to London. I had labelled it 'scientific material', and when I saw the look of suspicion on the postal worker's face, I told her that the particular primate skin enclosed was of the greatest importance for the advance of scientific knowledge. I elaborated; the skin, and its origin in the Vumba Mountains, would be described by one of the world's leading primatologists in his important series of monographs on the comparative anatomy and taxonomy of primates. She handled it with the care due to a national treasure. This skin of the Stairs' monkey *Cercopithecus albogularis erythrarchus* (this subspecies is now considered to be a variant of the Blue monkey *Cercopithecus mitis*), and some of the ecological observations that I had made in the Vumba Mountains, were subsequently recorded in W.C. Osman Hill's Vol. VI of his primate monograph.

Although my animal-collecting activities had ended in failure, the lush paradise of the Vumba Mountains was some of the most impressive and dramatic scenery that I had seen to date, so my time in Rhodesia's south-eastern districts had been, after all, a worthwhile adventure. When I arrived back at Douet Farm I told Robin and Pris of my disappointment in coming back empty-handed, although I added how well compensated I had been by seeing such a magnificent variety of scenery, and by being able to record so many fascinating observations about the wildlife diversity of the Vumba Mountains.

Chapter Six

JACKALS, SERVALS
AND HUNTING DOGS

At Dout Farm I employed an African helper, who had told Robin that he was a carpenter who could construct whatever travelling cages I required. His artisan's credentials were underlined by the fact that his name was John Carpenter. On a visit into Salisbury, I went to the Victoria Museum where I met the Director of the Rhodesia Museums, Reay Smithers, and his deputy, Dr Bob Brain. Reay Smithers had a size-able collection of waterfowl which I would be welcome to visit, while Bob Brain was studying the social behaviour of a family group of Vervet monkeys at his home, which he would be happy for me to see.

By good fortune, my visit to the museum coincided with that of a farmer delivering a live pair of Black-backed jackal, which he had trapped after they had killed some of his poultry. The museum already had a number of skins, and a mounted specimen, of this quite common jackal species, so Reay Smithers said that they would be delighted to present the pair to me providing I took the animals off their hands within a week. Without my either setting a trap or erecting a net, my Rhodesia collection had at last started.

Meanwhile, back at Glendale I had been contacted by a local farmer who had found a cat-like animal living in an old porcupine hole near his house. I promised to investigate. At a local farmers' co-operative store, I purchased building material; a variety of timber, weld-mesh, wire-netting, screws, hessian and binding wire. We had to construct a pen for the pair of jackals, as well as some secure travelling boxes for whatever animal that might flee from the porcupine hole. Once these tasks were completed, John and I loaded the pick-up with nets, spades and a pickaxe, and drove out along the twisting strip-roads through the rich tobacco lands of the European farmers. The waters of the Mazoe River were red and turbulent, six weeks into the rainy season. A pair

71

of Hammer-headed storks (Hammerkop) flew up from the riverbank to their big ramshackle nest of twigs. As we approached the farm, I felt a sense of occasion. There had been much talk about collecting animals, much preparation; now I was about to start catching one.

The farmer showed us the two old porcupine holes; clouds of midges hovered about them. In order to look as if I knew what I was doing, I rapped out a few business-like orders to John. We assembled and secured the nylon fishing nets over both holes, and I told John to cut a long flexible branch off a nearby tree, so that I could prod around the larger of the holes in the hope that any occupant would try to escape from the rear entrance. We heard a series of spits and angry hisses, and within seconds of this contact a clawing and spitting feline ended up tangled and fighting in the net that we had staked out over the smaller of the two holes. Eureka! – I had secured my first trophy. Even the farmer looked impressed.

My capture was a small African Wild cat, a creature not unlike the Wild cat of Scotland, with tabby markings on its light orange-yellow coat, black rings round its legs, and a tail shorter than that of a domestic cat. While the cat continued hissing and spitting furiously at us, I wrapped a further net around its clawing and biting form, and carried our prize to a nearby barn. Here we managed to untangle it into a large wooden crate, which had been furnished with a mound of wood-wool for it to hide in. Back at Douet Farm, Robin could not wait to ask me what we had managed to catch. He rashly peered through the wire mesh that provided ventilation for the crate, and almost fell backward when the enraged wild cat launched itself at the mesh, spitting and clawing its displeasure.

The next few days were devoted to preparing the accommodation for the jackals from the Salisbury museum. Although it soon proved that John's carpentry skills were as poor as my own, we did manage to wire off a section of the tobacco barn for the jackals, which included covering the floor with weld-mesh to prevent them from digging their way out. I was contacted by a newspaper reporter who had heard about my animal-collecting activities, and that I worked for the famous author, Gerald Durrell. I agreed to be interviewed by him before I picked up the jackals from the museum. When I met the young reporter I found to my considerable alarm that he had already jotted down a heading to the article: 'Ex-Rhodesia and Nyasaland Regular Soldier Turns Big-Game Hunter – "Bring 'em Back Alive".' I tried my utmost to persuade him to write about the conservation objectives of Durrell's Jersey Zoo, to mention the importance of captive-breeding programmes, the study of animals in both the wild and in captivity, and the importance of conserving Rhodesia's natural heritage. Regrettably, he was only interested in recording any amusing tale I may have about Gerald Durrell, the thrills and dangers of my quest, and any thoughts I may have about the lioness that I was to collect from the Okavango.

On the journey back to Glendale, just as we were approaching a small African settlement with its round, thatch-plumed mud huts, we hit a hen and killed it. The vehicle was almost immediately surrounded by a small crowd of aggrieved Africans. The group had assembled as quickly as if one of them had thrown the hen at the truck in order for them to protest about its death. An ugly scene appeared to be in the making. As the crowd got louder in their demands for compensation, I picked up the hen's carcass, handed it to the most vociferous of the men, and at the same time slapped the side of the jackals' wooden crates. This produced an eruption of fearsome noises and wild barking, and the crowd scattered as quickly as it had formed. I pressed a ten shilling note (50 pence) into the hand of a wizened old lady, who had been slower to retreat than the others, and was quick to drive away.

Once released from their cramped crates, the jackals didn't take long to settle down into their new quarters, and to bury themselves in the sizeable bundle of freshly cut reeds. They viewed the African Wild cat (which we had named Romeo), in its small den at the far end of the barn, with suspicious curiosity. Things were certainly moving: it was only the second week of my arrival in the country, and I had already acquired a pair of Black-backed jackal and an African Wild cat. Now I was almost beginning to believe in my assumed character as a professional animal collector, though this newly found confidence was soon to evaporate. After the article about me was published in the *Rhodesia Herald* I was asked to give a talk to the monthly meeting of the Glendale Farmers' Country Club. I had never given a talk in public and I started to be almost overwhelmed by apprehension. The date the after-dinner talk drew ever nearer, and my thoughts on the structure of the presentation became more and more muddled. If, without loosing face, I

73

could have got out of it I would have done so. I even contemplated feigning some tropical illness.

It was at this time that I decided to deploy some of my tunnel-shaped wire traps among the great granite boulders resting amid a nearby kopje, close to a tributary of the Mazoe River. I carefully placed the traps among the crevices and in addition to hanging a small piece of choice meat on the hook above the seesaw metal platform in the middle of each trap, I balanced a raw egg. When an intruder touches the platform a spring mechanism is released which simultaneously closes both entrances. I set three traps just before sunset on three consecutive evenings, but caught nothing. It was only after Robin suggested that I covered the floor of the traps with earth, and smeared their two entrances with some cow dung, that I had success. In the course of the next five days I caught four Slender mongoose; when I approached, they uttered a series of alarming-sounding growls, biting the side of the traps and emitted an unattractive musky odour. This agile stoat-like member of the family Viverridae has a rufous-brown wiry coat, and a long, conspicuously black-tipped tail. The species is particularly well-designed to prey upon small rodents, birds and their eggs, snakes, lizards, insects, wild fruits and berries.

Robin had accepted on my behalf a couple of African goshawks for the collection, 'They belong to a farmer who has hand-reared them from a nest that had been deserted by the parents. And another farmer has phoned; he saw the article about you in the paper and wants to know whether you would be interested in buying a female Cape (African) Hunting dog from him. I decided not to accept this until I had talked to you first. I told him that you would return his call tomorrow morning.' As I knew that Edinburgh Zoo was interested in acquiring Cape Hunting dogs, the following morning I accepted the farmer's offer. Two days later John and I, armed with nylon nets and one of the jackal crates, drove to a farm to the north of Que Que, bordering the Zambezi escarpment. As the Vauxhall pick-up spluttered its way along a dirt road, flanked by sparsely covered bush, we passed an old silver mine that had been last worked in the 1920s. We overtook an occasional pair of Africans, the man walking in front carrying a stout stick, the wife following some ten yards behind, a sizeable load balanced magnificently on her head, and, more often than not, a baby strapped securely to her back.

At the farmstead an Afrikaner farmer greeted me somewhat gruffly and thrust a bottle of Castle lager into my hand. He then immediately told me that the African who normally looked after the Hunting dog had not turned up, as he had probably drunk too much village beer on the previous evening. He then curtly continued: 'So if you want to take the Hunting dog, give me £10 for it, and you'll have to catch it up yourself'. He went on to tell me about the damage done by Hunting dogs in his area; that in the previous year they had accounted for the death of nearly eighty head of cattle. As a consequence, a farmer was allowed to kill any of this vermin (today classified as an endangered species!) and even realise some income, for the government offered a bounty of £10 for every tail handed in. The farmer had kept this female as a sexual lure. Each time she came into season she would be confined to a cage and hoisted into a tree. A poisoned heifer carcass laid below would kill all the male dogs that arrived in response to her calls.

After sharing such a horrific story with me, the farmer led the way to where the unfortunate Hunting dog was being kept, which was almost as depressing as the reason for her having been kept in the first place. She was in a pit-like trench, covered over with rusty chain-link and with a barbed wire entrance. Old bones and bits of skin were scattered over the earthen floor, while mounds of faeces in each corner swarmed with blowflies. It was sad to see a creature imprisoned in such an awful environment. As I started to talk to the Hunting dog she crouched, her black ears flickered, and she ran from one end of her trench to the other. She obviously expected to be caged and hoisted into the tree again. While I was trying to decide upon the safest way to extract the dog from its horrible quarters, the farmer said, 'I see that you have some nets in the back of your truck, so why don't you net her?' My heart sank at the prospect, but as I did not want to come back to Glendale empty-handed again, or to show my nervousness to the farmer or to John, I replied cheerfully, 'Of course; what a good idea.'

I tried to look as much like a professional animal-hunter as possible. I folded the net to create a sort of tunnel or bag and tied it at one end, so that if the animal could be persuaded to enter the mouth, I would be able to manoeuvre it to the closed end. The farmer yawned and appeared to be unimpressed by my resourcefulness, and he watched indifferently as I unwound the wire fastenings to the entrance of the

75

pit. I waited until the animal was at the far end of the trench before I dropped in. As I stood on the earthen ground under the roof's wire netting, armed only with a nylon fishing net, the bitch glared at me through her inflamed red eyes and watched my every movement. It was difficult to tell which one of us was the more terrified.

As the farmer was no doubt expecting immediate action, I worked my way along the narrow trench. I held the mouth of my net as open as I could, but even so it kept catching the debris on the ground as I advanced. The dog backed into the corner as far as she could go, then, choosing her moment, sprang forward. I swung the net in her direction, but unsuccessfully; although she became briefly entangled she brushed past me and ran to the other end of the trench – the end that I had just come from. Previously at the Jersey Zoo, whenever I had needed to catch up an animal in a confined space, I had made a practice of talking constantly to it. This at least bolstered my own confidence, but perhaps also helped to calm the animal. After reassembling the net and talking quietly to the bitch, telling her what a beautiful dog she was and that I had to come to save her from certain death, I crept back along the trench to challenge her again with the open mouth of the net. She faced me panting, with her red tongue hanging out, white teeth gleaming, and when I came within four feet of her she launched her brown and yellow mottled body at me. More in blind self-protection than in good judgment, I flung myself to the side of the trench and, like a matador with his cape, swung the mouth of the net in line with her attack. By great good fortune I managed to entangle the dog beyond the possibility of escape.

John was grinning broadly as he helped me out of the pit with my bundle of dog, and even the Afrikaans farmer appeared to have enjoyed the performance, although perhaps he would have preferred a more dramatic conclusion. We managed to untangle the net and transfer the dog into the jackal crate, I gave the farmer his money, and we drove back to Douet Farm triumphantly. I felt quite surprised with the success of my Hunting dog encounter. Back at the farm, we put the open crate in a sectioned-off wired-in area of the barn, at the opposite end to the jackals' pen, and adjacent to Romeo, leaving a generous dish of fresh meat and a bowl of clean water. It was sundowner time, and Robin, Pris and I and toasted the collection's new star. Some of my high spirits were alas diminished when Robin reminded me that this was the weekend for my talk to the Glendale Farmers' Club.

Saturday evening arrived and the sun appeared to set with sombre haste. I was introduced to the audience as if I were Gerald Durrell's prodigal son. After hastily downing a pint of Castle lager, I launched myself into the talk much as a cabaret artist would begin his act. At times I found myself getting out of my depth in subject matter and had to change the topic hurriedly, and no doubt flitted from one topic to another: the economic use of ungulate fauna outside game reserves; the destructive herd formation of domestic cattle; the social life of marmosets in captivity; the pros and cons of game eradication as a means of tsetse-fly control. Although my talk was disjointed, I somehow managed to keep going, relating as many stories about Gerald Durrell as I could recall.

When question time came, I was let off lightly. Although a middle-aged schoolteacher, well versed in the ways of birds and bees, commented that as I currently only had a female Cape Hunting dog to send back to the UK, what chance was there for it ever to reproduce? I responded that I planned to advertise for a mate, quickly adding: 'But not for me, for the Hunting dog' – a comment that at least was rewarded by a ripple of laughter. Then to my delight, and what made the evening worthwhile, a slim weather-beaten farmer in the second row said, 'Would you be interested in a pair of Serval cats?' I gulped. 'More than words can express!' What an offer! It was like asking a shipwrecked sailor if he'd be interested in meeting a flaxen-haired beauty.

The following morning I went over to the tobacco barn early to find John tending the animals. His cheerful grin soon disappeared when I told him about the newly expected arrivals – two bigger versions of Romeo. By midday, I returned to Douet Farm with the two African Goshawks that Robin had accepted, and left them in their two large wooden crates on trestles outside the barn, for I knew that they would not feel at ease in close proximity to the jackals, Hunting dog, Wild cat and Slender mongooses. I then set off to Combe Farm, to the north-west of the small farming centre of Banket. I could hardly get there quickly enough in my eagerness to secure the pair of Serval cats, for fear of the offer being withdrawn.

Mr Shattock invited me into his farmhouse with the usual Rhodesian

77

hospitality, and over a cup of china tea he told me how the orphaned servals had been found on his farm during the previous year. He and his wife had reared them indoors until they had become too boisterous with the children. They had tried to release them back into the wild, but the cats were used to humans and kept returning to the farmhouse. The male, Teja, ('beware' in the Biyla language) had proved too trusting and had almost been killed by a local villager's dogs. We went to the overgrown tennis court where they were kept; as soon as Teja saw his master he walked over to him, and allowed himself to be picked up and placed in one of my travelling boxes, accompanied by a freshly killed pigeon. The female, Tammy, was not going to be fooled so easily, for although she emerged from the undergrowth and walked over to her mistress, her bright eyes looked inquisitively at Teja's confinement, and it took a lot of coaxing with another freshly shot pigeon to tempt her into the second box.

Although I well knew that these servals had no chance of being successfully returned to the wild, I could not help feeling some compassion for them. For without being too anthropomorphic, the next few weeks would doubtless be incomprehensible for them. Confinement, the stress of air travel, and being put into a totally new environment in the Northern Hemisphere would no doubt represent a similar degree of suffering to that of a young conscript experiencing his first bewildering days at an army training camp.

There were now only ten days to go before this Rhodesian collection was due to be flown to England, and for the various travelling crates to be made to conform to IATA Regulation design for air freight. Sliding metal trays had to be fitted under all of the crate floors; double safety wiring on the doors; small accesses to water bowls; and a series of ventilation holes, covered by protective gauge on the crates outside. While this work was being carried out by John with the help of a local blacksmith, I was contacted by the museum with the great news that they had just been offered a male Cape Hunting dog for £5, and that it would be available for me to collect the following day. This was a stroke of luck, for I knew that Edinburgh Zoo particularly wanted to acquire a pair of this species, and realised that I would be saving another life by accepting it as a mate for the lone female.

When I arrived to collect the male from the museum, he looked a most dejected and frightened creature. John and I brought him back to Douet Farm and manoeuvred his box to the entrance of the female's pen. The bitch immediately started to growl at the newcomer, and when we had almost to tip the box up on end to get the dog out of it, the female immediately flew at him; after a short scuffle, the male cowered in abject submission. Such a skirmish made the jackals run about their pen yelping excitedly, their dorsal hairs standing almost on end, whereas Romeo and the servals retreated to the safety of the reed nests at the rear of their pens.

By this late stage of my stay at Douet farm, the news of my animal-collecting activities had reached the more distant parts of the locality, but unfortunately produced the notion that I was glad to purchase any kind of animal offered. It took some time before I could dissuade the local people from delivering a variety of forlorn looking birds and a selection of sullen looking reptiles. Any unsought animal delivered to me was immediately released among the safety of the bushes and boulders behind the farmhouse. An environment that probably had not had that particular species living in it for many a year, but at least I knew that the animals would now not be eaten by their captors.

I did however feel pity for a wizened old Mdala tribesman, who looked as though he had been journeying for a week or so to meet me, when he produced a 50–cigarette box that contained a small green snake. Not really thinking properly I picked the snake out of the box, and more by chance than skill, just managed to prevent it from biting me by holding it by its neck, before dropping it back into the cigarette box. I firmly closed the lid and put an elastic band around the box. The old man had come a long way with what he was sure would be one of the crown jewels of my collection, so I pressed a £1 note into his hand and he left with a face lit up as contented as a harvest moon. I returned to the farmhouse to consult one of my reference books.

After some searching, to my considerable alarm I identified the snake as a Striped skaapsteker, which is the Afrikaans for a 'sheep killer': a poisonous species. I had broken an elementary rule and handled a snake without first having identified it. I went over to the barn to collect one of the small boxes that I had originally intended for frogs. John offered to help in transferring the snake into this, but hastily changed his mind when I told him that the snake was poisonous and had been known to kill sheep. I returned to the pick-up and opened the glove compartment carefully, only to find the cigarette box open and no sign of the small snake in the compartment. I hurriedly exited the cab and peered in through the windscreen and side windows, searching every corner in sight, but to no avail. Then, as John had approached to see what I was doing in such an alarmed manner, I plucked up courage, opened the driver's door and gingerly lifted the bench seat cover, but still saw no sign of the escapee.

Wearing some thick gloves, and after using a stick to poke around under the seat and elsewhere, I decided that the best thing to do was to leave both the doors open throughout the afternoon and night, in the hope that the snake would vacate the vehicle. I decided not to drive the pick-up for at least 24 hours, and Robin lent me his battered Land Rover, so that I could collect the daily rations of meat for the carnivores and birds of prey, and eggs and vegetables for the mongooses. On my next visit to Salisbury, to finalise the export documentation and to check on the airline requirements for the day of the animals' departure, I couldn't help keeping a wary eye out for the snake; fortunately, it must have made good its opportunity to escape.

During the final few days my wire live-traps had secured two Rock monitors, two chameleons, and some more Slender mongoose; these latter I released. I also collected from a nearby pond a cross-section of 24 amphibians that I knew the Jersey Zoo would be interested in. When the day of departure arrived, I was up by first light and started to catch up or guide the animals into their respective tailor-made travelling crates. Roselle said a tearful goodbye to Romeo whom she had befriended. After all the crates had been loaded, Robin banged on the roof of the cab in farewell. The hired vehicle drove away from the buildings, Pris and Roselle waved from under the shade of a tree, and the jackals raised their heads and howled their lamentations at having to leave the security of their pen in the tobacco barn.

In Salisbury John and I had to wait for the veterinary office to open before the necessary health certificates could be issued. While we waited, a crowd of inquisitive Africans gathered, and it was difficult to stop some of them pulling back the hessian covering the cages to see what was inside; some even tried to climb on to the back of the vehicle to investigate further. The noisier the animals became, the larger the crowd grew, and I was relieved when an African policeman arrived to help control matters. When a European veterinary officer came to inspect the collection and peered into the crates, he narrowly escaped a sharp claw through the wire from Romeo, and a nip from the female Hunting dog. After one of the jackals launched itself at him he decided he had had enough, and issued a comprehensive health certificate forthwith. The export permit from the Game Department was also quickly acquired, for Reay Smithers had kindly written to explain that majority of the animals were bush orphans and would in all probability have had to be destroyed had they not been taken into my collection.

Out at the airport each crate had to be weighed and placed on a loader, and I carefully went over with a member of the BOAC Afro-Cargo crew the individual needs of each animal. When they were all well bedded down, fed and watered, I was confident that they would be all right for the period of the journey. Through the airline I confirmed with the RSPCA Animal Hostel at Heathrow their arrival time in London, and that they would be met there by Ken Smith from Jersey Zoo. Even after all of this careful planning, it was not easy to leave the animals, for during the past weeks they had all been much in my thoughts. I went from crate to crate bidding my farewells, checking on each water dish, and becoming sadder and sadder, eventually tearing myself away from this very special cargo. Perhaps on such occasions, when one has invested so much energy, planning and devotion to creatures that have been totally dependent on you, it is important to be as dispassionate as possible, and only after leaving them allow sentimentality to surge up. So I was relieved to hear from the airline representative, before I left Salisbury, that all the animals had arrived safely in London in apparently good condition. Apart from the Hunting dogs and jackals, which had been sent on to Edinburgh and Chessington Zoos respectively, the rest of the collection was now safely accommodated and cared for at Jersey.

As John had by now become accustomed to my ways and daily routine, and had served me well, I decided to take him with me to the Bechuanaland Protectorate. At first he was alarmed at travelling so far away from his native village to the wilds of the unknown, but I gave him my promise that I would bring him back to Glendale safely, and that if he did well he would receive a bonus to his weekly pay. Robin had kindly told me that whatever animals I collected and brought back from Bechuanaland, even if this included an adult lioness, he would be only too happy for them to be rested at Douet Farm, before the final part our journey by air to the British Isles.

On leaving Salisbury, we stopped for 48 hours in Bulawayo. It was in the 1890s that Cecil Rhodes had insisted that the new town be laid out in the grid pattern of an imperial Roman settlement, and that the main highways be wide enough to allow a wagon and a full span of 16 oxen to make a complete turn. This gave the city a spacious uncongested character, and one could quite easily imagine what life there must have been like for the early settlers at the end of the nineteenth century. After this short respite, and relieved of the tension of getting the animals away from Salisbury, I was now ready to leave Southern Rhodesia and move on to my next adventure.

However, just before departing from my Bulawayo hotel, I was alarmed to see a bold headline in the Sunday newspaper: THIS WEEK A FLYING ZOO TOOK OFF FROM SALISBURY.

Mr Mallinson should right now be somewhere out in the wilds of the Okavango Swamps region of Bechuanaland Protectorate: lean, bronzed, going after his quarry with the age-old excitement of the hunter out in the open, but with the added zest of knowing that what he is doing is infinitely worthwhile.

The reporter couldn't leave it at that:

How many Rhodesians must envy these fortunate characters that come out to Africa on assignments to film our wildlife or collect specimens for zoos and disappear on safari for months. He may of course be swatting mosquitoes as I write this, and wishing to high heaven that he, too, was somewhere in a city within reasonable distance of long cool one with ice chinking in his glass. But for all that, I'd still like to be with him, and I am aware of no small degree of envy. Good luck to you, Mr. Mallinson, as yours is the kind of 'hunting' that warrants a salute.

Gerald Durrell, 1983. © Durrell Archives.

Infant male Lowland gorilla, Mamfe, born Jersey, October 1963. © Philip Coffey.

The author with six year-old female Lowland gorilla, G-Ann, at Jersey Zoo, 1985. © Robert Rattner.

Left: Gerald Durrell with female two year-old Lowland gorilla, Bamenda, born Jersey, October 1975. © Philip Coffey. Right: The author with European Red fox vixen, Pufelli, on board RMS *Warwick Castle*, Gulf of Aden, October 1961 © 'The Lamp Trimmer'.

Conservateur Adrian Deschryver communicating with the Silver-back Eastern Lowland gorilla, Kasimir, in the Kahuzi Biega National Park, Kivu, Zaire, October 1975. © Jeremy Mallinson.

Two male cheetahs in the Kafue National Park, Zambia, October 2007. © Jeremy Mallinson.

Left: Aye-Aye at Jersey Zoo.
© Mark Pidgeon.

Below: Taken after the author's retirement lunch at Les Augrès Manor, June 2001. (left to right): Miles Mallinson, Sophie Dixon (née Mallinson), Advocate Keith Dixon, Julian Mallinson, Peter Olney, Air Chief Marshal Sir John Cheshire, Lee Durrell, The Princess Royal, Jeremy and Odette Mallinson, Dr Michael Brambell, Robin Rumboll, Dr John Knowles, Professor Roger Wheater. © Stuart McAlister.

Above: Golden Lion tamarins. © Philip Coffey.
Below Left: Black Lion tamarin. © DWCT Archives
Below Right: Golden-headed Lion tamarin. © Mark Pidgeon.

Above: Official opening of Bristol Zoo's 'Zona Brazil' by BBC Producer, Philippa Forrester, and the author in July 2002. In the company of Bristol Zoo's Director, Dr Jo Gipps, and some appropriately attired school children. © Bristol Zoo.

Left: Gerald and Lee Durrell at their tenth wedding anniversary, 24 May 1989. © Durrell Archives.

Sir David and Lady Attenborough with the author at the time of Sir David's official opening of the Jim Scriven Orang-utan Home Habitat, May 1994. © DWCT Archives.

The Sumatran Orang-utan Home Habitat at the Durrell Wildlife Conservation Trust. © Gregory Guida.

Above: Sir David Attenborough, Lee
and Gerald Durrell, Sarah Kennedy and
Dr Desmond Morris, 1993.
© Durrell Archives.

Left: The author with his wife, Odette,
after receiving an Honorary Doctor of
Science (DSc) degree at the University
of Kent, Canterbury, July 2000.
© University of Kent.

Feeling embarrassed at reading such a dramatic appraisal of my activities, I left the article face-down on the breakfast table; the last thing I wanted was to be identified as a Superman/Tarzan. I felt an urgent need to leave the city quickly and get to the Okavango Delta, where an introduction to two tame lions and a host of other members of Africa's diverse animals was sure to be enjoyable. John and I made some final purchases and left Bulawayo for the border town of Plumtree.

Chapter Seven

OKAVANGO'S TREASURE-CHEST
OF WILDLIFE

We arrived at Francistown mid-morning, with the temperature well into the mid 30s C (mid 90s F). After I parked the exhausted pick-up in the shade of a fig tree to let its engine cool off, and gave John one South African Rand (50p) with instructions to return in two hours, I set out to explore the small township and find a place to have lunch. The dusty pavements were shaded by the corrugated iron verandas of shops and houses, and I found my way to the small hotel on the town's main street. Seen from the balcony of the hotel, Francistown resembled the perfect setting for a Western movie and, sipping an ice-cold lager, I half expected to see a posse of cowboys riding wildly by, firing-off their six-shooters in all directions.

A mastiff-sized man sat beside me at the lunch table, shovelling his food down greedily. I took the opportunity to ask him the best route to take to drive the 515 km (320 mile) or so distance to Maun, the administrative centre of Ngamiland that embraced the Okavango Delta. 'Whatcha got?' he asked between mouthfuls. I told him about my Vauxhall pick-up, admitting its limitations, but explaining that it always seemed to get there in the end. He stopped eating and looked at me as if I had just been let out of a lunatic asylum. 'If I was in yer shoes mate,' he said, 'I wouldn't even bother to start.' This was hardly encouraging, so after lunch I sought a second opinion at a nearby garage. When a European mechanic appeared I asked, 'Do you see any reason why I shouldn't drive this to Maun? He viewed the pick-up disdainfully and told me that I must be joking. 'The police wouldn't let you even point a thing like that in the direction of Maun. If you're thinking about driving it there, you can forget about it. A four-wheel drive is mandatory for a trip along the northern edge of the Kalahari.' Reluctantly, I realised that I would have to accept his opinion, leave the pick-up with him to sell for me on a commission basis, and take his advice to book a couple of places on the back of a Riley's Transport truck that happened to be leaving that evening for Maun.

Fortunately, there was also room on the truck for all my equipment and personal baggage, although stowing it in the space available, on top of new galvanised dustbins, sacks of rice and bags of onions, was no easy task. When it came time for the truck to depart, John and I were joined under the canvas awning in the back by several Africans, male and female, with their bundles of clothing, pots and pans, grimy blankets, and even by some squawking poultry, whose legs were tied to prevent them escaping. As the diesel engine roared into vibrant life, the whole truck shuddered, the dustbins rattled and the bruised onions gave forth their savour.

According to the map, this was a 'secondary' road, but when I peered out from under the green canvas roof it more resembled a rough corrugated track of sand and stones. Just before the sun set over the dusty dry horizon of the northern Kalahari the truck came to a standstill. The African passengers were quick to alight with their cooking pots and eating utensils; fires were lit and a party atmosphere soon developed. I feared that there would be little chance of the truck making any further progress toward Maun that night. Fortunately I was wrong, for soon after the driver had blasted the vehicle's horn a few times, my fellow passengers hurried back to the lorry with their pots and pans and settled down for the onward journey.

The truck ploughed on through the loose sand of the track, trailing swirling clouds of sand in its wake and providing the passengers with a generous covering of the Kalahari's main ingredient. Due to this, the general noise of the clattering dustbins, and the difficulty of stretching out fully without invading another person's personal space, I slept very little. I was relieved when I began to see the sun rising from behind the truck in the east, which was hailed by one of the trussed cockerels giving an impressive dawn crow. Before much longer we left the sandy terrain and travelled through more thickly vegetated land before arriving at the Thamalakane River, which is the eastern border of the Okavango Delta.

Here the truck stopped for half an hour, and I remembered some of my reading about this isolated region of southern Africa. The more I did so, the more enthusiastic I became about the environment I was about to enter, and the adventures that I would be sure to meet. I could well imagine how in the late nineteenth century the explorer, Frederick Courteney Selous, must have rejoiced at arriving at the Delta after having trekked across the uncharted territory of what he called the 'thirst lands' of the northern Kalahari. For such an environment as the crystal-clear waters of the Thamalakane River, and the lush vegetation of its banks, must have been not only his party's salvation, but a paradise that would be difficult to surpass in this part of southern Africa.

The Okavango River rises in the Southern Angola Highlands and flows south-east through the Caprivi Strip and enters Ngamiland on its north-eastern border. The river never finds its way to the sea, but flows into the great depression of south central Africa comprising the Okavango Swamps, Lakes Ngami and Dow, and the Makarikari Salt Lakes. The Swamps in their turn drain into the Thamalakane River which when full flows into the northern Kalahari. The Swamps are an intricate maze of clear water and white Kalahari sand. The waters take no single course as they find their way among the papyrus, reeds and sedges, ever merging with other hippo-dredged channels, only to separate as little streams into lagoons and backwaters before becoming lost again in tangles of hippo grass and reeds.

The Okavango Delta covers an area of about 16,000 square kilometres (c. 6,178 square miles) and provides sanctuary to a treasure-chest of wildlife. Lush flood plain grasslands fringe the reed beds, ideal habitat for a host of species ranging from herds of elephant, buffalo, wildebeest, waterbuck, Sable and Roan antelope, tsessebe, Greater kudu, impala, reedbuck, zebra, to small family groups of warthog and troops of baboons. The Delta is also well known for its diversity of bird life, and even on my first viewing of the Thamalakane River, I saw the diminutive yet spectacular Malachite kingfisher diving on to its prey, and pairs of stunningly coloured Pygmy geese swimming among the abundant white water lilies. The ringing, far-carrying call of an African Fish eagle, often called 'The voice of Africa', seemed to welcome me to the Swamps. How fortunate I felt in being about to enter such a wildlife paradise.

There was no barrier on the crudely constructed bridge to prevent a vehicle sliding off into the water, and I was surprised that a vehicle as laden as ours should be able to pass over it safely. The bridge creaked loudly as it took the full weight, and I was thankful when we slowly managed to manoeuvre onto the security of the Thamalakane's western bank. Eleven kilometres (seven miles) further on along the sandy road we reached Maun, the tribal and colonial administrative centre of this region of the Bechuanaland Protectorate. There was nobody to meet me, and I was glad of this, for I must have looked more like a scruffy gypsy than like a keen young British naturalist. John looked comparatively fresh, but he was used to travelling in the back of crowded trucks. He collected my luggage and equipment while I entered the small Riley's Hotel to shave and shower. I thought nostalgically of the motoring trip through the Swiss Alps that I had enjoyed some eight months earlier, and I tried not to think that, sooner or later, I would have to return to Francistown by the same mode of transport.

I was driven out to the Kays' camp by an officer of the local Tsetse Fly Control Department. The track ran along the bank of the Thamalakane, winding its way among fallen trees and patches of boggy ground. Soon I saw a copse of impressive figs, and three cocker spaniels and a white bull terrier came out to meet us, barking and wagging their tails. 'You've come to a proper menagerie here,' said the officer, and before I could think of a reply, Robert and June Kay emerged from the shade to greet us. Robert was a large man with a booming laugh. His head was topped by a sizeable bush hat and, in his smart khaki bush jacket and well-creased shorts, he conjured up the image of a typical 1920 East African Big Game Hunter. June was petite, feminine and vivacious. John was introduced to the Kays' boss boy Kisi, who helped him unload the luggage, and who then took him away to meet the other members of the camp's African staff.

Over a mug of coffee Robert turned to me. 'I expect you're dying to meet Chinky and Timmy,' he said, and led me off to meet the Kays' two pet lions. Timmy was tied to a tree by a long chain. He was a dwarf male lion that they had reared from a cub, having taken pity on him at a circus that was visiting Bulawayo. When he stood up, his short front legs suggested a bowlegged and plump bishop in gaiters. From this first moment of introduction to him, I sensed an uneasiness between us, which during my time with the Kays proved impossible to overcome.

With Chinky, however, it was love at first sight. She was accommodated in the back of a Bedford truck, since the elders of the local Batawana tribe had insisted that she had to be secured in this way during the Kays' safaris in Ngamiland. She was the largest lioness that I had ever seen. Her hazel-coloured eyes were big but slit-like, somewhat oriental. Her enormous body was fawn coloured, and her forcefully shaped muzzle sported a powder-puff chin of snowy white fur. Part of the side of the truck had been cut away to allow cleaning, and she reached out of this narrow slot with one of her paws to play. After Robert had demonstrated how to play 'patty-paw' with Chinky, I offered her my hand, which she licked with seeming affection; I immediately felt that I had successfully bonded with her.

The 1944 Normandy landings DUKW-amphibious vehicle, named Shaka Zulu had been adapted by the Kays for their travels around the Okavango Delta. Nearby, in the open centre of the copse, stood their living tent, its canvas veranda serving as both a sitting and dining area. Freshly cut water reeds carpeted the ground to keep down the dust. The chairs were covered by the skins of various animals that Robert had shot for the pot, and a large Basuto war drum added to the camp's safari atmosphere. To the left of the living quarters was a small bathroom tent, with a canvas hip bath hanging on a nearby tree. Twelve respectable looking brown hens scraped and foraged around the reed covered floor, but were soon moved on by the spaniels if they encroached too close to where their master and mistress were sitting.

At sundowner time we sat under the largest of the fig trees, and with a gentle breeze fanning us from the river we watched, in this Garden of Eden, the reddest of suns sinking softly over the reed beds. Then Robert suddenly announced, 'Jeremy, I have some most exciting news for you from Gerald Durrell, which we received via telegram from his superintendent, Kenneth Smith. The Jersey Zoo has made the decision to accept Chinky; you can take her back with you to Jersey with any other animals that you may be able to catch here.' Knowing that neither John nor I was capable of constructing anything that could possibly safely contain an adult lioness, I stammered rather apprehensively 'Wh– what in?' 'Oh, I've thought about that. I've arranged for a firm in Bulawayo to make a metal travelling cage for her, with a drop-slide entrance, which could also be used as a trap. Riley's Transport will be able to bring it up from Francistown before the month is out.' As I was on an unpaid leave of absence from the zoo and was completely financing myself, I knew that Chinky's passage would have to be paid for by others. However, both Robert and June appeared to be most relieved to have Chinky's future settled. Whether I wanted to have a three-and-a-half-year-old lioness as a travelling companion back to Jersey was no concern of theirs, and I obviously had no alternative but for her to be the first member of my Okavango collection.

Robert had served in the British Army, in the Palestine Police, and during the Second World War had been in Southern Rhodesia, serving as a flying instructor in the RAF at a base near Bulawayo. June had been born in South Africa and brought up in Bulawayo. Here in the swamps they seemed wonderfully contented, subject only to occasional fits of irritation when the subject of wildlife conservation cropped up, for this was the time that East African Big-Game safari firms had started to take out hunting concessions in the northern regions of the Delta, without any apparent control or enforcement of conservation legislation. It was in connection with this that the Kays had formed a fund-raising NGO, The Friends of Okavango, to highlight the threat to Ngamiland's wildlife. The object of this charity was to create an African-sponsored game reserve to the south of the Kwaai River, and for this to be operated by the Batawana tribe itself.

In Gerald Durrell's introduction to June's first book, *Okavango*, he had written that he had wished that he could have been with her to see the magnificent wildlife that she had written about with such sympathy. Now June was devoting her spare time to writing her second book, *Wild Eden*, and directing her journalistic talent to newspaper articles promoting the fund-raising and conservation activities of The Friends of Okavango. In collaboration with the Batawana Tribal authorities she was working on forming a Bechuanaland Fauna Preservation Society.

Robert told me that he was on good terms with the Queen Regent of the Batawana tribe, Mahumahati Moremi. As I would have to get her permission to take live animals from the tribal territory of Ngamiland, he had arranged a meeting with her the following morning. The Queen Regent had told him that she had heard of Gerald Durrell and had enjoyed reading one of his books, the *Bafut Beagles*. Before I set out from Jersey, I had not fully realised how internationally well known

Gerald Durrell was, and how useful my involvement with his Jersey Zoo was to be; this connection had already borne some most beneficial fruit.

When the time arrived for our audience with the Queen Regent, Robert was dressed for the occasion in an immaculate white shirt, white shorts and white long stockings, with a pair of highly polished brown shoes; whereas the best I could muster was a rather crumpled khaki bush-jacket, a rather creased silk neckerchief, long trousers and well-travelled jungle hat. All I could hope for was to give the impression that I represented a rather forgetful but earnest young British naturalist, who spent the majority of his time wandering around the bush looking for animals.

The Queen Regent occupied a couple of whitewashed bungalows, which looked out of place amid the thatched mud huts of a typical African village. As I rather nervously approached the entrance to her office, I felt like an ambassador to the Court of St James, about to present my credentials to the Sovereign. When we entered the room, Mahumahati Moremi turned out to be a small plump lady dressed in European style, sitting behind a large mahogany desk. Feeling that I should follow some type of credible protocol, I bowed my head slightly and, for some reason, accompanied this with a Germanic clicking of my heels. The Queen Regent smiled at such an uncalled-for gesture of respect on my part and pointed toward some seats.

Robert started the ball rolling by telling the Queen Regent that I was seeking her permission to both study and collect certain species of animals within her tribal territory, at the same time emphasising that my chief reason for coming here was to learn about the measures being taken to conserve the Okavango Delta's unique wildlife. He was also quick to say, and to score an important political point, how interested I had been to learn about the conservation objectives of the Friends of Okavango, and in particular how impressed I had been with regard to the potential of there being established in her royal family's honour the Moremi Nature Reserve in the northern region of the swamps. After Robin had mentioned my work with the famous British author Gerald Durrell, she granted the necessary permission for me to take animals from Ngamiland, although I would be expected to pay a nominal fee to the tribal treasury for each animal taken. She also added that I would have to obtain export permits from the District Commissioner and health permits from the local Veterinary Department, in order to export the animals from the Bechuanaland Protectorate to Rhodesia. On taking our leave, Mahumahati Moremi expressed her particular pleasure to learn from Robin that Chinky was to be included in such an exportation from her tribal lands.

On our way to the British District Commissioner, Robert told me that the Commissioner was not a supporter of the establishment of the Moremi Nature Reserve; he would prefer to boost the coffers by the sale of licences to big-game hunters. In the early 1960s few administrators recognised the benefits of eco-tourism to wildlife conservation and to the economy as a whole. The DC, Mr Eustace Clark, seemed pleased to meet me and to see a new face in Maun. He told me that he had been at school with Peter Scott, had read some of Gerald Durrell's books, and had always been a keen bird-watcher. He, like the Queen Regent, was particularly pleased to give me the necessary permission to move Chinky from the territory, and any other animals that I may have in my possession at the time of my departure, providing the region's Veterinary Department had given all the animals a clean bill of health.

Back at camp, Robert made suggestions regarding the best use of my time with them in Ngamiland, particularly with my animal-collecting activities. He had arranged a trip to Lake Ngami, which was well known for it abundance of bird life. He had also accepted an invitation from one of the Queen Regent's advisers, called Benjamin, to spend a weekend with him and five Africans from the tribal administrative offices, as they travelled to an area some forty-five miles to the north-west of Maun. The area had been set aside for members of the Batawana tribe to 'hunt for the pot'. Robert thought such a weekend would be good for my general education.

I accepted Robert's recommendations with enthusiasm, and before leaving for the weekend with the tribal hunters, I set John the task of making a number of wooden frames of different sizes, covered with wire netting and protected externally with hessian, that could be easily assembled to serve as cages for a variety of animals. I also ordered two sizes of baskets from some local reed basket makers, for I considered that these would be ideal to carry any birds that we may manage to net on Lake Ngami.

The track to Chuchubegha looked like any other sandy route through mopane bush habitat and in some places, where the hard-packed ground gave way to soft sand, the vehicle had to take it at speed to gain the other side. After we passed through a Tsetse fly control post there was no definable track at all, and we followed the lead truck driven by Amos, which threaded its way through the light bush, between small copses and thickets, across tracts of parched yellow grassland, with the tracks of our vehicles stretching behind. I then had my first sight of a small herd of graceful impala who stopped grazing as we approached, sniffing the air and trying to catch our scent. To my astonishment, the sound of a rifle shot came from Benjamin's truck, and I clearly heard the horrible smack of the bullet as it tore into the buck's flesh. The animal was knocked sideways and staggered before managing to gather itself and limp off some way behind his harem of half a dozen does.

The leading truck drove on, making no attempt to follow up the wounded animal, so Robert in disgust swung aside and drove in search of the poor creature, and within five minutes had put it out of its misery. The other truck soon arrived to benefit from the kill, but Robert forestalled them with some angry words directed to the trigger-happy African who had fired his casual and pointless shot. It is one thing to shoot for the pot, but it is quite another to use small game for target practice. Robert made it quite clear that he would report such an unacceptable act to Mahumahati Moremi, should this type of shooting occur again.

The episode left a nasty taste in our mouths, but we were consoled by the spectacular and rewarding drive during the next hour. Three Reticulated giraffes towered above the long grass, browsing from the tops of stunted trees until, hearing the truck, they cantered away with their ungainly gait. Eight warthogs, disturbed from wallowing in some damp cotton-soil ran away in zigzag disorder, with their tails held upright, seeking the nearest cover. A herd of rich chocolate brown tsessebe, some twelve in number, viewed us suspiciously before crashing through the high grass to a nearby stream. Their paler rumps made ideal targets as they vanished, but not one of the hunting party was going to risk Robert's anger for a second time – it was wildebeest and buffalo that they were seeking for the pot.

It seemed that round almost every corner we would come across herds of zebra and various species of antelope, which snorted and swished their tails in indignation of our intrusion into their peaceful domain. Family flocks of the vivid blue-necked Helmeted guineafowl ran through the sparse grass habitat, adding their much repeated 'ker-bek-ker-bek-bek-ker-bek, krrrrr …' calls, in similar protestation at our presence. Then, once more, the tranquillity of the scene was destroyed by the deafening noise of a gunshot, and a nearby wildebeest stumbled to the ground. I felt a desperate desire to intervene, although of course it was too late, and the animal was lying motionless on the earth. I still thought in terms of innocent life and the brutality of sudden death, without fully recognising the necessity for local people to be able to live off their land and obtain valuable protein for their diet. It didn't take long for the animal to be skinned, the meat to be loaded onto the back of Benjamin's truck, and for the vultures to start circling the carcass.

An hour before sunset Benjamin halted his truck by a copse, which was flanked on the west by a small stream and surrounded by open grassland; here we pitched camp, the Africans lit a fire, and we arranged our bedrolls around it. The meal was cooked over the campfire and was delicious – boiled rice with grilled wildebeest steak, which tasted like well-hung venison. After darkness fell with its tropical suddenness, we listened to some old hunting tales and then took to our sleeping bags under a clear, cloudless sky studded with a galaxy of stars. The sounds of the bush were all around us; every so often the cough and hoarse grunt of a leopard could be heard, and the more frequent gurgles, howls and cackles of the Spotted hyena.

By seven next morning we had breakfasted and struck camp. I learned with mixed feelings that the hunt for a buffalo was next on the agenda. We spotted a herd of buffalo in a small clearing, but they dispersed before a shot could be fired, into vegetation too thick for the trucks to follow. So we went after them on foot, Benjamin leading, his .375 rifle carried at the trail. For some 20 minutes we pressed on through the mopane woodland, following the spoor of buffalo. When their fresh droppings became more numerous we spoke in whispers and I could sense the tension and, to my surprise, the excitement of the occasion: the hunter seeking his prey. Benjamin suddenly held up his hand and we stopped in out tracks. The herd was upwind of us and we communicated through sign language, advancing as quietly as possible. Then Benjamin crouched, levelled his rifle, and the silence was shattered as his bullet exploded from its breech and found its mark somewhere in the buffalo's body. At once the herd could be heard snorting and thundering through the undergrowth in our direction; as they emerged from cover and saw us, they swerved away at the last moment, leaving the heavy horsy smell of their bodies in their wake.

We were now in the classic tense situation, for the African buffalo is considered by some hunters to be the most dangerous of all Africa's big game. The buffalo is extremely cunning when wounded, and can survive many bullets – carry a lot of lead – and frequently hides up to the last moment before charging his assailant. Robert unslung the rifle he had brought along for self-protection, and we watched as Benjamin crept forward with every fibre of his body alert. He must have been almost upon the wounded animal before the buffalo broke cover and came charging at him with head lowered and horns outstretched, with all the tenacity and anger of a bull in a Spanish bull ring. As coolly as James Bond, Benjamin dropped to one knee and fired. The buffalo fell to the ground like a ton of rocks, shot through the heart. A few feet further on, and his body would have crushed and killed his assailant.

I congratulated Benjamin warmly for his tracker's skill and his marksman's composure at such a moment of danger. And against my usual feelings, I had to confess to myself that I had found the whole episode of the buffalo hunt, when the odds of survival between hunter and the hunted appeared to be almost evenly matched, had been exhilarating. We left two of the Africans to guard the carcass and returned to our vehicles, where Robert and I made our farewells. With sizeable haunches of wildebeest meat we made our way slowly back to Maun, and to the base camp on the banks of the Thamalakane. That evening, Chinky and Timber benefited from the meaty bones of the wildebeest, and the spaniels and bull terrier enjoyed generous portions of meat, while the rest of the camp feasted upon tender portions of antelope.

When the time arrived for Robert and me to visit Lake Ngami, June was busy writing another article for the South African Press – a condemnation of the growing trade in cheetah, leopard and serval skins – and she was rather glad to have us away from camp so that she could enjoy the peace that every writer needs. After collecting the specially made reed baskets, Kisi and John helped to load the truck with the equipment and food.

At Sehitwa we visited a small store owned by a Greek trader who lived with his African wife and their children. When he learned that I had come to Ngamiland to collect animals he took me round to the back of the store to show me an ostrich and an impala living together in an old chicken run. 'They can be yours for ten rand each,' he said. I told him that I wouldn't be able to take the impala, but would be interested in the ostrich if he could hold on to it for me for another six weeks. She was a fine sub-adult bird, almost four feet high, and as I looked her over appraisingly she appeared to simper bashfully, as if she were a young beauty in a Middle East harem. Her pale neck was striped with delicate broken lines in pastel shades, her large eyes were overshadowed by long flirtatious lashes, and her flightless dark wings sat on her body like large powder-puffs.

I agreed to pay the Greek an extra six rand to keep the Ostrich for me, and we drove on to the lake some 19 kilometres (12 miles) further to the south. This part of Ngamiland has little or no Tsetse fly, and represents the major cattle-rearing area of the region. Most of the African population here were of the Damara tribe, who had fled from German South-West Africa (Namibia) after the massacres at the beginning of the twentieth century. We could see that we were indeed in cattle country, for we passed four Africans wearing cowboy hats and riding agile-looking horses, as they herded some 300 head of beef cattle away from the lake to a nearby corral. The moving cattle had raised a great cloud of dust, making it hard for Robert to see the track, but eventually we emerged from the dust and the scrub-trees and on to an open flat terrain and, like a mirage, the lake itself appeared on the horizon. As we came closer we heard the increasingly deafening tumult of thousands of birds.

At home, in my book collection of nineteenth century African explorers, I had read with fascination Charles John Anderson's *Lake Ngami; or Explorations and Discoveries During Four Years of Wandering in the Wilds of South-Western Africa*, as well as his later book *The Okavango River*, so I could hardly have been more excited at having this opportunity to see this place just over a hundred years later. The sun was sinking fast as we stopped to set up camp for the night on the lakeshore. A camp-fire was lit, and Robert and I spread out our ground sheets and sleeping bags in the open near the fire, whereas Kisi and John preferred to sleep in the back of the truck. The sunset was the most breathtaking of any that I had previously witnessed. The whole horizon became a vast red furnace, into which the sun sank like a fireball. Then the night cooled, refreshing us after the heat of the day. We dined agreeably off steak and rice, washed down with some rather warm beer. In my sleeping bag I soon fell asleep under a ceiling of radiant stars.

When full, Lake Ngami covers an area of some 72 square kilometres (28 square miles). Most of the lake is only a few feet deep; it is rich in plankton, and has a matted forest of oxygen-producing plants growing from its muddy bottom. It is because of these water plants, and due to the saltiness of the water that results from evaporation, that the lake plays host to such a concentration and diversity of bird life. Perhaps the most eloquent description of Lake Ngami is given in Johnson, Bond and Bannister's book *Okavango; Sea of Land, Land of Water*, which records:

> From the lake shores it looks like a cloud of smoke, tossed by the wind, twisted into spirals in the sky. Then the smoke tumbles in a sunburst of wings, a spinning, flickering tornado that mark the flight of a million of birds dispersing from the water's edge. When the quelea [finches] are flying it sounds as if rapids have appeared on the placid lake.

Soon after dawn we breakfasted on fried sausages and eggs, with some refreshing watermelon that we had bought from the Greek trader, and a mug of coffee. We reloaded our kit onto the truck and drove along the east bank of the lake, with the sun starting to heat the inside of the cab like an oven. We passed groups of ecclesiastical-looking Marabou storks, Sacred ibis, Wood ibis, African avocets, Blacksmith plovers, Saddle-billed storks, Spur-winged geese and numerous species of ducks and terns. In the distance, through our binoculars, we could pick out the pink pastel shades of both the Greater and Lesser flamingo, and congregations of Pink-backed pelican, feeding in the middle of the lake. This entire treasure chest of bird life was an unremitting orchestra of calls and bird song. When we arrived at the lake's southern shore we chose a dry grassy stretch of ground for our base. For more shade, we erected a canvas awning that stretched some three metres (10 ft) away from the vehicle, supported by a series of aluminium poles.

In the afternoon, with the help of both Robert and John, we waded into the muddy shallow lake, positioned two telescopic aluminium poles, which Reay Smithers had kindly lent me, and put up the nine metres (c. 30 ft), five cm (c. two inch) mesh mist-net between them, the top of which stood some 2.7 m (nine feet) above the water. If ornithologists are engaged in ringing birds as they fly up and down a rural English stream, all they need to do is to stretch their net across the waterway concerned, and the birds will be almost certain to fly into it. Here, on the shores of such a vast expanse of water, it could not have been more different, and we would just have to rely on good luck for a bird to fly the net's way.

It was not until the following morning that the mist-net secured its first occupants, not single birds, but three to seven at a time. The Blacksmith plover was a species that I was not seeking for my collection, and because of the small carpal spurs they have on their wings, the more they struggled, the more entangled they became. It took three of us up to half an hour to release them all. Within three days we had caught two pairs of Red-billed teal, and three pairs of Hottentot teal. These I accommodated in the newly woven reed baskets, with dampened hessian under the lids. At first some of the waterfowl presented me with a feeding problem. Not that I did not know what to give them, and a mixture of corn millet and mealy-meal, with some finely chopped lettuce, was certainly adequate. The difficulty was to get some of the teal to eat at all, and I had to coax the obstinate ones by holding them gently and dipping their beaks into a bowl of floating seeds and lettuce. This usually worked, but when it failed, I made small moistened mealy-meal pellets, opened the bird's beak slightly, and inserted a pellet carefully onto the lower mandible. I would then close the beak, point it upwards, and at the same time stroke the teal's neck until it swallowed the food. This was a similar procedure to giving domestic dogs or cats their worming pills; a technique that I had first learnt at the Basil Kennedy Boarding Kennels.

When it came time to leave Lake Ngami, we drove round to the western side of the lake to go north. During the journey we saw no fewer than eleven individuals of the large, majestic Wattled crane, in pairs or groups, foraging along the shoreline. Their distinctive wattles hung beneath their chins, and their white bodies and light grey wings were highlighted as they danced from one tasty morsel to another. Wattled cranes are an endangered species, and if I had had rocket-nets, as were starting to be frequently used by the Wildfowl Trust, such sightings would have been an ideal opportunity to try and secure some for a captive-breeding programme. I recognised how fortunate I was to observe this rare crane in its natural habitat.

At Sehitwa we called in at the Greek's trading store to finalise my arrangements for collecting the ostrich when we had returned from the Swamps. The trader came out of his store to see what I had managed to net on the lake, and seemed disappointed not to see flamingos and pelicans. When I told him that we had managed to secure only a handful of duck, any thought that I was a talented British big-game hunter evaporated. He became slightly more enthusiastic about me when I decided to buy a roll of wire netting from him; I knew that before our departure for the northern part of the Swamps we would have to construct a couple of waterfowl pens on the banks of the Thamalakane for the newly captured teal. On the final part of our journey back to base camp we stopped at regular intervals to sprinkle water on the hessian over the reed baskets, to keep the teal cool and damp.

June, the lions, the dogs and the hens all seemed glad to have us back with them. I went over to greet Chinky, who generously gave me one of her affectionate and welcoming 'wowws'. During our absence, June had accepted from a local fisherman a three-foot African python, which had been put in a crate behind the DUKW and had already devoured a small rat that one of the kitchen staff had caught for it. A local trader had offered a young pair of the darker-phase Spur-winged geese, which June had also accepted on my behalf. I was more pleased to hear about the geese, because snakes had never been my favourites. The travelling crate for Chinky had been delivered by Riley's Transport, a heavy metal cage, which even when empty needed four men to carry it, and Robert demonstrated how the drop-slide could be used as a live-trap. He would bring the cage with us up to the Fig Tree Camp on the banks of the Kwaai River. He obviously couldn't wait to try the apparatus out, and concluded his enthusiastic explanation of its operation by cheerfully informing me, 'There will be no end to the variety of animals that I shall be able to catch in such a trap for you.' A statement that filled me with some apprehension.

I had so much enjoyed my first two weeks in the Okavango Delta. The buffalo adventure; the days on the shores of Lake Ngami; and staying in this pristine environment of the Kays' Thamalakane base camp; these were experiences as heaven-sent as I could imagine. Now, very much thanks to Gerald Durrell's introduction of me to the Kays, I was realising so many of my long-held ambitions to visit such unspoilt exotic places, as well as having direct contact and exposures to the animal kingdom, and to the unspoilt wilds of the African continent. Here was the adventure that I had dreamt about.

Chapter Eight

A LIONESS IN MY LUGGAGE

We left for the Kwaai River in the northern regions of the Okavango in a hybrid convoy comprising the DUKW driven by Robert and loaded up with all my equipment, Chinky's future travelling cage and Timmy as a cabin-passenger. June drove the diesel truck, with Kisi and two other Africans as her companions, and I followed in an old Dodge truck, with John as my passenger, Chinky in the back, and a metal dinghy strapped on top. We also had a Masarwa tracker by the name of Mrewa, riding the old grey gelding that in a rash moment Robert had swapped for a bottle of whisky with a local Batawana, in the belief that he could get good game photographs from horseback in lion country. The horse, appropriately named Whisky, seemed immune to the bites of Tsetse fly. I left the waterfowl enclosed in three small fenced-in ponds on the banks of the Thamalakane, where they could readily feed from passing vegetation, and I had instructed one of the Africans remaining at the base camp to provide them with a daily handful of millet.

It took two days for our noisy convoy to find its way off the beaten track, through the thick mopane scrubland and tall grasses to what Robert and June called Fig Tree Camp, situated on the east bank of the Kwaai, or Machabe, River. The Kays had first visited this region two years previously, and it was where Chinky had been taught to hunt in the bush, so it was sad that the tribal authorities had refused to allow her to be released back here. The two big fig trees that had given the camp its name stood alone in the middle of some open veldt, a most pleasant change from the scruffy disorder of the mopane terrain that we had just travelled through. We set up camp under the shade of the trees, with the DUKW acting as its centrepiece. A stretch of lush grassland sloped down to the reed beds and the clear waters of the river. It was a beautiful location, and it conjured up memories of my school days at Newton Hall, looking out over the Home Park and down to the lake, with its population of ornamental waterfowl.

Robert lifted Timmy from the DUKW and took him on a length of chain for a walk, before tethering him to a peg in the shade of a nearby tree. While I cleaned out Chinky, I tried to explain to her why she had not been granted a similar degree of liberty. During this conversation I became more and more anthropomorphic, telling her that her confinement was only temporary, as was her celibacy, for she had been betrothed to a very handsome lion waiting for her at Jersey Zoo, who no doubt had all the charm and blarney of the Irish, as he had been born at Dublin Zoo. She licked the back of my hand with her rough tongue as if she fully understood what I was telling her and uttered some of her quiet 'wowws'.

During the two nights on our way up to the Kwaai River, Chinky had, as if she recognised that she was returning to the unfettered wilds of paradise, started uttering a series of muted roars. On the second night, these calls were rather alarmingly responded to by a pride of lions some distance away; and closer to we heard the more familiar soft howl of a jackal, and the cackles from a pair of hyena. After our arrival at the Fig Tree Camp, Chinky's nocturnal calls increased, and it was on our second night there that she came into season. She roared persistently for about half an hour, as if she were determined to make quite sure that every male lion in the vicinity was aware of her condition. At first Chinky's roaring was answered only at intervals, and from a long way off. Then the interwoven roars of a pair of lion just on the other side of the river broke the darkness, and her calling became more compelling and urgent. To our alarm we heard the reply from another male on our own side of the river. It was apparent that Chinky was acting as a magnet to any male lion in earshot. Robert picked up his rifle and June climbed quickly on to the roof of the DUKW to switch on the 80–watt arc lamp mounted there. The beam of light picked out two pairs of eyes on the opposite bank of the river.

Kisi, John and the two African staff members clambered into the safety of Shaka Zulu the DUKW, and Robert led a worried-looking Timmy closer to it. He then took an even more concerned and snorting Whisky to a safer area upwind of Chinky's truck. Then he walked up to the Dodge truck to show Chinky the rifle, rebuking her sharply for her provocative behaviour, and fired a shot into the air, which had the effect of silencing everything around us. Such a scheme worked for a time; Chinky had found the deafening report of the rifle shot an unnerving experience and after this it was enough to show her the rifle to stop her roars.

Robert and I were standing close to the campfire, which we had kept well ablaze, when we heard a loud deep-throated woof of fear from Timmy. June shouted, 'Robert! There's a lion in the camp!' We immediately moved toward the rear of the DUKW and, in the beam of the arc light, we caught a glimpse of a lion retreating into the long grass. It momentarily gazed back at us through its rounded burnt-orange eyes, and we saw perhaps the largest lion I had ever seen, a fine black-maned male. This lion had been expecting to find a receptive lioness, but instead must have almost tripped over Timmy, to the horror of both animals.

With June keeping the beam of the searchlight on the spot where the lion had been, I revved the diesel truck with its headlights on full beam and created as much noise as possible by keeping my hand on the horn, while Robert fired a warning shot into the air in the direction of the intruder. Carrying his rifle at the ready, Robert walked directly in front of the vehicle and, on reaching Timmy, he untied him and brought the terrified dwarf animal back into the middle of the camp. I then moved Chinky's Dodge truck closer to Shaka Zulu where Robert took up his position, so that he could show Chinky the rifle whenever he feared she might again start her roaring. He said, 'If a lion comes into camp again I will have to shoot to kill; he would be a danger for us all.' We kept up the lion-watch until a pale jade sky heralded the first light of dawn, and the roars of the male lions had faded into the distance.

After the drama and excitement of the night, we spent most of the following day building a kraal-like fortification out of tree branches and thorn bushes. This surrounded the three vehicles, which were arranged in a defensive triangle. Two safer places were found to tether the dwarf lion and the grey gelding; although in order to minimise stress they were kept out of sight of each other. Before sunset that evening, Robert gave Chinky an extra large lump of meat in the hope that after her exertions of the previous evening she would soon fall asleep. In fact she did behave rather better, and her few enticing roars were only half-heartedly answered from afar. Robert decided not to take any chances, and for the next three nights we took it in turns to stand watch, showing Chinky the rifle whenever her roars became too vociferous. Kisi and John took turns to keep the fire well ablaze.

My first capture – perhaps I really mean my first find – was a Bell's Hinged tortoise that I stumbled across on my way down to the river to fetch some fresh water. I selected a lush patch of grass behind DUKW, and John made a small wired-in enclosure. When I found that the surface of its under-shell (the plastron) was distinctly concave, I identified the animal as a male. This concavity is said to accommodate more easily the convex upper shell (the carapace) of the female, when mating takes place.

I had told Robert about the lone Nile crocodile that we had at Jersey Zoo, and he offered to show me the best way to catch a crocodile in the Swamps. This was a demonstration I would gladly have avoided, but I was afraid of losing face. That evening we manoeuvred the dinghy through the reeds into the river. I was in charge of the outboard motor, Kisi sat amidships with a boat hook, and Robert knelt in the bows to guide us by the beam of the powerful torch that he had strapped to the front of his bush hat; this left both his hands free to grab the crocodile. A refreshing breeze kept the ubiquitous mosquitoes off our skin as we made our way through the reeds of one of the smaller channels. Startled frogs leapt from the saucer-sized water lily leaves to the security of the waters beneath.

Soon Robert started to gesticulate furiously like a French policeman in the Place de la Concorde, for he had seen a pair of reptilian eyes reflected in the beam of his torch. I glided the dinghy gently up to the seemingly hypnotised crocodile and Robert plunged his arm into the water. There was a slight struggle, a spraying of water from a flailing tail, and he swung the crocodile into the belly of the dingy, narrowly missing Kisi, before dropping it neatly into the waiting box. 'Your turn now,' he said triumphantly, and in dread I changed places with him. 'Remember, if the eyes are far apart, leave it alone, because it will be too big to handle.' I prayed that the commotion we had just caused had sent a signal out to any other crocodile in the area to make itself scarce.

Forests of reeds slid by on either side, and the pale moon peeped out from behind a blanket of rain clouds. Just when I was starting to feel that I would be spared from having to perform such a dangerous act, the beam of the torchlight picked out two icy green eyes, quite close to each other, and immediately ahead of us. I flapped my hands wildly, rather hoping that this would scare the crocodile, but it remained in its hypnotised state as Robert guided the dinghy just to the left of it. I had no option but to take a deep breath and to plunge my right hand into the cool water, aiming at a point about two inches behind the eyes and hopefully allowing correctly for the refraction of light. My hand made contact with the reptile's cold slimy shoulders, and my fingers closed over them tightly. As the crocodile took fright and started to flail around, I clung to it desperately. I then swung it over the gunwale of the dinghy where it managed to wriggle from my grasp and fall into the bottom of the boat. Kisi very nearly abandoned ship but Robert, with the focus of a leopard hunting its prey, managed to trap the angry little crocodile under one of the duckboards by his seat. I opened the box containing the first one, Robert dropped it in, and I closed the lid.

In spite of my clumsiness in dropping the animal in the boat, I had at least caught a crocodile without losing any of my fingers, and thereby ending my potential career as a bar-room pianist. The next morning I gave John the task of making holding cages for the now very stern-looking crocodiles. The cages were designed so they could be placed among the cool of the reeds, with the crocodiles having the choice of being either partially submerged or being on dry land.

I now turned my attention to trying to net some of the carrion-eating birds that I had noticed around a lion kill. Through my binoculars I had observed three different species of vulture, some Marabou storks and a Tawny eagle; all species that I knew a number of British zoos were interested in acquiring. Unfortunately, whenever I erected one of my nets near some carrion, the raptors gave it the widest berth. Undaunted by initial failure, we collectively came up with the idea of using a reel of strong nylon fishing gut, which we thought would be too thin for the birds to see, and from this to make a number of loops and nooses. These were then attached to a number of tin cans, filled with earth to give them weight, which in turn were buried and arranged in a big circle around a place that we had baited with a haunch of wildebeest. The plan depended upon the birds' usual habit of landing some nine metres

(30 or so feet) away from the carrion and then approaching with their customary ungainly, prancing motion. We hoped that their feet would become caught up in some of the loops and nooses, and that when they tried to fly away, they would be handicapped by the weight of the tins. I would then rush forward and secure the bird for my collection.

Regrettably, this capture strategy was also a complete failure. Through our binoculars we watched the first flock of vultures inquisitively approach the site, their great dark wings flapping slowly as they circled above the carrion before gliding down to the ground. The first arrivals pranced awkwardly over to the meat, and the foot of an immature White-headed vulture became entangled in one of the nylon loops. The bird immediately leapt in panic into the air, dragging the unearthed clanging tins beneath it, but immediately managed to shake them off. Although we continued with this strategy at a number of different locations, it soon became evident that the raptors' clear eyesight could spot any alien objects like the man-made nylon fish gut. Eventually Mrewa, the bushman tracker, told Kisi that if the white man wanted to catch the birds, Mrewa could easily catch as many as he required. He would charge four rand (£2) for each of the specimens. I accepted Mrewa's entrepreneurial proposition.

Kisi, who has been learning Mrewa's Sasarwa language, night-school fashion, from a bushman girl, laboriously translated the tracker's capture technique to us: 'Use just sticks and string made from entwined lengths of grass, for it is important for all such materials to be natural.' He went on to describe: 'You can see how he is putting a long strong sapling into the ground, and is tying one end of the grass string to the top of it. Then he is making a circle of small sticks and is looping the other end of the string round them, but is leaving a small length at this end so as to tuck it under a staple-shaped piece of stick, embedded in the middle of the circle, where a piece of carrion can be attached. He is then straining the string to bend the sapling, which in turn acts as a trigger when a bird takes the bait. It collapses and the circle of sticks and the noose goes round the bird's foot or neck. The strong sapling holds the bird to the ground so that it cannot fly away.' Although the whole mechanism sounded rather Heath Robinsonish, we could hardly wait to put it into practice.

The following day, under the guidance of Mrewa, we set up five of these gallows-like traps around a big chunk of carrion, and baited each with a piece of meat. As before, we then retreated into the cover of some nearby mopane and watched the slow, cautious assembling of the vultures and Marabou storks. They landed heavily, and with wings outstretched pranced awkwardly toward the array of bent-over saplings. One, hungrier or bolder than the others, pushed forward and pecked at the bait; the trap sprang itself at once, and a White-backed vulture struggled as a noose tightened around its broad neck. I sprinted forward, grabbed the bird's neck, cut the noose, and then controlled its struggling body and strong flapping wings by tucking it under my left arm, with its head to the rear, at the same time making its talons ineffective by holding the legs together. Back at camp, I put the vulture in our largest lidded reed basket, and John and I together set about fixing six of our medium-sized wire frames together, lining all but the bottom and the front side with a protective padding of hessian. Across the middle of this prefabricated cage I set a thick perch, in order to accommodate the width of the bird's talons. We put the cage on top of a large wooden bench that we had already made for the purpose, and tipped the basket to make the vulture go in. Over the next two weeks we caught five White-backed vultures, three White-headed vultures, one Eared- or Lappet-faced vulture, three Marabou storks and an African Tawny eagle. Three of the White-backed vultures showed no signs of settling down and would often regurgitate their daily rations, so I decided to set them free. I paid Mrewa 20 rand (£10), which no doubt made him the wealthiest of his peers.

The carrion-feeding raptors were located downwind of our living quarters for, in spite of their cages being cleaned out and serviced daily, the smell was anything but pleasant. Because of the perpetually hunched forms of the vultures and marabous, this area became fondly known as 'Death Row'. Undoubtedly, the prize of the collection proved to be the Lappet-faced vulture, the largest raptor of this region, with a wingspan of over three metres (nine feet). June named him Paris after Helen of Troy's lover, since she thought he looked so magnificent. It was soon after this that Mrewa came to my rescue again. He showed me how to make and set small grass nooses, and put a number of these in a nearby thicket. To my joy, by sunset of the same day the nooses had caught five members of the pheasant family, the attractive Red-billed francolin.

The cock birds have much larger spurs on their legs than the hens, so I could see that I had caught four males and only one female. The following two days Mrewa and I managed to catch a further three females for the collection, and from a different location in order to secure unrelated birds. Mrewa didn't ask any reward for his additional advice, but seemed pleased to be now held in such high esteem by the camp's Bwanas.

As my relationship with Chinky had progressed into one of mutual trust and respect, and it was obvious by her welcoming 'wowws' that she looked forward to my daily cleaning-out procedure with her, Robert put her care totally in my hands. She would play 'patty-paw' with the rake, and would lick my hand as I replenished her bedding reeds. Sometimes, as I bent down to the open hatch to kiss her paw, she would sneak a generous but gentle pumice stone lick on my cheek. June said, 'Jeremy, the way you talk about Chinky, if I hadn't known that she was a lioness, I would think that she was a beautiful girl that you had just fallen desperately in love with!'

I erected a mist-net at various different locations to try to catch a pair of friendly hammerkops. Although the birds seemed happy to walk around and beneath the net, they flatly refused to take wing anywhere near it; they almost appeared to enjoy the game of outwitting my attempts to catch them. However, during this time I netted a variety of single birds, including Giant kingfisher, coucal, Long-tailed starling, African skimmer, avocet, and a Barn owl; all of which I immediately released. There was no point in removing single specimens from the wild unless they could be paired up with mates back in Jersey, or if I knew, as with the raptors in my collection, that a specific UK zoo was interested in acquiring them.

Robert was determined to try out the effectiveness of Chinky's future travelling cage as a live-trap, although the last thing I wanted was to add any large mammal to my collection, for those animals we had were already taking up most of John's and my time. With a lot of effort we got the heavy metal crate to a suitable site and covered its floor with soil, raking this across the threshold to make a continuous surface with the ground outside. Robert fastened a piece of freshly killed meat to the far end of the trap, and I crawled inside to test the effectiveness of its mechanism. The drop-slide was pulled up to the maximum, where it rested on two small metal swivels, which in turn were attached to a cable that ran along the top of the trap and down to the bait. If anything tugged at the meat the cable would immediately dislodge the drop-slide, which thudded down and closed the trap. We camouflaged the trap under a good covering of branches and reeds, smothered its inside liberally with wildebeest dung to erase as much of our own smell as possible, and set the mechanism.

Just after dawn Robert and I drove to the trap, swerving between anthills, potholes and fallen branches, disturbing small groups of impala and warthog. Even Robert, usually so calm, seemed excited. As we approached the trap we heard the long mournful moans of a hyena and realised that this was our capture. As soon as the animal saw us it began to shriek and tear at the sides of sides of the cage. This was certainly not an animal that I wanted for my collection, so we would need to release it, without being attacked ourselves. We tied a rope to the handle at the top of the drop-slide, tossed it over a tree branch, and after backing our vehicle about ten yards away, fed the end of the rope into the cab. We then hauled on the rope to lift the slide, and the angry Spotted hyena vacated the trap and loped off into the distance.

As Easter approached, Robert received a radio message that Miles and Beryl Smeeton, with their daughter Clio, had just arrived in the territory and would like to visit Robert and June's camp on the banks of the Kwaai. I knew about the Smeetons as I had read about Beryl's journeys through China, Japan, Persia and Russia before the war (*Winter Shoes in Springtime*), and how she had ridden over the Andes into Patagonia, driven a van through much of the United States, and walked through Burma in the monsoons. The exploits and travels of Miles Smeeton were well known. His life in India where, as a regular army officer, he had regarded pig-sticking and big-game hunting as better training for jungle warfare than most of the official King's Regulations exercises. I had just read his recent book *A Taste of the Hills*, which described the light-hearted attempt that Beryl and he had made in 1939, with Sherpa Tensing (later of Mount Everest fame), to climb the 7,700 m (25,400 ft) Tirich Mir in the Himalayas. Although the story that had really captured so many people's imagination was of the Smeeton's two epic attempts to sail round Cape Horn, when on one occasion their yacht *Tzu Hang* somersaulted and, as Nevil Shute wrote in his foreword to Miles' book

Once is Enough, 'More ordinary people would undoubtedly have perished.' Perhaps Miles Smeeton's 20 years in uniform on four continents, which he ended as brigadier commanding the 1st Burma Brigade against the Japanese, gave him the tenacity to survive no matter what the odds.

The Smeetons were certainly no ordinary people. They arrived at our Fig Tree Camp on the Good Friday, and I had seldom met such a friendly family so keenly interested in everything that they saw. Miles was six feet six inches tall, and his wife Beryl and daughter Clio were both tall in comparison with the more petite June. On their first evening round the campfire, Miles told us how he had loved field sports for as long as he could remember. However over the years, in the course of their travels, he and Beryl had seen the consequences of all-the-year-round indiscriminate slaughter and come to realise how essential it was for a closed-season to be declared for big-game hunting safari operators. He was keen that viable conservation units be set aside for animal reserves and national parks.

As the Kays were trying to establish a society for fauna preservation in Ngamiland, they expressed their willingness to help in any way that they could to set up a conservation area in this northern region of the Okavango Delta. The best outcome would be if a game reserve could be established with the support of the local Batawana authorities, and thereby become the first tribal-sponsored game reserve in Africa. The results of these campfire discussions were significant, for on their return to Maun, the Smeetons spoke to the District Commissioner and influenced him to amend his previous opposition to the idea of a Batawana tribal-sponsored game reserve.

While I was preparing for the collection's journey back to base camp on the Thamalakane, thence by Riley's Transport to Francistown and by rail to Rhodesia, Clio had been very helpful in the daily tasks with the animals, and in helping plait reeds through the wire walls of the cages. She too loved talking to Chinky, which I must admit made me almost jealous.

Near the end of our stay at the Fig Tree Camp, gathering clouds warned us that the first storms of the rainy season were close at hand, and that it was important to get back to Maun before some parts of the track became impassable. We erected a tarpaulin on branch supports above the cages on 'Death Row', moved the reed baskets of the francolin and the tortoise under the DUKW, and left the crocodiles to enjoy a tropical drenching. Just before the first storm broke, everything became still and almost breathless. A silence, as deep as that of a cathedral crypt, hung over the veldt and the reed beds. Chinky swayed to and fro restlessly, Whisky gave a few stifled snorts. A gentle breeze fanned the ground and threw up eddies of dust and the first big plops of rain began to fall. From the north-west, the sky was slashed by laser-like beams of forked lightning, quickly followed by dynamite explosions of thunder as the full power and magnificence of a tropical storm reached us. Clusters of inky clouds moved overhead, releasing their reservoirs of water that cascaded like waterfalls on to the red soil around us. Due to the hardness of the earth the water was unable to soak in, and instead turned into muddy streams that found their way under the canvas lean-to, where we were sitting with our camp beds. Gradually the thunder crashed and rumbled away, and the lightning flickered over the far horizon. The dusty aridity of the dry season was over, and the rich moist smell of the earth was as agreeable as nectar is to a sunbird. I was thrilled to experience such a full-throated and dramatic African tropical storm in this way; I appreciated the diverse elements that make up the immense powers within our world.

During our last night at camp Chinky decided to give her final performance as a 'damsel in distress', but if the local lions heard her calls, they were not fooled again by her flirtatious enticements. We rose an hour before dawn so as to make a daybreak start. As the first light of the morning was just making the water sparkle on the tops of the tall grasses, we looked like a travelling circus leaving a gypsy encampment. The DUKW was piled high with the vulture and marabou crates, the metal trap, with Timmy tied to one of the bunks inside. June's diesel truck accommodated the bulk of the reed baskets and boxes; Chinky's truck had the aluminium dinghy strapped on top of it, and she lay comfortably in her reed-upholstered quarters, with far more space available to her than to anybody else.

So as to minimise the stress for the animals, the convoy retraced its route to the base camp at much the same pace as Whisky. In spite of this, it was difficult not to feel some anxiety for my wards, so that when we stopped for the night I checked every individual, filling up their water dishes and feeding them where necessary. Regrettably, all the raptors had regurgitated their final meal at Fig Tree Camp and showed no interest in taking any food. Another early start enabled the convoy to reach our Thamalakane base camp in the late afternoon of the second day, and three hours later the whole collection had been offloaded. I found the Red-billed and Hottentot teal looking contented in their river-fed pens.

I now had five days to wait until the Riley's Transport truck took John and me with the collection to the railhead at Francistown, and I found that I needed every minute of this to finalise things and make some additions to the collection. A second ostrich had been offered by somebody at the South African weather station outside Maun, a male. One of my metal live-traps had caught a young male Vervet monkey, which I was going to keep, for I knew we had a lone female Vervet in Jersey that had been presented to Gerald Durrell from Uganda. I named him Maunensis.

Robert kindly collected the female ostrich from the Greek trader at Sehitwa, and the pair of Spur-winged geese locally. My traps caught three delightful small green squirrels which, from the black speckles on their backs, I was able to identify as the local sub-species of the Bush squirrel *Paraxerus cepapi*. John was kept fully busy making two metal-lined boxes for them, and I ordered two large reed baskets as travel quarters for the Spur-winged geese.

Only two days now remained before my departure from Ngamiland. It took me an hour in Maun's post office to send a cable listing the collection of animals I needed transit permits for, and then I had to arrange the hire of a freight truck from Rhodesia Railways, to convey the animals from Francistown to Salisbury. I visited Riley's Hotel for a snack, and as I tried to decide upon my next task, my sandwich was suddenly snatched out of my hand from behind. I spun round, expecting some kind of bar-room brawl, but there on the next bar stool stood a shaggy olive-brown Chacma baboon, bobbing up and down as it enthu-siastically devoured my lunch. Most unlike my usual conservative and reserved behaviour, I snatched the remains of the sandwich back, and when the baboon flattened her ears in a threat posture, I slapped her across the muzzle; an act that immediately made her subservient to me as the Alpha male.

It turned out that this tame female baboon was owned by a government driver who had recently been forbidden to have her riding with him in the truck. The owner could see that I was showing interest in his pet, and offered her to me for 10 rand (£5). The bargain was struck, and after I took her leash, the baboon appeared to recognise that an ownership transfer had taken place, for she jumped into my arms and we exchanged an embrace. She turned out to be the most worthwhile purchase I had made for a long time, for she was remarkably tame, and through her possessiveness of me, her new master, became an excellent security guard to my collection.

As Clio Smeeton had provided me with so much help in looking after the collection at the Fig Tree Camp, I decided to name the baboon after her. I received an enthusiastic radio message from Clio to say how honoured she was, and I wondered just how many other British girls would have been happy to have a baboon named after them.

On my last afternoon I had some official calls to make. First I went and paid my respects to Mahumahati Moremi, and thanked her for allowing me to make an animal collection in her realm. After her assistant had looked over the list of animals that I was about to take out of Ngamiland, I was asked to contribute a sum of 24 rand (£12) to the tribal treasury. My next call was to the Protectorate's European colonial administration. The DC's office filled out various export permits in triplicate, stamped and adorned them with imposing blue and red wax seals, and enclosed them in a sizeable envelope with the solemn heading 'ON HER MAJESTY'S SERVICE – BRITISH BECHUA-NALAND PROTECTORATE'.

In the late afternoon I helped Robert transfer Chinky from the back of the Dodge truck to her travelling cage, which had been purged of its odours of wildebeest dung and hyena. Chinky lay stretched out on the mattress of reeds in the metal crate, but her eyes were narrower than usual, seeming to follow every movement that Robert and June made, as if she knew that farewell was imminent. Chinky had been almost like a child to them, and her departure would leave a painful gap in their lives.

After all the animals had been carefully loaded on to the Riley's Transport truck, and we had said our farewells, John's face shone like the rays of the rising sun, for he could not wait to leave the wilds behind him and return to the security of his Glendale village. Our journey across the northern Kalahari was uneventful, and we arrived in the goods yard of Francistown railway station almost to schedule. The Afrikaner stationmaster took us to a waiting goods wagon, into which we transferred the animal crates. Then I left John and Clio (the sandwich-snatcher) to guard the goods wagon, and to keep the gathering crowd of inquisitive Africans away from the animals, and went to the Veterinary Office to pick up the required export/import permits for the Bechuanaland /Rhodesia leg of the journey, which had to be endorsed by the head of the District's Game Department, Major Patrick Bromfield.

The train journey to Salisbury, via Bulawayo, was far more comfortable than the bumpy trip on the back of the Riley's truck, and most of the animals were now relaxed enough to eat their rations; even the vultures and Marabou storks stopped their regurgitating. We arrived at Salisbury in the early hours of the morning, and our wagon was detached and shunted into a siding. After attending to the animals, I visited the headquarters of Rhodesia's Veterinary Department to secure permission to transport the collection out to Glendale, in order to rest the animals for the three days before the Africargo flight to London. I then hired two lorries to convey the collection out to Douet Farm where we received an enthusiastic welcome from Robin, Pris and Roselle, who were keen to meet Chinky and rest of the Ngamiland collection. John was cheered by a group of farm workers with as much enthusiasm as Julius Caesar returning from a successful campaign.

A *Rhodesia Herald* article recorded my departure from Southern Rhodesia with the bold heading:

LIONESS IN THE CITY ... A lioness roared in Fourth Street, Salisbury, yesterday when a crowd of excited Africans gathered round a three-ton lorry parked outside the District Veterinary Office. The lioness, Chinky, was part of a consignment of wild animals which will be leaving Salisbury by air today en route for [Gerald Durrell's] Jersey Zoological Park in the Channel Isles. Besides Chinky, who has been reared in captivity for three years, and who will be the first fully grown lioness to make a scheduled flight from Rhodesia to Britain, are several maribou storks, vultures, ostriches, pythons, monkeys and crocodiles. FEW SNAGS ... At the veterinary office to collect a clean bill of health for the animals and supervise their

114

loading on the aircraft, was their hunter and captor, Mr. J. Mallinson. 'We have had few snags so far,' he said. 'The 800–mile road [and train] journey from Bechuanaland was quite uneventful and I am not anticipating much trouble on the air trip.' Mr. Mallinson said he would be feeding the animals on the air trip and was expecting to arrive in Jersey on Thursday.

The aircraft was a DC6 freighter, and I was the only passenger and I was listed on the flight manifest as an animal attendant – yet another new title for me. I checked that all the crates and Chinky's cage were strapped down firmly, and I wired up a small hole in the door of Clio's cage which she had been busily at work enlarging to get a better view. The engines spluttered into life. Chinky crouched on a thick mattress of wood-wool, her ears flickering as she was bewildered by the alien noise; her eyes became more slit-like and her body did a sudden shiver as the aircraft at full thrust rose into the starlit night sky. I raised the sliding door of her cage slightly to scratch her reassuringly under the chin. She seemed grateful for this contact with me, and lowered her head, with my hand inconveniently trapped between her powder-puff-like chin and the top of her plate-like paws. I kept my hand in this posi-tion until the plane had climbed to 35,000 feet and the engines had settled to a steady dull roar. Chinky became more relaxed and, as if in gratitude, started to lick the top of my hand with her rough, sandpaper tongue. I gently closed the slide, at the same time telling her that even the most experienced air traveller sometimes feels a shade nervous during take-off. Clio gave a couple of barks as if she totally agreed.

At Heathrow, the collection was transported to the airport's RSPCA Animal Hostel, where it had to have veterinary clearance before its onward journey to the Channel Islands the following morning. Odette Guiton, a Jersey girl that I had become extremely fond of before my departure from Jersey some seven months previously, and with whom I had corresponded from Africa, happened to be in London at the time of my arrival. Odette, with no mention of how nice it would be to see me again, did say how much she would like to meet the lioness that I had written so fondly about. So it was at the Animal Hostel, while intro-ducing her to Chinky, that I realised how she had to be the most desir-able mate for me. Almost as if the lyrics of the popular tune *Zambezi* had been written for me in the stars, the first verse of the song stated: 'I never thought I'd have the luck to fall in love, when I was bringing home a lion to the zoo ...'

Back in Jersey, the local media, Channel Television and the *Jersey Evening Post*, photographed the animals and interviewed me. On 14th May 1962 they printed an impressively captioned article with photographs, entitled: BACK FROM BECHUANALAND – MORE SPECIMENS FOR JERSEY ZOO which, among other things, recorded:

Just back from a private visit to Bechuanaland and Rhodesia where he renewed old acquaintances, is Jeremy Mallinson. Working at the Jersey Zoo, who gave him leave of absence for this trip, blond Jeremy Mallinson has brought back a superb collection of animals, most notably of which is 'Chinky' a lioness, which it is hoped will provide a mate for 'Leo'. This fine looking tawny beast showed great affection for Mr Mallinson when he entered her cage for an 'Evening Post' reporter on Saturday, demonstrating just how tame she is. Mr Mallinson patted and stroked 'Chinky' as if it was a domestic cat.

Chapter Nine

MENAGERIE TO CONSERVATION CENTRE

Back in Jersey, my first priority was to ensure that my African collection was adequately accommodated, and to find suitable zoos for those animals that Jersey Zoo was not interested in keeping. The latter included the pair of White-backed vultures, the three White-headed vultures, the Lappet-faced vulture, the pair of Black Spur-winged geese, and two of the four pairs of Red-billed francolins. I recognised that I was very much responsible for the future of the animals that I had taken from their African homeland. I went to the Bristol, Clifton & West of England Zoological Society (Bristol Zoo), the North of England Zoological Society (Chester Zoo) and the Zoological Society of London (London Zoo), in the hope that these respected establishments would be interested in adding some of the birds to their collections.

I went first to Bristol, which had been the first zoo that I had visited as a ten-year-old. There I saw my first Lowland gorilla, the famous Alfred, and had my first elephant ride. I had also been impressed by Gerald Durrell's comment in the foreword he wrote for Robert and Anne Warin's book *Portrait of a Zoo*:

Before I started my own zoological collection here in Jersey ... I was a professional animal collector for zoos and so I became familiar with behind-the-scenes of many major English zoos. Many of them, I regret to say, were not very well run in those days, and many zoo directors were sadly lacking in zoological knowledge, so much so that I had to choose with care the institutions that my precious animal cargoes went to. However, I never had any worries on this score when it came to letting Bristol have specimens. Under the

117

kindly, knowledgeable and efficient directorship of Reg Greed ...
I always knew my animals were in safe hands and would get the
best of treatment and attention.

So, what better recommendation could I have had for Bristol Zoo to
be given the first choice of the birds that I had to offer from my
Bechuanaland collection?

Reginald Greed could not have been more welcoming or to have
shown greater interest in my African travels. Unlike so many of his
peers at that time, he was a man who, no matter what position you held
at a zoo, be it distinguished or humble, would spare you much of his
time if he detected a genuine enthusiasm for animals. He had had a
long involvement in zoos, being appointed as Bristol's Superintendent
in 1929, before becoming its Director in 1957. He told me that even
before the war Bristol started a renaissance and revived one of the original concepts of a zoological society, that of providing pleasurable visits
for adults and children. In those days animal conservation was hardly
associated with the zoo world; they were mostly menageries aimed at
exhibiting a comprehensive range of species, and tried to display as
many different kinds of animals as possible – they were often 'stamp
collections' of exotic species. After the death of Reg Greed his son
Geoffrey, who soon became a good friend, served as Bristol Zoo's
Director during 1974–2001.

At Chester I met the zoo's Director-Secretary, George Mottershead.
Before my visit here I recalled that Gerald Durrell had told me that
when he was 24 he had landed a sizeable cargo of animals from one
of his West African collections at Liverpool docks, and that while London
Zoo had taken some of the rarities of special scientific interest, Chester
Zoo took over a third of the collection, with the proviso that the rest
of the animals be accommodated at the zoo before their further dispersal.
As a humble zookeeper, I was expecting to meet a rather inhibiting and
forbidding Zoo Director, so I was relieved to find a large bear-like and
most amicable man; his friendliness may of course have been due to
another of Gerald Durrell's generous letters of introduction. As its
founder took me round the zoo, I thought that I had never met anyone
so incredibly proud and knowledgeable of what he was showing me.
Chester Zoo had opened to the public in 1932, and Mottershead kept

proudly telling me that 'his' zoo was the first in the United Kingdom and Ireland to be a 'Zoo Without Bars'.

I was astonished to learn from him that it was not until 1950 that he and the Director of Dublin Zoo, Cedric Flood, discussed the lack of personal communication between zoos. They proposed, along with fellow zoological society directors, the establishment of an annual conference as a forum for the exchange of ideas and the furtherance of cooperation among collections. Dublin Zoo hosted the inaugural conference in late 1950, and, according to George Mottershead, it was an occasion where a number of directors met for the first time ever.

Furnished with a further letter of introduction, my final call was to London Zoo and to meet John Yealland, the Zoological Society's Curator of Birds. Yealland was an old friend of Gerald Durrell, who had accompanied him on his first collecting expedition to the British Cameroons (Cameroon), as described in Durrell's first book *The Overloaded Ark*. The book is dedicated: 'for John Yealland – In Memory of Birds and Beasts and 'The Beef That No Fit Die'. In 1959, when I had just joined the bird section at Jersey Zoo knowing so very little about exotic species, I had purchased John Yealland's *Cage Birds in Colour*, whose excellent illustrations so well helped me to identify the many species the zoo had at that time in its Tropical Bird House. I spent most of the afternoon being shown behind the scenes in the aviaries at Regent's Park. In spite of John Yealland's encyclopaedic avicultural knowledge, I found him to be a most modest, self-effacing and sensitive person, with a quiet and subtle sense of humour. As London Zoo had not been interested in acquiring more raptors for their collection, I had sold the White-headed and the Lappet-faced vultures to Bristol for £130, and Chester had paid £60 for the pair of White-headed vultures As London Zoo had not previously had the Red-billed francolin species represented in its collection, I decided to present the two available pairs to them.

With none of the three zoos interested in the pair of the darker-phase Spur-winged goose, on my return to Jersey I arranged for them to be sent to a great friend of Gerald Durrell's, the internationally known ornithologist Dr Jean Delacour, owner of Parc Zoologique de Clères, near Rouen in France. Jean Delacour had carried out zoological collecting in French Indo-China (Vietnam), and in Madagascar during the 1920s and 1930s. He was a prolific author of scientific papers and other publications, including the monograph *Pheasants of the World*.

Back in Jersey for the summer of 1962, I was delighted to renew my friendships with many of my previous wards, in particular with the Lowland gorilla N'Pongo, Lulu the chimpanzee and Peter the cheetah. Chinky seemed overjoyed to have my companionship again, and Clio displayed enthusiasm at being taken out of her cage on a collar and lead for a daily walk around the grounds of Les Augrès. She did alas become most possessive of me, and unfortunately bit the leg of a new young secretary, Betty Boizard, who I noted never came close to me again. As I got so much personal satisfaction in being surrounded by such a stimulating diversity of animals, I took up the zoo's offer of returning to my previous duties in the mammal section. Ken Smith did, once more, make it quite clear that my employment could only be on a temporary basis, for unless gate receipts greatly increased over the summer months, he doubted whether the zoo would be able to survive financially much longer.

While I was away in Africa, 'Shep' Mallet had been placed in charge of the bird section, and now had my ostriches, marabou storks, Yellow-billed kite and the two remaining pairs of Red-billed francolin under his care. John Hartley had been put in charge of the Small Reptile House, and had for the last five months been looking after the Rock monitors, chameleons and the assortment of amphibians that I had sent to the zoo from Southern Rhodesia. Now he had the added responsibility of the slender-snouted Nile crocodiles, pythons and Albert, the Bell's Hinged tortoise, from my Bechuanaland collection. During this time, due to the great success of Gerald Durrell's publications, he received a constant avalanche of letters from people seeking jobs at his zoo, and during the summer of 1962 a most attractive bevy of schoolgirls and some young university students joined the staff for their holidays. The overall enthusiasm and team atmosphere at the zoo was contagious, and it made an environment that was a joy to work in.

Soon after my return to the zoo, Trudy Smith stepped down from being responsible for the zoo's mammals, and Ken Smith put me in charge of that section. Although I was quick to inform N'Pongo, Chinky and Clio about my promotion, it totally failed to provoke enthusiasm on their part. Ken Smith, as the Superintendent, was still in charge of the day-to-day running of the zoo, but since my return from Africa it had become quite evident that the previous close relationship between the Smiths and the Durrells had broken down; most of the communication between them appeared to be through their secretaries, in challenging notes and memoranda.

It was during the autumn of 1962 that I decided to study Gerald Durrell's objectives and vision for the future of his zoological park. That was, of course, if the zoo was able to survive the financial crisis that was beginning to loom so threateningly. I also became interested in researching the history of zoos, to see how much they had contributed to the welfare, understanding and survival of the species that they had on exhibition. Whether, in fact, zoos were just devoting their efforts and resources to being places of entertainment and recreation.

Perhaps my chief reason for undertaking this research was that now I had reached my mid-twenties. I wanted to weigh up the pros and cons of taking animals from the wild, and to be satisfied that I had embarked on the right track in devoting my future to working in the zoo community for the welfare and conservation of wildlife. I had already been privileged to observe a great variety of species in their wild state, but I had also seen how their habitats in Africa were shrinking, and the threats that they were now facing. However I still had certain qualms about confining wild animals in zoos; particularly those that were kept in totally unsuitable conditions, with little consideration for their psychological and physical well-being.

During these 'peace of mind' and 'current state of play' investigations, I recalled how in the early 1960s Gerald Durrell had recorded in one of his programmes:

I wanted a life with animals, and I wanted to see the world. The only thing that presented itself to me at that time was to become an animal collector. And it was by becoming a collector that I learnt about the world and the destruction of the earth; which gave me the motivation to start the Jersey Zoo. Up to then, I thought zoos were simply convenient places that contained a lot of animals for my edification. I didn't realise that they had a purpose. And, in those days, even the majority of zoos didn't realise that they had a purpose.

121

Durrell had also often said that it had never been his intention that the small collection of animals that had been established at the Jersey Zoo, most of which he had collected during his expeditions to Africa and South America, should remain a straightforward zoological menagerie. His particular aim was to help in the preservation of animals, although he recognised from the outset that in the majority of cases it was the larger animals that were receiving the most attention from other zoos. Yet, scattered throughout the world, fascinating smaller creatures were being ignored. His ambition therefore, even during those early days of the Jersey Zoo, was to establish breeding groups of some of the smaller and lesser known animal species that shared this planet with us; studying their behaviour and needs would aid their conservation in the wild.

As I read more, it became evident that, in spite of the poor image that so many zoos had in the 1950s and early 1960s, a few trail-blazers like Gerald Durrell recognised that the overwhelming threat to wildlife arose less from the activities of hunters or zoos, than from the fact that a growing human population, and the spread of civilization, were making increasing inroads into natural habitats. Few members of the international conservation community considered that zoos could help them with their mission to avoid further extinctions. Gerald Durrell's philosophy was far more pragmatic; he recognised that zoos had their part to play in animal conservation and it was important to utilise all resources available. Success would come only when conservationists, zoo personnel, academic zoologists and educationists in their various fields co-operated wholeheartedly.

I found it fascinating to read accounts of some of the earliest zoos, which first appeared in Egypt and China several thousand years ago. In China, they were known as Gardens of Intelligence. Trade and exploration during the Renaissance brought Europe into contact with the new and wondrous worlds of Africa, the Americas and Asia. Improved trading connections supplied new collections with exotic species. Up to the beginning of the nineteenth century, little changed in Western collections; nearly all were the province of the nobility and the wealthy. Animals were kept for human amusement and as symbols of status and power. With few exceptions, animals were displayed for 'The gratification of curiosity and the underlining of the magnificence and power of their owners'.

The Royal Menagerie at the Tower of London, established by King

John in the early thirteenth century, was a good example of this. During these early times it was common for kings and other grandees to gift exotic species to one another. Richard Sabin, Curator of Mammals at the Natural History Museum tells us: 'Radiocarbon tests of a skull from one of the lions that terrified and delighted royalty, nobles and minions in the Tower of London, was dated between 1280 and 1385, and was found to be a representative of a form of lion from the Barbary Coast that was driven to extinction by hunters in the early twentieth century.' In those days it did not occur to people to try and set up self-sustaining captive populations, and the wild populations were simply there to be plundered. It was not until the Duke of Wellington acted in 1835 that the animals from the Tower were transferred to the new London Zoo.

I was interested to read that historians have called the nineteenth century 'the Century of Science' because of the major advances in those fields; within the study of natural history, this was the golden age of museum development and, by extension, zoo development as well. Also, with the publication in 1859 of *On the Origin of Species by Means of Natural Selection, or the Preservation of Favoured Races in the Struggle for Life*, it was the era of Darwinism, with all of its ground-breaking evolutionary ramifications.

As Gerald Durrell had decided upon the extinct dodo as Jersey Zoo's symbol, I made it a priority to read about how this turkey-sized flightless bird of the Mascarene Islands became extinct in about 1681, less than a hundred years after its first being described by a European. Hachisuka's book *The Dodo and Kindred Birds, or the Extinct Birds of the Mascarene Islands* so well summarises how the species' direct extermination resulted from the nourishment it gave to hungry seafarers and the destruction of its eggs by introduced rats and pigs. All that remains of the bird is represented by a mounted specimen in the Museum of Zoology, Cambridge, an almost complete skeleton in the British Museum, a head and a right foot in Oxford, a small upper mandible in Slovakia, and some skeletal fragments in both Prague and Mauritius; there are also some contemporary Dutch still-lifes.

What may be the last record of a person having a live dodo in their possession was shown to me by Professor Janet Kear, who had discovered a reference in the brochure of Berkeley Church in Gloucestershire. This refers to the Chief Mate of the East Indiaman *The Berkeley Castle*, homeward bound in 1681, who recorded in his diary (now in the British

Museum) eating a dodo that had been previously caught in Mauritius. And according to Christine Jackson's *Dictionary of Bird Artists of the World*, Roelandt Savery (1576–1639) made two paintings that include dodos, which were based on live specimens in the menagerie of Maurice of Nassau, Prince of Orange (1567–1625).

I found a number of records relating to other extinct species whose last representatives ended their days in zoological establishments. For instance, the Passenger pigeon of North America was once so prolific that its migration in dense flocks darkened clear skies like storm clouds. By 1850, due to the popularity of the pigeon's savoury flesh, several thousand people were employed solely in its capture and marketing. In 1855 one New York handler alone had a daily turnover of 18,000 pigeons. 1n 1879 a billion birds were captured in the State of Michigan. The last nest was observed in 1894, the last wild specimen was shot in 1900, and the last captive bird died in Cincinnati Zoo in 1914. In *A Passion for Natural History*, edited by Clemency Fisher, it is recorded that a population was kept in the zoological collection at Knowsley Hall near Liverpool, the home of the Earls of Derby. These birds were originally part of a gift of American birds and mammals sent to Lord Stanley (later the 13th Earl) by his friend and admirer the French-American artist and explorer Audubon. The birds thrived and the first chicks fledged in 1832. However, when the 13th Earl died in 1851 the animal collection had to be dispersed, and though 70 Passenger pigeons were included in the auction they were split into small groups or sold separately; had they been kept as one group, this colonial breeder could possibly have survived.

The story of the once common (though of restricted range) zebra species, the quagga, represents another wasted opportunity for zoos to secure a self-sustaining captive population of a now extinct animal. It is reported that in 1861 a London Zoo collector in South Africa published advertisements asking specifically for 'zebras – not quagga'. Between 1865 and 1878 the quagga had disappeared from throughout its range of Cape Colony and the Orange Free State and, like the dodo, was extinct within a century of the species being first described. As with the Passenger pigeon, the last known quagga died in a zoo, a mare that had lived in the Amsterdam Zoo from 1867 until 1883. A number of European zoos exhibited quaggas during the mid-nineteenth century, including Antwerp, Amsterdam, Berlin and London, but in spite of the opportunity to form a breeding population, the need for such an important requirement had yet to dawn on the zoo community.

It was evident from my reading that until after the Second World War zoos were predominantly museums, exhibiting as many different species as possible; the more dramatic the animals were, the more financially profitable the zoos would be as places of recreation. I found a few examples of far-sighted people establishing captive breeding programmes for species that were threatened with extinction in the wild. Perhaps the earliest example of this was the Père David's deer. In 1865, the French missionary and naturalist Père Armand David described the large handsome deer species that he saw in the Chinese Emperor's Hunting Park near Peking, though by this time the species was already extinct in the wild. A few individuals from the Imperial Hunting Park were sent to various European zoos. Peking's last female died in 1922, and it was thanks to the foresight of the 11th Duke of Bedford, who in 1900 acquired 18 animals from various European Zoos for his park at Woburn Abbey, that the species survived. This herd prospered; so much so that some deer were sent back to Beijing in 1956 and the first calf was born there in 1957. In November 1985 a herd was reintroducd to the Dafeng Milu Reserve near Beijing.

The European bison or wisent is another species that owes its survival to a captive population. At the beginning of the twentieth century the only surviving truly wild herd was in the Bialoweiza Forest in Poland. In 1914 there were 737 animals in the herd, but all were slaughtered during World War I. In 1923 the International Association for the Preservation of the Wisent was founded, and the following year recorded a total of 33 males and 33 females, all of Bialoweiza origin, distributed among various European zoos. It was not until after the Second World War that international cooperation began to produce any real signs of breeding success. The turning point came in 1952 when a free-living herd of wisent was re-established in the Bialoweiza primaeval forest, and since free-ranging herds have been established in a number of Eastern European countries particularly Poland and the Russian Federation.

Another example of a species that owes its survival to a scientifically managed cooperative captive breeding programme is the Przewalski horse. The first Asiatic wild horses to be brought out of the wild were captured between 1899 and 1903, and today's population of this species traces its ancestry to just eleven animals captured at the turn of the twentieth century, and a single male brought out of the wild in 1947. Zdenek Veselovsky recorded, however, in the first international stud-book for the Przewalski horse, that the captive bred stock was descended from twelve founders and one domestic Mongolian mare. Subsequently, it has been through scientific management, good cooperation and coordination of the zoo population that the species' survival has been assured; most importantly, with the help of many other bodies, since 1985 a number of free-living herds have been released into the wild in Mongolia.

When Gerald Durrell gave me his letter of introduction to London Zoo, he had mentioned that when John Yealland was Curator at Peter Scott's newly formed Wildfowl Trust, it was he who had brought back the first two Hawaiian geese to Slimbridge in 1950. This critically endangered species had declined from an estimated population of 25,000 in the Hawaiian Islands in the eighteenth century to fewer than 30 birds in the 1950s. Now, thanks largely to the success of the extended captive breeding programmes at both Slimbridge and in Hawaii, and an extensive reintroduction programme in Hawaii, the future of this species looks encouraging. Durrell also told me that it had been the conservation mission of Peter Scott's Wildfowl Trust that had originally inspired him; Scott's conservation objectives were a template for the type of establishment that he dreamt of founding one day.

After reading so much about the history of menageries, it had been marvellous to learn about recent successes, and to recognise the potential conservation role of a modern zoo; this, in my opinion, justified taking animals from their native habitat. With this in mind, I came to appreciate Gerald Durrell's aims for his zoo as a place of education, research and captive breeding, particularly of those animals threatened with extinction in the wild. It was impossible not to have become inspired by my mentor's contagious enthusiasm and his determination not to allow his Noah's Ark in Jersey to collapse, in spite of the serious financial difficulties it was facing. So, having been successfully converted to such a noble cause, I had no alternative but to tie my flag firmly to the Ark's mast and to remain working at the Jersey Zoo until Providence directed otherwise. With an almost missionary zeal I became one of Gerald Durrell's most dedicated disciples.

In September 1962, Gerald and Jacquie Durrell returned to Jersey after six months and 25,000 miles through New Zealand, Australia and Malaya, making a series of television films for the BBC. In the introduction to his book about the trip, *Two in the Bush*, he writes: 'it was a glorious trip and I enjoyed every moment of it'. Alas, on his return to the zoo he found anything but enjoyment. In spite of a record summer season through the turnstiles, the zoo's finances had reached a point of crisis, and morale was low. Drastic action had to be taken to prevent the zoo from folding.

On 8th November 1962, Gerald Durrell announced to the local press that he would be asking the States of Jersey (the island's government) to furnish Jersey Zoo with a grant to help establish it as a Trust for the breeding and preservation of endangered animals. He told the *Jersey Evening Post* that the zoo was now getting 100,000 visitors a year, and he felt it could justifiably expand its activities as a scientific organisation for the breeding of rare animals. 'It was an expansion,' he said, 'which would go far beyond the Island; it could grow into a worldwide affair, for if successful, the zoo would be the first in the world to take such a major step. It was of vital importance, especially in the light of the recent upsurge of interest in the preservation of wildlife.'

Four days later, the *Daily Mail* published a short article entitled DURRELL ZOO IN THE RED:

> Mr Gerald Durrell, author and wild animal collector, is £12,000 in the red with the zoo he opened in Jersey four years ago. His appeals that the zoo should become a wild-life preservation trust partly subsidised by the people or Government of Jersey have met with protests.

In exasperation, and almost as a final throw of the dice, Gerald Durrell terminated the contract that he had had with Ken Smith, and took over as the zoo's Director. He advertised for a professional company administrator and troubleshooter, who it was hoped could sort out the mess that Jersey Zoological Park Ltd now found itself in. When interviewing Catha Weller (an interview referred to in Douglas Botting's excellent biography of Durrell), Gerald Durrell recorded:

127

She waltzed into my office ... diminutive, round, with sparkling green eyes and a comforting smile. Yes, she knew how to do book-keeping, shorthand and typing – the lot. I looked at Jacquie and Jacquie looked at me. We both knew instinctively that a miracle had happened.

Catha Weller started work a few days later, and after seeing the books and the drastic financial state that the zoo was in, she formed the impression that she had been brought in simply to wind the place up, and gave her job no more than six months. But fortunately for all the animals and the zoo staff, thanks to her expertise, far-sightedness and persuasive ways, she was able to make enormous economies. By reorganising the zoo's administration and operation she reduced the financial burden on the zoo's founder. It was not long before she optimistically declared that, with prudent future management, it could be possible to operate the zoo as a viable concern.

In January 1963 an appeal was launched to raise £15,000 with the intention of making the zoo the headquarters of a Trust. Gerald Durrell stated, 'There will be created, it is hoped, an amenity of tremendous importance, and Jersey Zoo will become a power in the world with regards to its conservation activities.' He went on: 'The Trust has worked out a ten-year programme of development and it is hoped by the end of this period that a great many breeding colonies of threatened species will be established at the zoo. By attempting this extraordinary conservation project, it is considered that the Jersey Zoo will be the only zoo in the world to devote all of its resources to the cause of conservation and so, as a zoo, will be unique in so much as all the species on display will be those threatened by extinction in their natural state.'

Steps were now taken to wipe out the zoo's outstanding debts. As Gerald Durrell had kept all his fan letters, Catha Weller set about writing to the fans requesting their help. Donations soon poured in, from cheques for £1,000 to a child's pocket money. Also, through the zoo's friendly bank manager Ray Le Cornu, a benefactor was introduced who presented the zoo with a cheque for $2,000. However, Durrell's own financial contribution was by far the biggest; he was so determined to bring his dream to fruition that he agreed to shoulder the whole bank loan, waiving any right he might have to reclaim the money. As Douglas

Botting records: 'thus, in effect, donating it (£20,000) to the zoo. Since his only income was from writing and television – unreliable livelihoods both – he had condemned himself to unremitting toil for years to come. But he was adamant.'

Although I was enjoying my daily work with so many different species of mammals, some of which I treated almost as my personal pets, I started to look into other ways to earn money, should the zoo's finances fail. Because it had become one of my ambitions to study as many different species in their native habitat as possible, I started to look into organising an 18–month trip to take me back to Bechuanaland for another animal collection in the Okavango Delta. Instead of flying the animals back to the British Isles, I meant to take them by boat from Cape Town to New York, and through the advice of Fred Zeehandelaar, who was reputed to be the largest and most respected supplier of exotic species to North American zoos, to find the most appropriate zoos to receive them.

After this United States venture, I would follow the footsteps of my mentor by undertaking a collecting expedition in British Guiana (Guyana), for this had been the first country in South America that Gerald Durrell had visited in 1950. Recently, he had kindly inscribed a copy of his book *Three Singles to Adventure*, about his activities in Guyana, writing: 'For Jeremy, in the hope that one day he may take a Single to Adventure – Gerry Durrell.' What an idea! And how foolish it would be for me not to try and realise such a hope in the future!

I was also considering having Clio accompany me on these trips. I could arrange to have her photographed on Westminster Bridge, with the backdrop of the Houses of Parliament, in the presence of the press. I felt confident that journalists would be keen to meet her and to hear about the baboon's imminent return to her African homeland, and to learn about the type of adventures that she was sure to have back in Africa and during her time in North and South America. We could have a series of articles about Clio's travels, with photographs of her on top of Table Mountain; at her birthplace in Ngamiland; on top of the Empire State Building; at the test cricket ground in Georgetown, Guiana; all this could help the overall finances of my proposed travel plans.

While I was fine-tuning the planning of such an extensive expedition, Catha Weller told me that Gerald Durrell wanted to see me in his flat the following morning; I immediately worried about what I had done wrong. Had I been spending too much time playing with N'Pongo and Lulu on the front lawn? Too frequently exercising on a lead the zoo's new female cheetah Paula, recently arrived as a gift from the Johannesburg Animal Orphanage as a mate for Peter? Devoting too much attention to grooming and talking to Chinky, who was still being rather beastly to her Dublin mate Leo? Whatever it might be (and as I went to bed that night various other scenarios started to occur to me, including the thought that my services were no longer required), I tried to occupy my mind with the comforting thought that at least I now had a potential second string to my bow.

The following morning when I entered the room I recall being immediately relieved to see the welcoming smile on the face of the zoo's founder. He ushered me to a chair and, without a second of small talk, said, 'Jeremy, would you do me the honour of becoming my deputy – the Deputy Director of Jersey Zoo?' I was almost speechless, and I probably stammered that I would indeed 'be most proud', but I asked him, as I had gone so far in organising my African and American trips, whether he would give me 48 hours to come back to him on such a magnificent offer; and fortunately he agreed to this. When two days later I returned to his office, smiling as if I had just won the football pools, I told him how very proud I was to accept the honour of becoming his deputy. Whereupon Gerald Durrell kicked away any degree of formality and, in what I imagined was the Corfiot way of expressing pleasure, came out from behind his desk and embraced me by kissing me on both cheeks. With my customary British reserve I foolishly blushed, though I knew that his action stemmed from genuine emotion.

After my mentor had informed me what he now expected of me in my new supportive role as his Deputy, and the responsibilities that I would have to shoulder, he asked whether I had any questions. As going to South America had become one of my ambitions, I asked whether, when the running of the zoo had reached a satisfactory level and he was happy about its day-to-day management, he would allow me to take two to three months' leave of absence, so that I could undertake a trip to countries like Bolivia, Brazil and British Guiana? Durrell kindly responded by saying, 'Of course, dear boy, you must be given the opportunity to visit such a magical continent in the future, but let us decide on this later; the time could be right in a couple of years.' There was no formal contract to sign, although I knew that when we shook hands on the terms of my appointment no securer contract between boss and deputy could ever have been achieved. So I left his office feeling as gratified as if I had just received a major award from the Queen.

Soon after my acceptance, my boss recalled: 'Jeremy, with his Duke of Wellington nose, his buttercup-coloured hair and his bright blue eyes, was as devoted to our animals as if he had given birth to each of them personally. His habit in referring to human male and female acquaintances as "fine specimens" was an indication that his job tended to creep into his everyday life.'

On 26th March, 1963, the fourth anniversary of the zoo's opening, The Jersey Evening Post announced that I had accepted the post as the zoo's Deputy Director, and that I would be taking up my duties on 1st April. The article showed a photograph of me holding the hand of an extremely timorous looking two-year-old female Bornean orang-utan, whose free arm grimly hung on to her mate for reassurance. These juvenile examples of an endangered species were called Oscar and Bali, and had just arrived, having been presented to Gerald Durrell by the Government of Singapore after their confiscation from illegal animal traders. Two other important birthday presents had arrived; an extremely tame young male Black ape from Celebes (Sulawesi) called Hitam, and a pair of attractive Blue-crowned pigeons from New Guinea.

On April Fools' Day I formally dedicated myself to the development and success of Jersey Zoo's conservation mission. Three months later, on 6th July 1963, the official deeds of the Jersey Wildlife Preservation Trust were incorporated at a formal sitting of Jersey's Royal Court, and the Trust became legally registered as a charity. This was due to the support of some of Jersey's prominent residents: the Earl of Jersey; James Platt (a Director of Shell International); Lady Coutanche (wife of the ex-Bailiff of Jersey); Senator Wilfred Krichefski; Deputy (later Senator) Reginald Jeune; and the owner of Les Augrès Manor, Major Hugh Fraser. Gerald Durrell had handed the ownership and management of his zoo to the Trust, with himself as its (honorary, unpaid) Director and Lord Jersey as its President; with a Zoological Park Management Committee comprising the President, the Director, an accountant, an ornithologist, Catha Weller as Secretary and PRO, and myself as Deputy Director. The establishment of the zoo as a Trust marked a significant milestone in the realisation of one of Durrell's ambitions for his 'Stationary Ark'. It was no longer a dream but a registered animal conservation charity.

David Attenborough, who was already well-known for his BBC television *Zoo Quest* series that had included programmes of his expeditions to the Argentine, New Guinea and Madagascar, visited Jersey in August. An article in the local paper recorded:

DAVID ATTENBOROUGH AT JERSEY ZOO. Two of the country's leading raconteurs and expert broadcasters on animals and animal life, this morning recorded a BBC sound radio programme in the natural history series. This will be heard at 1.10 p.m. on August 18th and will be entitled *Island Zoo*.

An accompanying photograph showed Gerald Durrell introducing Hitam to Attenborough, with the monkey's hand covering the microphone as if he personally had no wish to be interviewed.

At the time of my marriage to Odette Guiton on 26th October 1963, the zoo recorded the first breeding in captivity of the Red-billed francolin, and a sub-species of the Bush Squirrel, the parents of whom had been a part of my Okavango Delta collection. Also, a litter of kittens had been born to the female Serval cat Tammy, who had been part of my Southern Rhodesia collection. Our first child Julian was born on 24th May 1965, and Gerald wrote the following note to Odette:

Can it be that you succeed where PANDAS fail?
For this – you know – you could be put in jail?
Instead of yet another squalling brat
Why not a pigmy marmoset or vampire bat?
Why not at least, a beast that we can show?
Not something pink that goggles, croon and crow.
These sexual orgies we don't mind the least –
But next time 'try' and have a beast.

With love,
Gerry and Jacquie

Chapter Ten

EXTINCTION IS FOREVER

The Durrell's Christmas card for 1963 was one of Gerald's caricature sketches of him hauling a Noah's Ark, which he had renamed: *THE OVERDRAFT ARK*. The boat was crowded with an assortment of Jersey Zoo's mammals and birds; while accompanying the Director on the river bank were two tortoises, the first with a torch, its companion with a box of sandwiches, strapped to the top of their shells, as they walked in the opposite direction towards a signpost that proclaimed: *To Extinctionville*. Under the sketch was written: *May we wish you what we wish Ourselves*, and beneath this was a drawing of the juvenile pair of Orangutans Oscar and Bali, holding a placard that said:

Freedom From Hunger, Freedom From Fear
But, Above All Freedom From Extinction This Year.

In June 1964 I accompanied Gerald Durrell to my first wildlife conference, entitled: 'Zoos and Conservation Symposium', held at The Zoological Society of London (ZSL) and sponsored by The International Union for the Conservation of Nature (IUCN, now the World Conservation Union); The International Union of Directors of Zoological Gardens (IUDZG, now World Association of Zoos and Aquariums – WAZA); and The International Council for Bird Protection (ICBP, now Birdlife International). Perhaps this meeting can claim to be the first of its kind in assembling under one roof zoo personnel, animal dealers, research institutions, game departments, conservation societies and other organisations concerned with the welfare of wild animals. In welcoming the delegates and observers, The Duke of Edinburgh, in his capacity as President of ZSL, stated that he felt that the symposium marked a

133

new stage in the general progress of zoos by securing widespread recognition of the fact that zoos not only have a special part to play in the conservation of wildlife, but also a particular responsibility to ensure that conditions in zoos are such as will enable them to play this part effectively. He emphasised that conservation and the public interest must be long-term objectives.

Professor François Bourlière (President of IUCN) who, with Peter Scott, Dr Osman Hill and Dr Ernst Lang, became founder members of the Jersey Wildlife Preservation Trust's Scientific Advisory Committee, highlighted how the modern zoo was essentially different from its forerunners. Whereas at the beginning of the century zoos were predominantly museums exhibiting single specimens of as many animals as possible, or were mere amusement parks, some of them had now become research and educational centres and could be regarded as the link between the modern world and the receding domain of nature. In his summing up, Professor Bourlière echoed Gerald Durrell's 1950s belief that zoos could well adopt the function of saving threatened species from extinction, by affording refuges for animals whose natural habitats were disappearing under the pressure of increasing human population. At best, it might be possible to develop populations in captivity from which, in the course of time, wild populations could be reinforced, or even new populations established in suitable areas.

Dr Ernst Lang, the Director of Basel Zoo, Switzerland, who was considered at that time to be one of Europe's foremost zoo directors, touched on the subject that I also considered to be of paramount importance. How, if the human relationship with the animal is one of interest and sympathy, the animal is likely to thrive; otherwise it will not. He also emphasised the importance of creating conditions of captivity in which animals can be contented, for without contentment it is unlikely that satisfactory breeding and the rearing of young will be successful.

In this context I knew from my own hands-on experiences with animals the importance of getting the balance right. Through a degree of sympathy and mutual respect exceptional relationships can develop between human and those animals placed under one's care. Perhaps my first real experiences of such relationships with adult exotic species had been with Peter the cheetah and Juanita the female Collared peccary at Jersey Zoo. And later with Chinky, when I had held the lioness's paw in order to comfort her while the DC6 Africargo engines were noisily taking the plane to its cruising height; and with Clio my pet Chacma baboon. However, I shall always remember two occasions when I am sure that my affection for, and personal relationship with, animals under my care was responsible in one case for the survival of a mother and infant, and in the other, satisfactory post-operative recovery of another animal.

The young male Vervet monkey Maunensis, that had entered one of my traps on the banks of the Thamalakane River just before I left the Okavango Delta, had grown into a fine adult, and had paired success-fully with his Ugandan born female Mary. Although I was Gerald Durrell's Deputy Director, I was still doing a good deal of routine animal work in the zoo's Mammal House; caring for anything from the anthropoid apes to the newly arrived Ring-tailed lemurs. While checking the primate cages early one morning, I found Mary lying motionless on the floor with an infant lying at her side, its umbilical chord still attached to the placenta. I quickly coaxed Maunensis into a small 'shut-off', and with the help of a keeper, Michael Armstrong, wrapped the cold bodies of mother and infant in blankets and conveyed them to the zoo's small animal hospital where we put them both into a human incubator.

The zoo's consultant veterinarian Nicholas Blampied was called and he gave Mary some injections and detached the umbilical chord from the infant. We then submerged most of the infant's body in hot water, and once it revived and became quite lively, we dried it with a hair-dryer. After this I was left to try to bring some degree of life back to the still motionless mother. I must have held Mary's hand, gently pulsating her fingers, for well over an hour, before I detected a slight response from one of her fingers. She slowly opened her eyes and, on seeing a friend, started to tighten her fingers around mine. From then my subcon-scious told me that provided I stayed with her for another hour or so, she would be sure to make a full recovery. This she did, and during her time at the zoo she successfully reared 14 young in less than 13 years, thereby providing one of the first examples of the reproductive capacity of a species of guenon.

Over the years, my relationship with N'Pongo matured into one of deep friendship and mutual respect. Whenever she saw me approaching she would utter her 'rumbling' noises of affection, which I considered to be a more genuine and flattering greeting than one often received from a human. The spoken word of a human sometimes only represents polite deception, but with gorillas there is no such mendacity. N'Pongo had to be examined by a team of medics which included two consultant anaesthetists, a consultant paediatrician, a general practitioner, a maternity hospital sister and two consultant veterinarians. They in turn were assisted by the person in charge of the gorillas and orangutans, Richard Johnstone-Scott, and the zoo's biologist. When N'Pongo's examination was over, she was returned from the zoo's Animal Hospital to the heated inner den of her accommodation where Richard and I remained sitting on either side of her prostrate body, which we had comfortably propped up on a deep bed of wood-wool.

We each held one of N'Pongo's rough cold hands until they gradually became warmer; she slowly regained consciousness and we encouraged her with comforting words. When her hands started to respond to our flexing of her fingers, her sunken eyes blinked opaquely before managing to focus on her two favourite human friends. Her grip tightened, almost digging her fingernails into the palm on our hands, as if to show her appreciation of our concern for her plight. Seeing N'Pongo's surfacing from the bewilderment of an anaesthetic and her recognition of us, seeing the transformation of her strained wizened countenance to that of the face of a totally relaxed young female gorilla in the prime of health, was a privilege for me. After this experience, I often reflected on the degree of trauma an animal as intelligent as a gorilla would have had to deal with, if such a relationship of bonding between human and ape had not been so successfully nurtured and been so evident, as had been the case with both Richard and myself.

However, such traumas can sometimes work the other way. For when Chinky became pregnant letters had flowed between Jersey and the Okavango Delta with as much excitement and intensity as if I had married the Kays' only daughter. But just before the lioness gave birth her cubs died, peritonitis developed and before it was possible to do anything she also died. I recall informing Gerald Durrell about Chinky's death and he, listening to my shaking voice and seeing the tearful state that I was in, quickly thrust a glass of brandy in my direction. At the time of this loss I recognised that there could never be a replacement in the animal world for Chinky, for she had become a part of my life and had taught me so much about trust and the true understanding of animal friendship. Ever since leaving the Okavango with her I had felt totally responsible for her welfare. Now that she was gone, I doubted whether I would ever again be as devastated at such a loss of an animal; particularly with that of such a sizeable, powerful, but gentle creature as Chinky, whom I had spent so much time in cultivating and gaining her respect and friendship.

In May 1965, Gerald Durrell, John Hartley and a BBC television crew, with its producer Chris Parsons (who later became Director of the BBC's Natural History Unit), returned from a four-month animal-collecting expedition in Sierra Leone. Two tame leopard cubs, a young chimpanzee, Black-and-White Colobus monkeys, Bosman's pottos, porcu-pines, a variety of squirrels, White-crested hornbills, African Wood owls, African pythons, were among the 90 animals in this West African collec-tion. The expedition had acquired such a diverse collection of rare species that the BBC was able to produce a series of six 30–minute programmes which were screened during the course of the year. It also provided the material for a part of another of Gerald Durrell's best-selling books, *Catch Me a Colobus*. All such events were incalculably valuable publicity for Jersey Zoo, as well as providing some essential personal income for the zoo's director. As Gerald Durrell had steadfastly refused to take any financial remuneration for his iconic leadership of the recently estab-lished Trust, his title was appropriately changed from Zoo Director, to that of Honorary Director of the Jersey Wildlife Preservation Trust; he had always been the contributor and provider, as opposed to being the recipient.

Gerald Durrell showed me a letter that had arrived at the zoo during his absence in Sierra Leone; a school teacher from Wanganui in New Zealand wrote: 'Having read all your books, I started to read other authors who you had done forewords to in the travelogue field, and I was delighted to renew acquaintance with Jeremy Mallinson, whom I met in Southern Rhodesia very many years ago. You can tell him I was very pleased that the rumour which had passed around my friends in Rhodesia that he had been shot in the head and killed in the Congo was obviously untrue.' After reading this, I remarked to the Honorary Director that when he replied to the letter could he say how equally pleased I was that the rumour had not been true, and that the story had probably germinated from my scooter crash and my time on the danger-list at the Potgietersrus Voortrekkers Hospital in the Northern Transvaal, in March 1958.

After the excitement of settling-in, and getting to know the animals from the Sierra Leone collection, the zoo was delighted to record its first birth of a Brazilian tapir from Claudette, who had been presented to the zoo by Armand and Michaela Denis, and had been successfully paired with Claudius from Gerald Durrell's collection from Argentina. I recalled that it had been just over three years previously that I had had tea with Michaela Denis at Meikles Hotel in Salisbury, Southern Rhodesia, while I was undertaking my first collection of animals, which coincided with the Denis's filming of *Operation Noah* in the Zambezi Valley near the Kariba Dam.

During our conversation at Meikles about the aims of Gerald Durrell's zoo in Jersey, and the plight of so many threatened species, I remembered when I had first seen Michaela in one of Armand's renowned East African TV programmes. In particular, when one minute he would be dramatically describing a Kenyan landscape, and then the camera would swing on to Michaela appearing from behind an acacia tree waving enthusiastically to Armand; whereupon he would announce, as if he had been taken totally by surprise, 'Ah, there's my beautiful wife, Michaela.' She was undoubtedly a most interesting and charming person to talk to, as well as a dedicated conservationist with a real love for Africa's wildlife. However I did find it rather disconcerting when our conversation was frequently punctuated by Michaela giving one of her famous friendly waves to yet another person who had recognised her on their entering Meikles spacious lounge.

Thanks to the excellent administrative management of the zoo by Catha Weller, and the professional team of animal staff that had been employed, Gerald Durrell was now happy with the standards being maintained and the overall operation. So on the strength of the agreement we had made at the time of my appointment two years previously, he told me that if it was still a compelling ambition of mine to visit South America, that the autumn of 1965 would be the most convenient time for me to be away from the zoo. My most supportive wife Odette was happy for me to get what she termed 'The South

American Bug' out of my system once and for all; I had been talking about my determination to undertake such an expedition before our engagement, and, like Gerald Durrell, she understood that the trip was important to me.

As I could only be away from the zoo for about ten weeks, I had to abandon my original plan to take Clio with me, and instead would spend half my time looking for a legendary animal, the mitla, that had been described by Colonel Percy Fawcett at the beginning of the twentieth century in Bolivia. This would give me the opportunity to travel on at least two tributaries of the Amazon, and to see some of the natural wonders of South America. The remainder of my time would be spent visiting British Guiana (Guyana) to bring a small animal collection back from Georgetown. I would also try to get to the small town of 'Adventure' on the west bank of the Essequibo River that Gerald Durrell had visited in 1950.

After I was interviewed on Jack Di Manio's BBC early morning programme *Today*, a national newspaper carried an over-dramatised article entitled:

ZOO MAN'S QUEST IN 'THE JUNGLE OF NO RETURN'
– A young British zoologist will make a one-man expedition into the Bolivian jungle to look for an animal that has only been seen twice. He is Jeremy Mallinson, 28–year-old deputy director of a Jersey zoo owned by television personality Gerald Durrell. He will spend two months looking for a 'Mitla' – described by the explorer Colonel Percy Fawcett in 1925 as a 'small black, dog-like cat'- in the forests of Rio Abuna. The area he will be exploring is near where Colonel Fawcett and his elder son disappeared while searching for South American 'lost cities'. Indian tribes, who have never seen white man, hunt in the forests. Mr. Mallinson said yesterday; 'This has been one of my most compelling desires for years.'

So, rather similar to the article that had appeared in the *Rhodesia Sunday Herald* some four years previously, about the dangers of my expedition to the Okavango Swamps, I was pleased to leave England to escape any further embarrassments.

When I arrived in La Paz, the British Ambassador to Bolivia, Mr David Crichton, had already learnt about my proposed Bolivian venture from various press cuttings that had been sent via the diplomatic bag. The contents of some of the articles had evidently made the Crichtons curious to meet me, as well as making them concerned about my ultimate safety. For, as they were to divulge to me at a luncheon that they gave for me at the embassy, their concern was: as I was a British citizen, if I did disappear in the forests of northern Bolivia, who would they send to look for me, and how would they know where to look?

Once more in my life, I benefited from the reflected glory of being associated with the Durrell family. For in the early part of the ambassador's diplomatic career he had replaced Lawrence Durrell at the embassy in Belgrade, so knew him reasonably well. Mrs Crichton told me that she had read most of Gerald's books, and should I plan to bring back any animals from the Beni province in Bolivia, she would be only too happy to accommodate them for a short time in the grounds of the embassy. Also, by coincidence another luncheon guest, who was in charge of the British Agricultural Mission to Bolivia, had spent some 20 years in Northern Rhodesia and had known the Vaughan-Jones family well.

Prior to my arrival in Bolivia I had been in contact with the Director of the Instituto Linquistico de Verano Boliviano (ILV) about my mitla quest. I wanted to travel to the Abuna forest region of northern Bolivia and he had agreed, for a nominal fee, to fly me to a jungle landing strip situated between the Rio Beni and the Rio Abuna. Therefore, after leaving La Paz, I spent a couple of days in the small township of Riberalta, which Colonel Fawcett had visited on a number of occasions at the height of the rubber boom days at the turn of the last century. When Fawcett visited Riberalta he described how two of the big rubber firms had kept forces of armed men to hunt the forest Indians and capture them for slave labour to work with wild rubber; wholesale butchery was commonplace, as well as the meting out of a lashing for anyone who attempted to disobey an order, or to escape from their enslavement.

Here I met Professor Gaston Bejarano, who was leading a small expedition to record for the United Nations Food and Agriculture Organisation (FAO) the many different types of trees found in this region of north-eastern Bolivia. The professor was a food and agriculture specialist, and I found him a most friendly and helpful person, as well as being a mine of information about animals and natural history in general. While visiting a trading store that specialised in animal skins, we saw those of jaguar, ocelot, various small cats, River otter and caiman, but nothing that resembled the legendary mitla. In one corner of the store lay a great pile of vicuna skins that we were told were in transit to another dealer. The skins had only just arrived, smuggled over the border from Peru. Gaston Bejarano told me that the vicuna together with the chinchilla were the only two animals listed by the Bolivian authorities as being on a restricted list; whereas indigenous animals like the increasingly rare Spectacled bear, the River turtle, and the Red-fronted macaw, could be freely hunted either for their skins, for food, or for the pet trade.

Although Professor Bejarano's party had travelled extensively within the Rio Beni and Rio Abuna area, they had neither seen nor heard reference to an animal resembling the mitla. From Fawcett's description his team considered that it could well have been a melanistic form of a jaguarundi, a small forest-dwelling carnivore. They recommended that I concentrate my search in the little known Rio Abuna region of northern Bolivia, of which Fawcett had been warned, over one hundred years ago: 'The fever will kill you, and if you escape that, there are the dreaded Pacahuara Indians.' Although I recognised that once on my river journey I would have to take reasonable care, I consoled myself by thinking of Peter Fleming's search for Fawcett in the 1920s when he had confidently written in his book *Brazilian Adventure*: 'Exploring in the Mato Grosso is a soft option compared with caravanning in the Cotswolds.' It had been Brian Fawcett, the colonel's surviving son, who had written the book *Exploration Fawcett* about his father's exploits and who, during a lunch that I had had with him at his home before my departure from the UK, had advised me to try and make contact with the Pacahuara, for those were the people most likely to be able to provide information about the mitla.

A detailed account on my river journeys on both the Rio Beni and the Rio Abuna in search of the mitla is described in my previous publication *Travels in Search of Endangered Species*. However, to summarise the final part of this quest: it had been after almost two weeks of travelling up the twisting jungle-clad Rio Abuna, in the company of a Bolivian boatman, that we came across, just upstream from the small river settlement of José Gormez, a small encampment of 'Districto Militer Boliviano'. It was here that a lieutenant, who had a smattering of English, showed me a crumpled photograph of the body of a youth with arrows embedded in his back, and having had both of his legs removed. The youth had evidently been tapping the wild rubber and had encroached upon the Pacaharara's tribal territory. His body had been conveyed to a nearby landmark to ensure that it would be found before it became too decomposed, in order to act as a warning to others not to venture into the Indians' hunting grounds.

After seeing the dreadful photograph, I was relieved to have the excuse to abandon my search for the mitla. During the previous weeks, as my only way of communication with the boatman Ilmar had been through sign language, I had started to feel the solitude of a Moses in the Wilderness. The further we had paddled upstream away from Ilmar's home, the more nervous he appeared to become, which affected me too, so that I started to worry that during the night he would steal our small wooden craft and return to his village, leaving me stranded. Now, on learning of my decision to give up my quest in search of the mitla, Ilmar could not have been more excited by my decision to return downstream to his home at Abuna.

Perhaps the only things that had managed to sustain me during my time on those remote tributaries of the mighty Amazon network had been seeing the diversity of the luxuriant vegetation, and the sights and sounds of a great variety of animal life. The large buttress bases of the trees had evolved to cope with seasonal flooding, while their lofty tops struggled for light, space and further moisture for their foliage. The lianas that twisted like cables among the roughened tree trunks were often festooned with an abundance of epiphytes, which flourished in the humid environment; all of which conjured up a veritable Garden of Eden.

Dawn and sunset were signalled by howling sessions of troops of the Black Howler monkeys; the volume had to be heard to be believed. Small family groups of the Weddell's tamarin could be seen busily foraging among the mosaic of green foliage. Many species of birds, from toucans to macaws, fed from the different fruits and berries adorning the moist dense forest walls of the river banks, and herons and kingfishers swooped down to Abuna's muddy waters to catch fish, gather up insects or refresh themselves. A multiplicity of butterflies of every shape, colour and size, fluttered like confetti through those shafts of sunlight that managed to filter through the forest canopy. The opportunity to see such wonderful tapestries of wildlife so much reminded me of the adventures of Henry Walter Bates, which he recorded in his book *The Naturalist on the River Amazons* almost exactly a century before. But perhaps the highlight of those few weeks in northern Bolivia was the feeling of having been an integral part of nature, and having had this opportunity to experience such an adventure into the unknown.

On our return to Abuna, and after giving Ilmar what was probably an over-generous payment as thanks for his strenuous paddling, navigation and the obvious degree of stress that he had experienced, I was fortunate to catch the Mamoré-Madeira Railway twice-weekly service from Guajara-Mirim to Porto Velho, a train locally known as the 'Mad Maria'. During this daytime journey from Abuna to Porto Velho I thought of how my previous enthusiasm for such an adventure, involving river travels within the forests of the Amazonas, had now been amply satisfied and was therefore no longer an unfulfilled ambition.

From Porto Velho I flew to Manaus on the banks of the Rio Negro, which provides the city with its lifeline to the Amazon and its 1,600 km (1,000 mile) journey to the Atlantic Ocean. The trans-Amazonian highway was still several years away from reaching its destination and the establishment of Manaus as a free-trade zone. On the east bank of the Rio Negro was the region inhabited by the Pied tamarin, a species of Neotropical primate that used to be abundant but which, due to hunting and the clearance of its habitat, had become increasingly scarce. As Jersey Zoo already had this threatened species represented in its collection, I was anxious to take the opportunity to see Pied tamarins in their wild state, before travelling north to Boa Vista and over the Brazilian border into British Guiana and its capital Georgetown.

I began making enquiries about travelling to an area where Pied tamarins could be observed and, in spite of their protected status, I was soon offered a pair for £8; in so many places in South America protective legislation was only a paper law, seldom if ever enforced. During my five days in Manaus, I was fortunate to see a family group of these

143

striking jet-black, bare-faced animals, with their contrasting snow-white shoulders and rufous hind-quarters, living in a copse of trees at Manaus's museum. Through the Director of the Research Institute (INPA) Dr Paul Anthony, I was introduced to a team of Americans from the Niagara Falls Aquarium, who took me to see individuals of the fresh water Amazon dolphin, and the smaller La Plata River dolphin, which they had recently captured and were acclimatising in a big muddy pond, before flying them to their North American aquarium.

A local scientist told me that a recent IUCN-sponsored workshop had drawn attention to the fact that, although the river dolphins' population in the Amazon and Orinoco was believed to be good, they were becoming increasingly vulnerable to the effects of commercial fishing, the development of hydro-electricity, deforestation and pollution. The marine biologist also told me that the lack of any closed-season to protect the taking of eggs, or the killing, of the Giant South American River turtle, was responsible for causing the disappearance of the species from all but its more remote jungle regions. During my trip on the Mamoré-Madeira Railway I had been saddened to see the way these giant turtles had been packed in on top of one another so that, on our arrival at Porto Velho, over a quarter of them had died during the trip, and were therefore thrown aside. A species that had once represented an important source of protein in the diet of the river-dwellers was being exploited to satisfy the increased demand in the Western world for such produce as tinned turtle soup. The Brazilian biologist concluded his depressing analysis of the future plight of an increasing number of threatened species, by repeating to me on several occasions that mankind has to recognise that 'Extinction is Forever'.

The flight from Manaus to Boa Vista had an alarming air of uncertainty throughout. Soon after take-off it was apparent that one of the port engines was in difficulty, and eventually the propeller stopped rotating. In Brazil, when domestic flights experienced a mechanical failure of this sort they had to comply with the Brazilian Aircraft Authority regulations, and follow the course of a river so that if a forced landing did occur it would be possible to find the plane. Due to this much longer route to Boa Vista the flight fell well behind schedule, and the pilot eventually announced that he would have to break normal practice and not fly over such remote forest after dark. When the plane did

144

eventually arrive at Boa Vista's small airport, in the high savannah lands that surround the Rio Branco delta, it managed to land after first circling the earthen landing-strip to clear the cattle off, and was then guided down by the headlights of two Willys jeeps. What had particularly impressed me throughout the flight was the cheerfulness and general nonchalance of my fellow passengers; as if something far more dramatic would have been even more entertaining and desirable.

Two days later I managed to get a flight to the Atkinson Airfield in British Guiana, and to secure a room at Georgetown's Park Hotel, which I was to make my headquarters. The hotel boasted of having South America's largest wooden veranda; it was like a massive stage crowned at the centre by a dome with an impressive railed gallery, all of which was amply fanned by the constant airstreams provided by the north-east trade winds. It had been the Dutch in 1782, who had moved their seat of colonial government from the Demarara territory down-river to the present site of Georgetown. As the land was 1.2 metres (4 feet) below sea level at high tide, the Dutch utilised their dyke-building skills in constructing a large sea-wall and a system of streets divided by canals, in the manner of their home country. These canals have been essential for drainage control, and smaller drainage channels skirted each street. From the nearby gnarled writhing beauty of the saman (Rain Tree), and other flamboyant trees of the Main Street, could be heard the *qu'est-ce que dit?, qu'est-ce que dit?* calls of the Kiskadee flycatchers; these starling-sized birds were given their nickname by the early French settlers because of the bird's magpie-like curiosity.

My first port of call was to meet Stanley Lee, the Superintendent of Guiana's National Zoo, which was situated in Georgetown's famous botanical gardens. These covered an area of 73 ha (180 acres) and were veined by pinkish granite paths and an elaborate system of irrigation and drainage channels. Neatly cut parkland lawns stretched generously between both indigenous and alien plantings. A variety of palm trees thrust their ostrich-like forms into the tropical blue sky, while a stand of towering eucalyptus was surrounded by dense clusters of bamboos and a few of the sharply spiked Sandbox trees. While both the temperature and humidity hovered in the mid-eighties, I saw for the first time the rubbery and stiff bristled muzzles of a small family group of manatees, feeding on grass cuttings in a muddy lake in the centre of the gardens.

Stanley Lee told me that these strangely supple aquatic herbivorous mammals were kept in the gardens as an educational resource. Parties of schoolchildren were given the opportunity to feed them and, at the same time, to learn how this once abundant sea-cow had now become threatened throughout its range. In spite of a degree of protection, they were frequently hunted for meat, caught up in fishermen's nets or, in heavily populated areas, increasingly struck by boats and injured. Later on in the day, while visiting Georgetown's fish and meat market, I was saddened to see manatee meat openly displayed for sale, which so well highlighted reality; the gulf between paper protection and the lack of law enforcement, a scenario that occurs daily.

Because I had spent more of my time in Bolivia than I had originally planned, I realised that my stay in Guiana was now limited, and I would have to rely on the assistance of Georgetown Zoo for any animals that I might take back with me. Although the zoo offered me species that ranged from White-collared peccary, Giant anteater to Martial eagle, I ended up purchasing only a small cross-section of the country's indigenous fauna, including the Two-toed sloth, Red-handed tamarin, Grey-winged trumpeter, Crested curassow, Teguexin lizard and anaconda. This was mainly because any animals accompanying me would be treated as personal luggage on a normal scheduled passenger flight; I would not be using a freighter, as I had with my two African collections. Also, as far as the offered peccaries were concerned, there was a total ban on taking members of the pig family either in transit through the US or into the UK. Nevertheless, the acquisition of the collection could not have been easier or more relaxing than my previous ones, for the zoo staff cared for the animals right up to the time of their departure, as well as having them adequately crated for the journey to the UK via New York.

During my 20 days in Guiana, I heeded the 'hope' that Gerald Durrell had inscribed in my copy of his *Three Singles to Adventure* – that one day I may take a single to Adventure. So in keeping with my mentor's wish I purchased a Transport of Harbours Department steamer ticket to the town of Adventure, and retraced his steps from Georgetown to the far bank of the Demarara River. From there I took the Parika train to the Essequibo River, from where a ferry conveyed passengers (and cattle) across its muddy waters to the west shore of the Essequibo and to

146

Adventure. It had been in 1950, 15 years previously, that Gerald Durrell had first visited Guiana to collect animals for various zoos in the United Kingdom, and made Adventure his headquarters.

The ornithological pageant that he had described – 'embracing dozens of military starlings, snowy egrets, jacanas, marsh birds and snail hawks' – were all very much in evidence, confirming that the environment he had written about as 'a landscape overloaded with birds' remained unchanged. Even the small stone grey jetty and the corrugated iron roof of the shed, with the bold printed white letters announcing to the outside world that the small trading landing place was indeed Adventure, had been left unaltered in this backwater of human activity. On my return to Georgetown I called at the country's National Museum and met its curator, Ram Singh, a delightful man who, with his considerable knowledge of the bird life of the territory, had provided valuable advice to the Durrell expedition, as well as helping with the identification of various specimens of the fauna that had been collected. I told Ram Singh about my Bolivian quest for the half-dog, half-cat, legendary animal that Colonel Fawcett had referred to as the mitla, and after further discussion, he took me to see a mounted museum specimen of a greyish-to-pale-brown jaguarundi; his opinion concurred with Gaston Bejerano's in that Fawcett's mitla could well have been a melanistic form of this nocturnal feline.

Outside the museum Ram Singh took me to see a young Spectacled owl that had just been brought to the museum as a potential mounted specimen for display. On seeing my enthusiasm for this attractive bird, and on hearing that Gerald Durrell's zoo in Jersey had a lone specimen of the species, he told me that as he had so many fond memories of the zoo's founder, he would be delighted to present the owl to him, with the proviso that I would collect it within 24 hours. On my way back to the hotel the taxi took me by way of Georgetown's colossal Gothic-styled wooden cathedral, which dominated the main square. The Victorian colonial houses boasted balconies made up of a lace-work of wrought iron, which had been originally brought out to Guiana from Great Britain as ships' ballast. The brilliant whiteness of some of the painted wooden buildings helped to dilute the solemnity of the large stone statue of Queen Victoria.

It was unfortunate that on my last night in Guiana, while I was enjoying a sundowner on the veranda of the Park Hotel, the country's Prime Minister, Forbes Burnham, leader of the People's National Congress (in six months time to become the first President of the renamed Guyana); and Dr Cheddi Jagan, leader of British Guiana's People's Progressive Party, had decided to hold a political rally using the hotel's huge veranda as a stage, to protest against the recent (11th November 1965) Unilateral Declaration of Independence by Ian Smith in Southern Rhodesia. After sunset it was mandatory for guests to wear a tie at the hotel, and unfortunately the only one that I had brought with me depicted the three assegais insignia of the Regular Army of Rhodesia & Nyasaland. As soon as I realised what the rally was all about, I had tried to hide such an identification behind a newspaper, in case the significance of the tie had the misfortune to be recognised by the protesting politicians.

The political temperature of the rally started to rise, with Forbes Burnham calling for volunteers to help liberate what he called the 'downtrodden slaves of British Colonialism'. I decided, with the newspaper clutched firmly to my chest, to leave the veranda as discreetly as possible, for the last thing I wanted was to be made an example of by way of redirected aggression from an unruly mob seeking vengeance. Therefore I had in effect adopted the mantle of a Judas Iscariot, and had to forfeit my last supper in Guiana by retiring to the security of my bedroom. Here, at least, I was able to communicate with the female Spectacled owl that I had collected from the museum earlier that afternoon. This most attractive of owls, whom I had named Jan, kept uttering a series of low hoots from inside her travelling crate, as if in gratitude for having been saved from death. Outside the windows, as the political shouting died away, the tropical evening was filled with the diverse calls of the ubiquitous amphibians, and the continuous shrill murmurings of the multiplicity of crickets.

Stanley Lee was kind enough to organise the transport to the airport of the animals that I had purchased from the National Zoo, and I joined him there at midday with the forever-blinking spectacled owl. As the Pan America inter-continental jet left South America bound for New York, the passengers were provided with an albatross view over the magnificent azure-blue waters of the Caribbean with its numerous atolls and islands. Several hours later the captain announced that due to heavy snow in New York he was diverting the aircraft to Boston, which meant that I would miss my onward flight to London. Although my small animal collection was held up at Boston airport for 36 hours, where there were no animal holding facilities, it was very much thanks to the enthusiastic and concerned Pan American ground staff, who generously accommodated all the animal crates in the warmth of their staff room, that none of the tropical animals suffered.

On my return to Jersey it was wonderful to be reunited with my very understanding family, as well as with my friends, both human and animal. The anacondas and the Teguexin lizards were delighted to have the opportunity to warm up sufficiently in the zoo's Reptile House to be able to feed again. The only incident that had given some concern during my absence was when Odette had had one of her letters returned to her from a Mr Perry Priest, in the Riberalta office of the Instituto Linquistico de Verano, with an accompanying note stating: 'The Institute's Cessna flew Mr Mallinson to a jungle landing strip between the Rio Beni and the Rio Abuna on November 8th, and since that time no sighting or word has been received from him.' Fortunately, the news-paper's prediction just before my departure from the UK, that my mitla expedition was going to take me into 'A Jungle of No Return', had been proved wrong after I made telephone contact with Odette from Manaus.

Among the letters that I had written during my time in South America had been one to Noël Coward. While in Manaus I and Antony McCammon, a Jersey friend who was working in South America, visited the city's magnificent Opera House, which had been built at the height of the rubber boom days of the late-nineteenth century. Antony knew the Director of the Opera House who kindly gave us a personal conducted tour, which included taking us at dusk on to the centre of its stage. On drawing back the faded maroon velvet curtains he switched all the lights on in the auditorium, where ornate chandeliers dramatically highlighted the opulence of the theatre, with all its marble, its gilded plaster work, and lavishly embellished State Governor's box. The Opera House, which had been constructed with choice marble imported from Italy, and windows made from the finest Venetian glass, appeared so incongruous in a city surrounded by the forests of the Amazonas. As I knew that Noël Coward had travelled to many different parts of the world, including some of its most out-of-the-way places, I asked in my letter whether he had had visited Manaus and witnessed such a dramatic sight; I thought such a fine environment would have provided an ideal setting for one of The Master's sophisticated productions. Noël Coward replied to the letter from an address in Belgravia, London, in May 1966:

> Dear Mr. Mallinson
> When I had at last met Mr. and Mrs. Durrell [lunch at the Savoy Grill] while they were over here I had every good intention in the world of sending you a message by them and am furious with myself for forgetting. I got your letter from Georgetown ages later – perhaps you had learnt in the meantime that my schedule had had to be completely changed and I flew direct to Bombay – Seychelles? I hope you did and realised what had happened. Anyway, I have high hopes of coming to Jersey later this summer – I finish my season on July 30th – and shall look forward so much to meeting you then.
> Yours sincerely,
> Noël Coward

At the time of his letter, Noël Coward had been performing in one of his plays on the London stage. As with many famous people that I had met, or was later to meet, through my involvement with Gerald Durrell, I found that no matter how insignificant one was, through their professionalism and attention to detail they would somehow find time to communicate with you. Most regrettably, due to illness Noël Coward never did visit Jersey; although along with David Niven, Lord Craigton and Sir William Collins, in January 1973 he had accepted Gerald Durrell's invitation to become an International Trustee of the Jersey Wildlife Preservation Trust.

Chapter Eleven

WORK, MORE FUN THAN FUN

In 1967 the Trustees and Council of the Jersey Wildlife Preservation Trust (JWPT) established a Garden Committee, chaired by Mrs Vi Lort-Phillips, a world expert on camelias, comprising a cross-section of Jersey's foremost garden enthusiasts, including Major Rollo Hawkins and his wife Ansell, Mrs V. Hope Platt and Lady Guthrie. This was followed by the formation of an international Scientific Advisory Committee that included such well-known scientists and naturalists as Jean Delacour (France), Peter Scott (UK), Gordon Williams (New Zealand), Dr Harry Frith (Australia), Dr Ernst Lang (Switzerland), Professor Françoise Bourlière (France), Dr Osman Hill (UK/USA) and Wahab Owadally (Mauritius). A Fund-Raising Committee was also established under the chairmanship of Lady Saranne Calthorpe.

In September 1969 Gerald Durrell set off on a six-month Australian safari with the intention of covering over 24,000 km (c.15,000 miles) in his well-seasoned Land Rover, to look at the conservation work being practised there. He was accompanied by his wife Jacquie, their secretary, and Saranne Calthorpe who, with her fund-raising hat on, hoped to raise money for the zoo from those Australian members who had written to say that they wanted to help. Like all similar expeditions, the Australian safari was financed entirely by the Trust's founder; and during his absence from Jersey he planned to devote some of his time to writing a sequel to his book *Menagerie Manor*. On their return to Jersey in the spring of 1970 he told the press that the expedition had been a great success, having visited most of the conservation areas of the continent, including the Great Barrier Reef. He had made valuable contacts and had been promised a number of rare marsupial species, should the Trust be in a financial position to develop an Australian section. At the end of the interview he couldn't resist adding, 'I consider it is a great credit to myself to have spent six months with three women in the Australian outback!'

In 1970, although the lease on Les Augrès Manor still had 15 years to run, the Trustees and Council decided that they should do everything possible to buy the property. They recognised that without security of tenure it would be impossible for the Trust to approach grant-giving bodies and scientific foundations to obtain the money required for the furtherance of its conservation mission. They also hoped that it might be possible for the States of Jersey to help in the acquisition of the property, if they could see that the Trust was making a determined effort to raise the money itself.

The first step was to send a letter, signed by Gerald Durrell and the Trust's President, the Rt Hon. the Earl of Jersey, to all Trust members. The positive response to this in turn gave the Council the impetus to present a proposition to various individuals in the States of Jersey. Sir Giles Guthrie, former chairman of BOAC who had recently become a Trustee, gave an interview to the press and said that, 'We must own our place of work if the zoo is to survive.' Sir Giles went on to say that he believed Jersey would benefit from the Trust's contributions to the conservation of wildlife, to science, education and tourism. In March 1971 the States agreed to lend the Trust half of the purchase price (£120,000) of the property on extremely generous terms. So very much thanks to the Trust's membership in all parts of the world, some grants from charitable Trusts, and the support of the States of Jersey, Les Augrès Manor was purchased from the Fraser family in April 1971, and the future of the Trust made more secure.

It was during the early 1970s that Gerald Durrell attracted a galaxy of famous people over to Jersey to meet him and to see around his very special zoological collection of threatened species. In October 1970 the actress, 81–year-old Dame Gladys Cooper, fulfilled one of her ambitions to meet the zoo's founder and Honorary Director. She was accompanied by actor and television star Peter Bull, who had recently published his book *Bear with Me*, which told the story of his collection of over 60 teddy bears. In April 1972 David Niven, dressed in wedding attire, and accompanied by his delightful Swedish wife, Hjördis, acted as best man at the introduction and wedding of Jambo, the Basel Zoo-bred male Lowland gorilla, to the zoo's two females

N'Pongo and Nandi, and officially opened the Brian Park Gorilla Complex.

Under the caption A VEGETARIAN WEDDING BREAKFAST *The London Evening News* published a photograph of David Niven presenting a huge bouquet of vegetables to the happy trio of Lowland gorillas. The article recorded: 'It's not everyone who can boast of having such a distinguished guest at their nuptials as David Niven … what's more he brought the wedding breakfast along too.' When I took the film star into the middle den to introduce him to the two females, I had not realised that Jambo was able to gain entry to the den by putting his 160 kg (352 lb) weight against the drop-slide and pushing it up with his massive hands to get in; I saw him do this only a month later. I could well imagine what the headlines in the national press would have been if the star of *Casino Royal* had come face to face with such a fine 'silverback' male as Jambo!

In May 1975, Miss Fleur Cowles, author, painter, philanthropist and a recently appointed Trustee of JWPT, persuaded James Stewart, who was in London starring in the stage version of *Harvey,* to accept Gerald Durrell's invitation for him to open the zoo's new Nocturnal House. James Stewart and his wife Gloria had a great interest in conservation, and I knew that their eldest daughter Kelly Stewart and her husband Sandy Harcourt were, at the time of the Stewart's Jersey visit, currently studying mountain gorillas with Dian Fossey in Rwanda. After the opening ceremony, while James Stewart was in Gerald Durrell's library signing the Visitors' Book he asked to have a look at an atlas, in order to see exactly where Jersey was in relation to the Cherbourg Peninsula. After viewing the map, he told us that the last time he had flown in this region was while he was serving in the US Air Force (as a colonel) during the Second World War and had been *en route* to Germany.

Undoubtedly the most significant person to pay her first visit to the Trust was Her Royal Highness The Princess Anne (now The Princess Royal). The Princess was on an official two-day visit to the Bailiwick, and as she had always been a fan of Gerald Durrell's books had asked, rather at the eleventh hour, to visit the Trust Headquarters to meet one of her favourite authors and to see his animal collection of endangered species. Although, at this time, Gerald Durrell was in the middle of writing another book at his house near Nimes in Provence, on hearing that Princess Anne had requested a visit to the zoo, he dropped everything to return to Jersey to meet her. In the Trust's Ninth Annual Report the Honorary Director wrote:

At 10.30 a.m. on Tuesday 23rd May, 1972 in the company of The Earl and Countess of Jersey and Mr and Mrs J.J.C. Mallinson, I escorted Her Royal Highness around the grounds ... Owing to a very busy schedule I was told that Her Royal Highness could only allow half an hour for the visit ... However, the visit was nearly an hour ... [she] seemed most interested in all she saw, and in the work that we are doing ... Before she left, Princess Anne graciously accepted a specially bound edition of the *Trust Annual Reports* and a copy of my latest book *Catch Me a Colobus*. In view of the great interest the Princess had shown in the Trust and its work, I then wrote to ask whether Her Royal Highness would be willing to become our Patron'

On 21st August 1972, Gerald Durrell received a letter from Buckingham Palace, signed by the Secretary to HRH Princess Anne's Office, which said:

Princess Anne has asked me to write and thank you, the President, Trustees and Council of the Jersey Wildlife Preservation Trust, so very much for inviting Her Royal Highness to become Patron of the Trust. The Princess asked me to convey to you Her sincere thanks and to say that she would be most happy to accept the Patronage.

This significant and exciting news was announced in a Press Release from Buckingham Palace on 12th September, and provided us all at the Trust with an enormous degree of encouragement in the work that we were doing and our faith in the future.

Due to what Gerald Durrell considered a lack of any meaningful contact, cooperation and collaboration between those working with endangered species in captivity, and those involved with studying the animals in their natural habitats, he had the idea of hosting a multidisciplinary international conference in Jersey, which he asked Peter Scott to chair. In his foreword to the proceedings of the First World

Conference on 'Breeding of Endangered Species in Captivity – As an Aid to Their Survival', which was published in *Breeding Endangered Species in Captivity,* edited by R.D. Martin, Gerald Durrell recorded how he was delighted that the Trust, with the Fauna Preservation Society (FPS now Fauna & Flora International – FFI), could be joint hosts to the 1972 conference. He considered that such a conference was of the utmost importance since it is now vital that zoos all over the world assess their contribution to conservation and make clear the part they are going to play in the conservation movement in the future. He added, 'I think that to a very large extent most zoos will have to rethink their future policies.'

The Marquess of Willingdon (then President of FPS) provided a brief summary of the work and interests of the Society, pointing out that the conference really amounted in some ways to a 'marriage' between Peter Scott and Gerald Durrell, symbolically combining efforts towards conservation in the field with attempts to maintain stocks of endangered species in captivity. The Earl of Jersey's welcome to delegates highlighted: 'What an appalling indictment it is, what a disgrace to mankind that the road to his so-called civilisation should be built on the memories of extinct species and species on the way to extinction.' Such expressions as 'Dead as the Dodo' and 'Extinction is Forever' were soon to become phrases frequently used in a zoo's conservation vocabulary.

During the period 1972–1999, seven world conferences on 'Breeding Endangered Species in Captivity' took place. In May 1992, the JWPT hosted the sixth conference and Roger Wheater (Director, Edinburgh Zoo) mentioned in his foreword to the published proceedings: *Creative Conservation, Interactive Management of Wild and Captive Animals,* edited by P.J.S. Olney, G.M. Mace and A.T.C. Feistner, how so much had been achieved in the sphere of breeding endangered species during the past two decades, and how our cooperative efforts had already borne much fruit; as well as identifying the tremendous future challenges and responsibility individual zoos and regional and international organisations have in spreading the conservation message.

In May 1972 Gerald Durrell appointed me as the Trust's Zoological Director, which prompted me to have placed in a prominent position on my desk the printed notice: **WORK IS SO MUCH MORE FUN THAN FUN** – *Sir Noël Coward* – (in 1973, was added): – *International Trustee of the Jersey Wildlife Preservation Trust*. When interviewing potential staff (in particular those for the zoo's maintenance department), I could see some of them thinking 'what a strange type of employer we have here'. But I considered that from the start it was important for new employees to recognise that work can be fun, if they adopt the culture of the organisation and enthusiastically join the team in helping the Trust to achieve its mission.

It was soon after the tenth anniversary of the Trust, in September 1972, when Gerald Durrell was away at his home in France busily writing another book, that the Zoo Management Committee, of which I was a member, recommended that a special committee of the Trust's Council should look into the future organisation and administration of JWPT. When the Special Committee produced its findings the document's bottom-line raised the issue: 'Who governs the Trust? – The Council or the Honorary Director?' When Gerald Durrell read the recommendations of the committee he saw a future of committees and sub-committees proliferating like mushrooms, with him as a kind of figurehead Director-General without any involvement in the day-to-day running of the organisation, and he returned immediately to Jersey to do battle. He wrote to Lord Jersey, The Trust's President, and to Sir Giles Guthrie, who had been mainly responsible for the drafting of the document, stating that he had found some aspects of the report 'exceedingly offensive', some 'laughable', some 'distasteful', some even 'immoral'. He concluded:

> What does not interest me is having to waste my valuable time constantly as a fund-raiser owing to the complete inertia of the Trustees and Council. If the committee seriously imagines that I intend to have my authority undermined in this way ... I would not dream of accepting any of these proposals. Should the Trustees and Council wish to implement anything like this then I am afraid they will have to ask for my resignation.

A final meeting between the Trust's founder and Trustees and Council took place at Les Augrès Manor on December 8th 1972, at which Gerald Durrell told everyone present exactly what he thought of their recommendations, using a colourful vocabulary that had probably never previously been heard at such an august gathering. This meeting was followed by one held at Lord Jersey's home, Radier Manor, which resulted in letters of resignation being signed by all but one (Brian Park) of the Trustees and Council. The objective of such a mass resignation was to bring Gerald Durrell to heel, but those of us who were a part of his team and knew him more personally, were well aware how he would react to such an insensitive confrontation, and that such an approach would have exactly the opposite effect to what was intended. The National Press was quick to pick up such differences of opinion. On 12th December 1972, *The Daily Mirror* printed under a bold heading:

BIG WILDLIFE ROW AT ZOO AS NINE WALK OUT – Author and animal expert Gerald Durrell was at the centre of a major row last night over the running of a famous zoo where he is the director. Nine of the eleven trustees quit ... the nine announced: 'The point of issue is who governs the trust – the council or the honorary director' ... Mr. Jeremy Mallinson, deputy director of the zoo, said later 'The members who resigned had worked extremely well with Mr. Durrell.' He was very surprised and regretted their resignations. But the objectives of the Trust will continue, and further trustees will be appointed.

During this whole most regrettable imbroglio, for both Lord Jersey and Sir Giles Guthrie had contributed so much to both the funding and the initial development of the Trust, I was called to several meetings with the major players. At these, it was always stressed that by their recommendations to have me appointed as the Trust's Executive Director, reporting directly to the council, this would take a great deal of pressure off Gerald Durrell and thereby give him, as Founder and Life President of the Trust, far more time for his travels and writing. The only response that I could possibly give to such an opinion was that as Gerald Durrell was my mentor, I could only go along with whatever he saw as the future of his creation. Perhaps such an unfortunate chapter in the Trust's early history would never have happened if communication between all parties had been better lubricated.

Although those who resigned *en masse* imagined that it would leave Gerald Durrell without a remit, and thereby a mandate to continue, they had failed to read the small print of the laws governing the make-up of the Trust's Council. For these included a loophole that provided for a quorum to take over, which meant that both Catha Weller and I, as members of the Board of Management, and John Hartley, as Trust Secretary, were legitimate Council members with a vote; thereby with Brian Park a quorum could be formed. So this was the time that Gerald Durrell invited his publisher, Sir William Collins, Sir Noël Coward and Mr David Niven to become International Trustees; Mr Ivor Chambers, Mr Brian Park and Mrs Kath Robinson, to be Jersey-based Trustees; and Lord Craigton, Senator Reg Jeune, Mr John Perry and Mr Robin Rumboll (Treasurer) became Council Members. So what has since become known as 'The Palace Revolution' was successfully forestalled. As Douglas Botting recorded in his admirable book *Gerald Durrell – The Authorised Biography*:

> Looking back with the gift of hindsight, it is clear that the Trustees were probably right to propose improving the efficiency of the organisation. But they set about it in the wrong way, provoking a defensive and hostile reaction from Gerald, who went right over the top. Nearly twenty years later, the Earl of Jersey wrote to Sir Giles Guthrie's widow, Rhona, wondering what all the fuss had been about. He reflected 'Looking through our Report with today's eyes it seems so very mild and to the point. I am amazed it resulted in all the kafuffle, and amazed that practically all of our recommendations have, bit by bit, been adopted.'

Apart from the unfortunate hiccup of 'The Palace Revolution' in the Trust's gestation, the previous two years had been most stimulating and highly satisfactory as far as I had been concerned, for not only had the Trust's headquarters been secured and its conservation work become more focused and acknowledged as a 'trail-blazer', but also I had been provided with the opportunity to travel to two different parts of the world; to Madagascar in 1970 and to Assam, India, in 1971. On my way to Madagascar in October, Odette, my brother Miles and I took the opportunity to holiday in Rhodesia, which resulted in my being asked to give a talk to the Zoological Society of Rhodesia, at Rhodesia's University in Salisbury. Due to a press announcement of my forthcoming talk about 'The Modern Role of Zoological Institutions', I received an invitation for sundowners from my Staff Corps commanding officer, Keith Coster, who was now the Lt General in charge of Ian

Smith's army. During this drinks session, a Brigadier from the South African embassy asked Coster what was this Rhodesian & Nyasaland Staff Corps that I had served in. Whereupon the General replied, 'Well, it sometimes recruited English public school people like Jeremy here, who was never quite sure why he had joined the Staff Corps in the first place; although I was told later that he had only enlisted in the Federal Army in order to come out to Africa to see as much of the continent's animal kingdom as possible.' The General was, of course, right!

Since that time I have lunched on two occasions with the now 90–year-old (2009) Keith Coster at the famous Lady Phillips Restaurant, near his home in Somerset West, Cape Province. He had been in the South African UDF and fought in North Africa during the Second World War. And, after his plane had been shot down, he had spent some three years in a prisoner of war camp in Germany. He had always acted as a perfect gentleman, and when I had recently asked whether Rhodesia's UDI had been worthwhile he reflected how sad the whole situation had been, for he had needlessly lost so many good friends, both European and African. He also told me that his grandmother had been born in Jersey, in the mid-nineteenth century, to the wife of a serving officer at the time that the Island was garrisoned by a regiment from the British Army; a commitment that ended in 1940 at the beginning of the Second World War.

The purpose of my visit to Madagascar was to represent the Trust at the First International Conference for the Conservation of the Flora and Fauna of Madagascar, which was held under the co-patronage of the Malagasy Government, UNESCO, IUCN, FAO, the World Wildlife Fund, the French Overseas Scientific Research Organisation and the National Natural History Museum of France. The chief objective of the five-day conference was to attract international attention to the scientific, cultural and economic importance of the island's unique fauna and flora. The conference was held at the Charles de Gaulle University of Tananarive and chaired by the past chairman of IUCN and a member of JWPT's Scientific Advisory Committee, Professor François Bourlière. It was at this important meeting of some of the world's leading conservationists that I met for the first time Dr Jean-Jacques Petter, Deputy Director of the French Natural History Museum, who had organised the conference and who had done much to further the study and conservation of Madagascan primates, and who was later to join the Trust's Scientific Advisory Committee. Also present were such prominent field workers as Dr Alison Jolly and Dr R.D. (Bob) Martin, who both became Council members of JWPT and significant supporters of the Trust's international conservation training and scientific activities, as well as becoming most valued friends.

Through Peggy Peel, a BBC producer friend of Gerald Durrell, I was provided with an introduction to Great Britain's Ambassador to Madagascar, Timothy Crosthwait who, with his wife, was kind enough to take Odette and me on a sightseeing tour of Tananarive and a Malagasy royal burial site on the outskirts of the capital. The embassy's official Land Rover had the Union Jack fluttering proudly from its bonnet, which reminded me of the Rolls Royce of the British embassy in La Paz that I had ridden in five years previously. As with so many members of the British diplomatic corps, it turned out that the Crosthwaits were old friends of the Crichtons.

After the Tananarive meetings, Odette and I visited, with other conference delegates, the forest reserve of Perinet which was chiefly known for representing the best remaining example of Madagascar's eastern rain forest, and being home to the largest member of the lemur family, the indri. Although we were not lucky enough to see this spectacular primate, we could easily hear the chorus of the indris' characteristic calls, four-syllable ululations, that seemed to be even louder than the vocalisations of the Howler monkeys that I had regularly heard enthusiastically announcing each dawn in the forests of the Amazonas. In an attempt to get closer to where the indris were, I left the main body of delegates and climbed to the top of a nearby hillock, in order to gain a better view of the forest canopy. On my return to the conference party I encountered a tall American who asked whether I had managed to see an indri, and if the route I was taking was the quickest way back to the vehicles. It was only when I saw him getting into a limousine flying the Stars and Stripes that I was told my recent companion had been Charles Lindbergh, who 43 years previously had flown the first trans-Atlantic flight of 33½ hours in his single engine monoplane *The Spirit of St Louis* from New York to Paris. Charles Lindbergh died in 1974, less than four years after my brief meeting with him, but it was not until some 20 years later that I had the opportunity to reflect on his incredible aeronautical achievement by going to see *The Spirit of St Louis* at the Smithsonian Institution's Air and Space Museum in Washington, D.C.

From Perinet our party flew to Diego-Suarez at the northern tip of Madagascar, which is one of the largest and most beautiful natural harbours in the world. Here, in a restricted area behind a camp of the French Foreign Legion we were able to observe a family group of five Crowned lemurs. These lemurs are mostly confined to this particular region, and have the military authorities to thank for their survival; if the restrictions governing this area were to be lifted, the vegetation would soon be cleared and the lemurs deprived of their sanctuary. Our final visit was to the isolated township of Maroansetra on the north-eastern coast, and from there by boat to the island of Nossi Mangabe. It was here that I saw an aye-aye, one of man's rarest and most primitive cousins; at that time it was considered to number possibly as few as 50 individuals. About the size of a cat, it is completely black, with large nocturnal eyes, bare bat-like ears, and a bushy tail like a splayed out brush. Its most striking anatomical feature is the hand, particularly the long thin third finger which is a highly specialised adaptation to the animal's diet; this elongated finger is used partly to detect the larvae which constitute the aye-aye's principal food, and partly as a probe. This species has the further distinction of being the only large lemur to construct a complicated nest, a feat that is usually considered in mammals to be the prerogative of the great apes.

Gerald Durrell beautifully describes in his book *The Aye-aye and I – A Rescue Expedition to Madagascar*, his first encounter with an aye-aye:

In the gloom it came along the branches towards me – its round, hypnotic eyes blazing; its spoon-like ears turning to and fro independently like radar dishes; its white whiskers twitching and moving like sensors; the thin, attenuated fingers on its black hands tapping delicately on the branches as it moved along, like those of a pianist playing a complicated piece of Chopin.

The rare collection of Malagasy fauna that the Durrell Expedition brought back to Jersey in 1990, on loan to JWPT from the Malagasy Government, included the Ploughshare tortoise, Madagascar Spiny iguana, Madagascar

Tree boa, Madagascar teal, Madagascar Giant Jumping rat, Aloatran Gentle lemur and the aye-aye. In 1992 the Trust was the first to record the successful births in captivity of all of the latter four species; and through an Accord with the Government the Trust is directly involved in a number of important conservation field programmes in Madagascar, including the reintroduction of captive bred Flat-tailed tortoises.

My first visit to Assam was due to the re-appearance of the world's smallest and rarest member of the pig family, the Pygmy hog, in the Himalayan foothills of northern Assam during March 1971. Captain Johnny Tessier-Yandell, a Jersey-born tea planter in Assam had, during a home leave in 1969, mentioned to Gerald Durrell that he had received reports that this once-considered extinct species was still alive in some isolated pockets of the tall grass savanna habitats bordering Assam, Bhutan and Nepal. Gerald Durrell, always fascinated about the small and forgotten animals on this earth, asked Tessier-Yandell to let him know should he receive any further information about the whereabouts of this rarest of pigs. An extensive fire that had swept through 50 miles of the tall grass thatch lands in the north-western region of Assam at the beginning of 1971 resulted in a number of Pygmy hogs being captured by the tea garden workers. And it was thanks to Tessier-Yandell's intervention that they had not ended up in the pot, but were being kept alive at the Attareekhat tea estate. Within a four-week period, March-April 1971, 17 Pygmy hogs had been rescued from the thatch fire. On behalf of the Fauna Preservation Society and JWPT I went out to Assam in the May of that year to advise on the conditions in which the animals should be kept, and to make recommendations for their future husbandry.

Pearson St Regis Surita, an executive of the Williamson Magor Group, which owned over 30 of the tea gardens in Assam, was well known for his regular commentaries on the Indian cricket team for both the BBC and All India Radio. He was also a regular contributor to the *Calcutta Statesman* and within an hour of our meeting had filed an account of my involvement with wildlife and the work of the Jersey Trust for his next day's column *On the Scene*. As I was to be the guest of the Williamson Magor Group, Pearson had been given the job of escorting me to Assam, as well as being my travelling companion throughout the duration of my Pygmy hog investigations. The first thing he told me was that he had been with Lawrence Durrell at the same school in Darjeeling, and that he was a fan of the writings of both of the Durrell brothers. Due to the political tension that had recently sprung up between India and East Pakistan (Bangladesh), Indian planes could no longer fly over Pakistani territory, and flights from Calcutta to Assam had to be routed to the north of West Bengal before turning to the east through the corridor bordering the kingdoms of Nepal, Sikkim and Bhutan to the north. Fortunately, although totally unwittingly, I had seated myself next to a window on the port side of the Dakota, so just after the plane had altered course to the north-east towards Darjeeling, I was afforded a breathtaking bird's-eye view of Nepal's rumpled foothills. As the monsoon clouds rolled by I could see the large formations of black rocks, lightly covered with snow, that rose in ribs to form an amphitheatre of peaks in the Everest chain.

From the lowlands of Nepal, the 9,100 m (30,000 ft) summit of Mount Everest lies at the northernmost head of a glacier-filled valley, surrounded by peaks swathed in snow; some of the summits fluted by ice-furrows before dramatically descending in great buttresses to the humbler Nepalese foothills beneath. As we flew closer, and as if responding to a prayer, the cloud broke and on a sunlit horizon was revealed the majesty of the snowy summit of the world's highest mountain, which undoubtedly was one of the most spectacular and exhilarating sights that a man could ever have the privilege to see. While the Dakota was still making its way some 9,100 m (30,000 ft) over the Himalayan foothills toward its destination in Assam, my excitement at having so unexpectedly viewed Mount Everest was momentarily forgotten. For the air stewardess prematurely switched on a recorded message which announced, in a calm and most matter-of-fact fashion: 'Captain Muckerjee and his crew would now like to say goodbye.' After this slight shock to the system I was relieved when some 40 minutes later the plane safely landed at Gauhati Airport, without its passengers having had to bid farewell to life due to an unscheduled crash-landing in the Nepalese foothills.

The Pygmy hog was first described by B.H. Hodgson in 1847, in his paper 'On a New Form of Hog Kind of Suidae' in the *Journal of the Asiatic Field Society, Bengal*. Since the turn of the twentieth century, the scarcity of records, and the fact that the species remained almost unstudied in the wild state, led some authorities to believe that the species was possibly extinct. So one could well imagine my excitement when I first saw the small group of Pygmy hogs at the Attareekhat tea estate. I needed to handle them in order to take weights and measurements (up to 9 kg [20 lb], and c.25 cm [10 in] in height); to take photographs; to study their behaviour; and to make recommendations on diet, accommodation and their future management. I also was given the opportunity to examine a seldom-observed rare species, the Hispid hare, another escapee from the extensive fires in the thatch lands of the Himalayan foothills. The last description of this species had been by a German zoologist when he had examined one in the Goalpara Division of Assam in 1956. Due to the paucity of published data about the Pygmy hog and the Hispid hare, I published my observations in two papers in the *Journal of the Bombay Natural History Society* in 1971.

During this first visit to Assam, I was fortunate to receive an invitation from the well-known Indian conservationist, Dr Robin Banerjee, to visit the famous Kaziranga Wildlife Sanctuary. Here we rode on an elephant; guided by its *mahout*, it ambled its way forward in a swaying gait, taking us through the tall grass that provided so many species with their life-line and sanctuary. After the elephant had managed to barge its way through denser vegetation on to the flat grassy terrain of the Brahmaputra alluvium, within minutes of breaking cover we came across the prehistoric-looking Indian rhinoceros, three-quarters submerged in a particularly marshy region. Riding on its armour-plated back were two snow-white Cattle egrets using their position as a vantage perch to spot ground insects disturbed by their host's feet. During this visit to Kaziranga I was privileged to see more than 20 rhinoceros, some of which were accompanied by their calves, miniature versions of their armour-plated parents. I was also given the opportunity to see for the first time small herds of the attractive reddish-brown Indian Swamp deer, pairs of Hog deer, family groups of wild boar, and a galaxy of bird life which included groups of pelican, Lesser Adjutant stork, and small clouds of Ring-necked parakeets that flew over us in protest at the disturbance. In spite of the presence of the Bengal tiger, elephant, Water buffalo, Barking deer, and all the winged beauty of the wealth of the animal kingdom that are to be found in Kaziranga, the concentration of the Indian rhinoceros undoubtedly represents the *pièce de résistance* of the sanctuary.

Finally, in order to give me a good insight as to the remaining habitat available to the fragmented populations of pygmy hog, one of the tea company's single-engine Cessna 180s took Pearson and me along the foothills to the east of the Mangaldai sub-division of Assam. We flew over and along some of the lesser rivers of the Brahmaputra to north Lakhimpur, Dibrugarh, as far to the north-east as the region of Sadiya. The foothill savannah belt was lightly forested and appeared to be about 8–24 km (5–15 miles) wide, and looked in places to be fairly discontinuous. In these regions it was only too evident how dramatic the transformation of the previous 'wilderness' had been by the progressive settlements of immigrants, replacing practically all the natural habitat, up to the boundaries of forest reserves. From such a bird's-eye view of the Pygmy hogs' remaining habitat, it was easy to understand how such continued pressure by immigrants from Nepal on their homelands, sandwiched as they were between the tea gardens to the south and the Himalayas to the north, could easily cause the animals' ultimate extinction.

During the period 1971–1976 various attempts to establish a viable captive breeding population in Assam, under the auspices of the newly formed Assam Valley Wildlife Scheme, as well as at the Gauhati Zoo, all failed. Because of these failures it was evident that if the Pygmy hog were to be given a real chance to establish itself viably in captivity, it would be important to take some of the captive stock to a scientifically managed site outside Assam. It was in pursuance of this goal that, on behalf of the Jersey Wildlife Preservation Trust, Sir Peter Scott, in his capacity as Chairman of the Species Survival Commission (SSC) of IUCN, wrote to India's Prime Minister, Indira Gandhi, on 15th March 1976. Sir Peter said:

It would be of great biological and conservation value if a breeding colony could be established in Europe and that, as Gerald Durrell's Jersey Trust had been formed for the express purpose of building up breeding colonies of various threatened species, I am satisfied that it would be a most suitable place for such a project.

After several months, a reply from the Indian Prime Minister's Office, New Delhi, was received by Sir Peter, which said:

165

Dear Sir Peter,

In your letter of 15th March you asked for two or three pairs of Pygmy hogs from Assam for the Jersey Wildlife Preservation Trust.

This animal has reached the very edge of extinction but because of our strict protection, it is now making good recovery and we are able to spare some for breeding. I hope they will do well in Jersey.

Indira Gandhi

As a result of this exchange of letters, in November 1976 I returned to Assam and escorted a pair of Pygmy hogs from Attareekhat to a quarantine station at Zurich Zoo. Although I had an export permit for up to three pairs of the species on a breeding loan agreement from the Central Government, the Territorial Government of Assam refused to honour this or to allow me to take more than one pair of Pygmy hog out of their immediate jurisdiction. This pair did successfully breed in Zurich on 1st May 1977, producing a litter of five (four male, one female), though by 1984 no individuals of the Pygmy hog species remained in Zurich. Due to the continuous systematic loss of remaining habitat, a field study was jointly instigated and financed by the Assam Valley Wildlife Society and the JWPT, which had the full cooperation of the Assam Forest Department. William Oliver, the Trust's Research Assistant, who was subsequently appointed chairman of the IUCN's Pigs and Peccaries Specialist Group (PPSG), undertook a survey in 1977. His comprehensive report, highlighting the vulnerability of the fragmented populations of the animal, was sent to the appropriate national and international conservation and forestry authorities. Four years later he returned to Assam to find that the Pygmy hogs' status had worsened dramatically. In November 1984, at the General Assembly of the IUCN in Madrid, the Pygmy hog was chosen as one of the twelve animals representing the world's most endangered species.

In 1996, William Oliver was responsible for capturing the remaining six (two males, four females) wild hogs from their last surviving population in the Manus National Park of Assam. Due to the formation of the Pygmy Hog Conservation Programme (PHCP), a collaborative project of JWPT (now, Durrell Wildlife Conservation Trust – DWCT), the

IUCN/SSC/PPSG, the Forestry Department of the Government of Assam, and the Ministry of the Environment & Forests of Government of India; and to the establishment of a captive breeding facility at Basistha, near Gauhati (now, Guwahati) under the professional super-vision of the PHCP Project Director, Goutam Narayan, the captive population at Basistha currently (2009) numbers over 70 individuals.

During a recent visit to DWCT, Goutam told me that there were three major breeding pens at the Basistha facility which have been named after Gerald Durrell, Richard Magor and Jeremy Mallinson – I could hardly have been more flattered! However, it is has been very much due to William Oliver's 30 years of dedication and foresight in his initiating of this international collaborative conservation programme, that the PHCP has now been able to release 16 (seven males, nine females) captive bred Pygmy hogs, belonging to three social groups, into the Sonai Rupai Wildlife Sanctuary, as part of a proposed series of rein-troduction projects in selected sites in Assam. Such a collaborative project represents an excellent example of what can be achieved by organisa-tions sticking to a conservation project long-term, and the adoption of a multidisciplinary, multinational and team-based approach.

During the 1970s and early 1980s I became involved on behalf of the Trust in an increasing number of national, regional and interna-tional zoo and conservation committees and organisations. These included the Conservation and Breeding Committee, and Council, of the Federation of Zoological Gardens of Great Britain and Ireland; the IUCN's Species Survival Commission (as alternate member to Gerald Durrell); the International Union of Directors of Zoological Gardens (IUDZG=WAZA); and the Council of the Fauna and Flora Preservation Society (FFPS). During my first participation at the Annual Conference of Directors of Zoological Gardens of Great Britain and Ireland, at Dublin Zoo in May 1972, I had the opportunity to meet informally and to get to know the characters of the different zoo directors at that time. It was particularly interesting to note that out of the eight directors present, only one of them had had a university background, and half of them had previously spent many of their working years in Africa. Of the 38 annual meetings, the Jersey Trust hosted those in 1977 and 1978, and it was at the last that it was recognised that, because of the proliferation of so many other zoological and conservation groups, these informal and friendly get-togethers had outlived their original usefulness, and this series was officially 'put to bed'.

Lord (Jack) Craigton and his wife Eileen had spent many of their holidays in Jersey, and had been given a letter of introduction to me from Richard Fitter, the Hon Secretary of FFPS, the international conservation society of which Jack Craigton was currently Chairman. Craigton had one time been the Conservative Party Minister for the Scottish Office, and more recently Chairman of United Biscuits. When I first showed the Craigtons around the zoo he told me that now he had retired he wanted to devote his time to the cause of conservation, utilising his political and business acumen. Odette and I soon became close friends of theirs and we met up with them both on a regular basis. And after Jack had accepted Gerald Durrell's invitation to join JWPT's Council in October 1973 he asked me to share a platform with John Aspinall, to present one of two talks to an All-Party Conservation Committee, of which he was chairman. This was to take place at one of the small meeting rooms at the House of Lords. My subject was to be 'Breeding of Rare Species in Captivity in Public Zoos', to highlight the work of Jersey Zoo; while John Aspinall was to talk about 'Breeding of Rare Species in Private Zoos', giving examples of breeding successes at his private zoo of Howletts, and at his nearby estate of Port Lympne.

At this time, John Aspinall's reputation with the popular press was that of a millionaire playboy and gambler with eccentric right-wing views, but with a passion for exotic animals, in particular for tigers and gorillas. Due to his colourful reputation I felt that to follow such an exuberant, enthusiastic and outspoken person as Aspinall would be an unenviable ordeal and an undoubted anticlimax for any audience, so thankfully my host acceded to my request to go first. During my school days I had been told that when giving any type of presentation it is important to try and start off well, and attempt to finish on a high note. It was my seven-year-old son, Julian, who gave me the idea of using a comment that he had made at a previous Sunday luncheon at a rather formal hotel in Jersey. It had been at the end of the meal when, attired in a well-tailored three-piece suit and leaning back on my chair, savouring a good glass of red wine that Julian, sitting opposite me, looked me up and down and said in a voice loud enough for the whole dining room, 'Daddy, why are you sitting there looking so important, when you only look after animals at a zoo?' So at least such a comment gave me a way to start my address and to spell out to their lordships how important the conservation role of a modern zoo now was. I provided many examples of the successful breeding of threatened species at the Jersey Trust. John Aspinall's talk was the sort that a Silverback gorilla would have given, had it been able to speak. Their increasingly startled lordships were left in no doubt that they were all wasting their time just sitting in the House of Lords pontificating, when they should be out in the cities, towns and villages of this great country of ours, raising both awareness and money for the conservation of the world's dwindling wildlife and wild places. After Aspinall's address I reflected that such a forthright presentation was so like the type of talk that Gerald Durrell would have given; he and Aspinall were both alpha-males who enjoyed 'kicking against the pricks' of society and the norm. These two 'Silverbacks' had a great deal in common.

After 25 years of personal friendship with the Craigtons, who could not have been more supportive of my role at the Trust, when Jack died aged 88 on 28th September 1993 Eileen asked me to present the formal address at his funeral, which was held on 5th August at St Andrews Church, Wraysbury, which I was most honoured to do.

During the 1970s much progress was being made at the Jersey Zoo with many new buildings constructed for the animals, including aviaries, marmoset complexes, a nutritional research laboratory and the Gaherty Reptile Breeding Centre, the gift of a Canadian millionaire with a love for reptiles and a great admirer of Gerald Durrell. This largest of the zoo's animal buildings was officially opened by the Trust's patron, The Princess Royal, on 27th October 1976. The animal breeding results were also going from strength to strength. These included the successful rearing of five Lowland gorillas, a Sumatran orang-utan, Mayotte Brown lemurs, Goeldi's monkeys, Golden Lion tamarins, Jamaican hutias, Rodrigues Fruit bats, Spectacled bears, Waldrapp ibises, Pink pigeons, Meller's ducks, Round Island skinks and Jamaican boas. In order for the Trust to further develop its mission of representing a centre of conservation, education and research, two new important positions were established and appointments made; an Education Officer, Phillip Coffey, in 1978, and a Research Assistant, William Oliver, in 1979.

During these formative years of the Trust, a great deal of the progress made had been due to the sizeable gifts and grants it received from across the Atlantic. This chiefly resulted from an extensive lecture tour that Gerald Durrell undertook in the United States at the end of 1973. During this time he met a great number of enthusiastic and influential people, some of whom became his lifelong friends and, with the help of Dr Thomas Lovejoy, Margot Rockefeller, Sophie Danforth and Emerson Duncan, a US wing of the Jersey Trust – Save Animals from Extinction (SAFE) (later renamed Wildlife Preservation Trust – WPTI) was established which, at the same time, took over JWPT's American members. Tom Lovejoy had written the mandate, which was originally conceived to assist Americans in making tax deductible donations through SAFE to the work in Jersey and overseas. The Zoological Society of Philadelphia donated office space to house the organisation's head-quarters, with Tom Lovejoy as chairman of the board and Jody Longnecker as the administrator in charge. It was also at this time that Tom Lovejoy realised the importance for the American Trust to have a patron who was a household name and thereby have an impact in the States. Jacquie Durrell suggested Princess Grace of Monaco, formerly Grace Kelly, one of Hollywood's greats. We knew that Prince Rainier had a zoo of his own and was enthusiastically interested.

David Niven, a close friend of the Rainier family, made the initial approach to Princess Grace which, in the spring of 1974, resulted in Gerald Durrell and Tom Lovejoy meeting Her Serene Highness in her office at the palace in Monaco, during which time they explained the conservation objectives of the newly formed American Trust. In recog-nising that Princess Grace had many other commitments, as far as Gerald Durrell was concerned his ace card had been his showing the Princess a photograph of Jersey Zoo's second-born baby gorilla, Mamfe, lying on his tummy on a snow-white towel, and adding, 'These are the sorts of animals we are trying to help.' Evidently, the Princess was over-whelmed by the baby gorilla's cuteness. Before Princess Grace agreed to become the American Trust's patron, a further meeting with her was arranged in Monaco in August of the same year, and this time I was invited to accompany the Durrells and Tom Lovejoy to an informal lunch in the gardens of the palace, with both Prince Rainier and Princess Grace present.

It was certainly the most memorable of four days in Southern France.

A night with the Durrells at their second home at Mas Michel, near Nimes; a lunch with Larry Durrell at his home in Sommières, where he gave me one of the oil paintings that he had been preparing for an art exhibition in Paris, under his pseudonym Oscar Epfs, of a Barn owl that inhabited the old tower overlooking his swimming pool; a night at the *belle époque* Negresco Hotel in Nice, on the Promenade des Anglais overlooking the Bay of Angels; and finally the luncheon with the Rainiers at their palace in Monaco. Although I had seen the exterior of the Renaissance-style palazzo several times before, for my parents-in-law had lived in nearby Cros-de-Cagnes, I never dreamt that I would ever have the opportunity to enter and, even more, to meet the star of two of my favourite films: *To Catch a Thief* and *High Society*. We were ushered through one of the impressive archways of the fairytale pink building by a liveried servant and guided to the lush gardens situated to the rear of the buildings for our lunch by the pool. We were greeted by Princess Grace, who asked us what we would like to drink. When I said that a lager would be most agreeable, you can imagine my surprise when the Princess plunged her arm into the heart of the sub-tropical shrubbery and brought out an ice-cold bottle from a fridge concealed within the leaves.

When we arrived Prince Rainier was swimming in the nearby pool, and Princess Grace explained that they had both had a late night at the annual Red Cross Ball in Monaco. We sat round a beautifully laid table, which had a magnificent colourful ceramic centrepiece which brimmed over with white lilies. I sat on the left of the Princess and while the white-gloved servants served the meal, we talked about the combined conservation objectives of the two Preservation Trusts, in Jersey and in the US, and in particular about the Jersey Zoo's first two gorilla births. Towards the end of the meal Prince Rainier beckoned an aide to tell him that in half an hour he would be showing his guests around the zoo, and asked that all visitors vacated the zoo before his visit. As this was the height of the tourist season, such a task could not have been an easy one to accomplish. From our tour of his zoo it was quite obvious that Prince Rainier was extremely proud, knowledgeable, and fond of his collection, and he took the opportunity to show us the small veterinary surgery that our colleague Dr Ernst Lang from Basel Zoo had designed for him. A few weeks later, Gerald Durrell received confirmation, via the palace private office, that Her Serene Highness Princess Grace of Monaco had graciously agreed to serve as the American Trust's patron. So now both Trusts, on either side of the Atlantic, had princesses at the helm.

Perhaps 1979 proved to be the most significant year in the Trust's history. The student training scheme was launched, and the nearby property of Les Noyers was purchased to accommodate the newly established International Training Centre for Breeding and Conservation of Endangered Species (ITC); the Trust participated at the inaugural session of the IUCN/SSC Captive Breeding Specialist Group (CBSG) meeting held at the Zoological Society of San Diego, that had been promoted by the chairman of SSC, Sir Peter Scott; and Gerald Durrell married Lee McGeorge in Memphis, Tennessee.

The creation of the Trust's training programme had been stimulated when Gerald Durrell and John Hartley were in Mauritius, discussing with Carl Jones a partnership arrangement in support of Carl's magnificent work with the successful captive breeding programmes for both the Pink pigeon and Mauritius kestrel, and the restoration of the endemic fauna and flora of the nearby Round Island. The first trainee was a Mauritian forestry officer, Yousoof Mungroo, who later in his career became the first director of the first national park in Mauritius. As Desmond Morris was to comment, 'There are scores of conservationists and what-not who sit around pontificating learnedly about this and that. What Gerry did was train local people to do it themselves in their own countries.' The Trust's first ITC Training Officer, Dr David Waugh, was soon appointed and became responsible for the development of a diploma course with University of Kent at Canterbury, and since that time the ITC has trained almost 2,500 students from more than 122 countries (August, 2009).

After the first official meeting of CBSG, held in Jersey in June 1980, under the charismatic and dynamic chairmanship of Dr Ulysses Seal, I was privileged to serve on the Steering Committee of this significant Specialist Group for a period of 21 years.

I had first met Lee McGeorge in January 1978, after my mentor had coaxed her over the Atlantic to Jersey from Duke University, North Carolina on the pretext that she carry out some scientific study on animal vocalisations at the Jersey Trust. Gerald Durrell, as mischievous as ever, had only one objective in mind and that was to capture such an enchanting and intelligent 'southern belle' from Tennessee, and to share the rest of his life with her. I was deeply flattered and almost speechless when I was asked to be the best man at their wedding at Lee's parents' home in Memphis on 24th May 1979. The wedding's rehearsal dinner and speeches took place on a paddle steamer cruising down the Mississippi on the previous evening. It was almost like a scene from *Gone with the Wind*; with the groom resembling Rhett Butler, in a blue striped blazer, white flannels, a straw boater and a bow tie; while the bride wore a bonnet with ribbons, hooped skirt and crinoline, which so well recalled the compelling Scarlett O'Hara. After a considerable amount of champagne, talking to a Federal Judge who officiated at the wedding ceremony the following day, and whilst the sun was setting on the western bank of the Mississippi, I delivered what I considered a well-thought-out and well-expressed best man speech. However, once I had finished, any feeling of achievement was soon dashed when an American lady came up to me and said, 'Gee, Jeremy, due to the paddles of the steamer being so noisy, only about half of the reception could hear you. And due to your quaint English accent, only a few people from these southern states could understand a word you said!'

In 1985, Gerald Durrell founded the Wildlife Preservation Trust Canada (WPTC), which took over JWPT's Canadian membership, and appointed Paula Harris as its Executive Director, a position later taken by Elaine Williams; and in 1999 Paula became Development Director at JWPT until 2005. In America, Dr Mary Pearl was appointed Executive Director of WPTI (now Wildlife Trust) in 1993, with Tom Lovejoy as the Trust's Honorary Chairman. With Gerald Durrell being the founder of both of the North American Wildlife Trusts, Dr Lee Durrell and I attended many of their Board meetings and served as Honorary Directors. Lee Durrell became Honorary Director of the Jersey Wildlife Preservation Trust (now Durrell Wildlife Conservation Trust) when my mentor died at the beginning of 1995.

Chapter Twelve

A PASSION FOR PRIMATES

Whether it be a mammal, bird, reptile, or an amphibian, it is always difficult to choose favourites. I found that as soon as I became directly involved with an animal, I would in most cases start some sort of enthusiastic relationship with it. During my 42–year career of working directly with exotic species, my passion for the order Primates was always present. When I was not totally preoccupied by my Zoo Director duties and responsibilities at the Trust, I would give my attention particularly to the welfare and conservation of gorillas, both in captivity and in the wild. And similarly, for over 30 years, I became part of an international team supporting the conservation of their diminutive Neotropical cousins, the endangered Lion tamarins, from the Atlantic coastal forests of south-eastern Brazil.

Gorillas

I first read about gorillas in Paul du Chaillu's book *Explorations & Adventures in Equatorial Africa*, in which he claimed that it had been his fortune to be the first white man to see gorillas in darkest Africa. He wrote: 'I can vouch that no description can exceed the horror of its appearance, the ferocity of its attack, or the impish malignity of its nature.' So the grossly maligned character of one of man's nearest relatives was very much imprinted on people's minds, prior to the first male gorilla being exhibited in the Berlin Aquarium in 1876. It was the aquarium's director, Dr von Hermes, who presented a more correct and generous description of the true nature of this anthropoid when he wrote: 'It seems as if he was born with a patent of nobility among Apes … In comparison to a chimpanzee, he holds his head higher, producing the impression that he belongs to a better class of society,' [quoted by Brehm, In *Life of Animals*].

Up to 1911 only 14 gorillas were recorded as being exhibited in Europe and the USA. Apart from a young female called Pussi, which had lived from 1897 to 1904 at the Breslau Zoological Gardens, Germany (now Wroclaw Zoo, Poland), and kept behind a glass screen to keep it away from human germs, none of these young gorillas survived their captivity for long. Such a lamentable record prompted Dr W.T. Hornaday, Director of the New York Zoological Society to state in 1915: 'There is not the slightest reason to hope that an adult gorilla, either male or female, ever will be seen living in a zoological park or garden ... It is unfortunate that the ape that, in some respects, stands nearer to man, never can be seen in [its] adult state in zoological gardens; but we may as well accept that fact – because we cannot do otherwise'.

There are many records of the unnaturally human diets given to the young gorillas at the beginning of the twentieth century, ranging from hot meals of roast beef, gravy and roast potatoes to ice cream and crackers, as well as reports of their vulnerability to various human diseases and their quick decline if not provided with constant companionship and friendship. The known anatomic and metabolic similarities between the gorilla and man should have prompted zoos to offer sick animals the benefits of human medication. Nutritionally, they should have been given a diet more in keeping with the food they would have found in the wild; and as the young gorillas were showing so much affection towards their keepers, their psychological requirements could also have been more seriously catered for.

Fortunately, over the years, the standard of management of gorillas in captivity has much improved, with far better accommodation, nutrition and human involvement. The conventional bar-fronted cage has given way to laminated glass and, with the consequent protection from human diseases and the provision of far more naturalistic outside environments, gorillas are now living in captivity for a much more acceptable period of time. To date the female Jenny who died at Dallas Zoo in September 2008 aged 55 years, holds the longevity record for captive gorillas; an age well over a gorilla's lifespan in the wild. However, it was over 100 years from the first live gorilla being seen in Europe, in the Liverpool area of England, exhibited by the Wombells Travelling

Menagerie during the winter of 1855–6, and a further 41 years after Dr Hornaday's pronouncement that mankind will never see an adult gorilla in captivity, that the first successful birth of the Lowland gorilla species was recorded in December, 1956 when a female infant, Colo, was born at the Columbus Zoo, USA. The next two births occurred in Europe at the Basel Zoo, Switzerland: the female Goma in 1959, and her brother Jambo in 1961. Jambo was the first male gorilla to be born in captivity, and the first to be fully reared by his mother.

In April 1972 Jambo arrived in Jersey accompanied by Basel Zoo's director, Dr Ernst Lang. He proved to be a successful breeder and in 1973 sired two male infants from his Jersey brides. The first was born to Nandi on 15th July and named Assumbo, and the second to N'Pongo on 20th October, and named Mamfe. Both these young gorillas had to be hand-reared, and three years later they were sent to Molly Badham's famous primate collection at Twycross Zoo. Here they were introduced to a group of adults, and here Mamfe eventually sired two infants.

After reading George Schaller's epic book *The Year of the Gorilla*, which so well described the characters and behaviour of free-living gorillas in central Africa, I became increasingly keen to undertake a return trip to the African continent in order to have the opportunity to see gorillas in the wild. In 1969 I joined The Scientific Exploration Society, which had just been formed by Major (now Colonel) John Blashford-Snell (also known as Blashers) and Richard Snailham. I had first met John and his wife Judith in Jersey soon after my return from the Okavango swamps in 1962, and Odette and I had stayed with them just before my 1965 'Mitla' expedition to Bolivia, when I had borrowed some expedition kit from his stores; at the time he was an instructor at the Royal Military Academy, Sandhurst. In the spring of 1974, when John heard about my ambition to study gorillas in the wild, he offered me a place on The Zaire River Expedition, an expedition to commemorate the centenary of Henry Morton Stanley's hazardous journey (1874–1875) down the world's seventh longest river. From its source on the Zambian border, the Lualaba River joins the Congo and flows 4,374 km (2,716 miles) to the Atlantic. Gerald Durrell saw my enthusiasm to undertake a further field trip, and most considerately gave me the green light to join the expedition for an approximate period of two months.

All expedition participants had a 36–hour stay at Sandhurst, and I was designated a member of the scientific team. Each member was issued with a military survival kit, khaki clothing, a waterproof cape, a jungle hat, a pair of US marine jungle boots, a panga, a mess tin, two woven expedition badges, and a specially bound Zaire River Expedition pocket-sized New Testament and Psalms, presented to all expedition members by the Naval, Military & Air Force Bible Society. We were also provided with a Zaire River Expedition 'Survival Map' which had, as its pragmatic bold heading: IF LOST – DON'T PANIC, MAKE A PLAN. A month later, at 5.30 a.m., 4th October 1974, a cold wet winter's day, over one hundred army personnel, scientists, explorers and students, with 20 tons of stores, assembled at Gatwick Airport to be flown to Zaire in a chartered Air Zaire DC 10, by the personal pilot of President Mobutu Sese Seko.

Although I was very much using the expedition as the means of returning to Africa and to have the opportunity to observe gorillas in the wild, I had also agreed to spend up to five weeks with the main river party. We would travel downstream in the Colorado River giant inflatable, or in the smaller Avon Professionals, via some minor rapids in the upper regions of the Lualaba River before it joined the Congo at the Stanley Falls. This part of the expedition is covered in my previous publication *Travels in Search of Endangered Species*, and in Richard Snailham's *A Giant Among Rivers*. However, during my time in the Kivu Province of Zaire, I was fortunate to be the guest of Adrien Deschryver, the Conservateur of the newly created (1970) National Park of Kahuzi-Biega, and to meet his tall, dark-haired, highly motivated (and most attractive) Californian female assistant, Lee Lyon. Lee had first met Deschryver while she had been part of Anglia Television's production team who, with Dieter Plage, some two years previously had filmed the Kahuzi-Biega gorillas for the TV company's *Survival* series. Their programme *Gorilla* showed the remarkable relationship between Deschryver and the family group of gorillas that he had befriended, especially his association with the Silverback male Kasimir.

From my base in Bukavu, I was able to visit Kahuzi-Biega on several occasions with both Adrien Deschryver and Lee Lyon. Perhaps my most memorable encounter with Kasimir's group had been after Adrien's Pygmy trackers found where the gorillas had been recently foraging on bamboo shoots. While following their spoor, walking in single file as

178

Durrell family reunion, Les Augrès Manor, Jersey, Christmas 1960. Gerald Durrell with Louisa (mother), Margo (sister), Lawrence (brother) and Claude (Lawrence's wife). © Durrell Archives

The author on his Lambretta scooter at King George VI Barracks, Salisbury, Southern Rhodesia, October 1956. © Jay Duncan

Left: The author with Dingo puppies at Jersey Zoo, 1961.
© Michael Armstrong

Below: The author under the discerning eye of Gerald Durrell, the Founder and Honorary Director of the Jersey Wildlife Preservation Trust.
© Rosemary Gilliat

The author and June Kay, with Roger holding a snared Marabou stork, Okavango Swamps, Bechuanaland Protectorate (Botswana). Easter, 1962. © Robert Kay

Clio, the author's pet female Chacma baboon, 1963. © E.D.H. Johnson

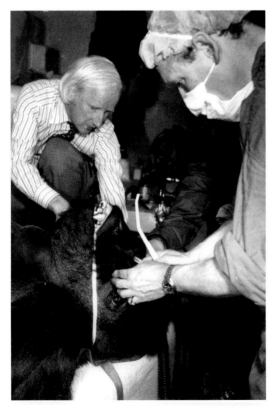

Above: The author with his favourite female Lowland gorilla, N'Pongo, at Jersey Zoo, 1968. © Philip Coffey

Left: Male Silverback Lowland gorilla, Jambo, under sedation at Jersey Zoo, 1981. © Philip Coffey

Female cheetah, Paula, taking the author for a morning run at Jersey Zoo, 1969.
© JWPT Archives

The author introducing Paula to his Basset hound, Scobie, at Jersey Zoo, 1969.
© Peter Le Breton

The author with the 3½ year-old lioness, Chinky, soon after her arrival at Jersey Zoo, May 1962.
© *Jersey Evening Post*

The author with a two year-old Bornean Orang-utan, Gigit-born Jersey, November 1990.
© *Jersery Evening Post*

Above: Pygmy hog sow with five
piglets in one of the three 'Breeding
Pens' named after Gerald Durrell,
Richard Magor and Jeremy
Mallinson, at the Basistha Centre,
near Guawahati, Assam, India, 2006.
© Michael Hammett

Right: The wedding of Gerald Durrell
and Lee McGeorge in Memphis,
Tennessee, with the pianist Mose,
and the best man, the author,
24 May 1979.
© Durrell Archives

Above: The Princess Royal, with Gerald Durrell and the author, at the time of the placing of a 'Time Capsule' in the foundations of The Princess Royal Pavilion, Jersey Wildlife Preservation Trust, December 1988.
© *Jersery Evening Post*

Left: The author, soon after his appointment as Zoological Director, Jersey Wildlife Preservation Trust.
© Robert Rattner

quietly as possible, and in some places having to bend, stoop and crawl, we started to smell the familiar musky body odour of gorillas. Suddenly, the cool tranquillity of the montane rainforest was broken by the roaring and chest-beating of an adult male gorilla. Deschryver remained facing the direction of the sounds saying quietly, over and over, 'Com, com, com, com', and then mimicking the gorilla's rumbling noise of pleasure. Soon after this we heard the snapping of a twig and a response to Deschryver's rumblings, and within minutes we came across the large bulk of Kasimir, who was lying down with six members of his family around him. A male, large though not a Silverback, lying on his back in a totally relaxed position, his attention divided between casually regarding the knuckles on his right hand and looking good naturedly in our direction. While Deschryver purposely chewed some leaves to demonstrate to the gorillas that he was no threat to them, two young siblings tussled together like friendly wrestlers, while other members of Kasimir's family contemplated us from a sitting position, occasionally waving their hands at the ubiquitous clouds of midges, while casually keeping an eye on our presence.

My time with this gorilla family had been like a dream come true, and I had found it the most humbling experience, particularly because I knew that gorillas throughout their range in equatorial Africa were being hunted for bush meat and trophies. We left Kasimir's family group to settle down for the night, when the adult females and younger ones climb into their nesting sites in the trees, while the senior males remain on the ground to slumber and keep guard. After such memorable and rewarding visits to Kahuzi-Biega, I reflected not only on my own good fortune but also how it was that Adrien Deschryver had shown that deep bond that can be developed between man and anthropoid ape, providing that such encounters can be based on sensitivity, understanding and mutual respect.

Soon after my return to the river expedition on the Lualaba River, at one of Blashford-Snell's late-afternoon 'Q'-meetings, during which time he would present a report on how the expedition was progressing, he read out a wireless message received from Gerald Durrell to inform Jeremy Mallinson that another baby of his had been just born at the zoo on 20th October. This was not of course to Odette, but rather to my favourite gorilla N'Pongo. Blashford-Snell announced, to a round

179

of clapping and cheers, that Gerald Durrell had named the female infant Zaire to honour the international make-up of the expedition. Later, when Zaire became an adult, she was sent to London Zoo where she still lives. It was at this time that Hugh Davies, who was covering the expedition for the *Daily Telegraph*, filed an article to his newspaper, based on the information I had given him about my first-hand experience with Kasimir's family in the Kahuzi-Biega National Park. This was published under the heading GORILLAS PLAY HOST TO ZAIRE EXPLORER, and recorded:

> The most interesting experience so far of any member of the scientific team of the Zaire River Expedition is that of Jeremy Mallinson ... For Mallinson, who has travelled throughout the world for over 15 years looking for various species of monkey and chimp, this visit to the home of the gorilla was the most exciting experience of his life.

After Odette had read the *Daily Telegraph* article, she told her friends that she was not aware that she was married to an explorer who had spent the first decade of his married life travelling throughout the world in search of other primates!

On 20th January 1975 the expedition achieved its objective of reaching the Atlantic Ocean, after having successfully navigated the rapids of the Lualaba and Zaire Rivers. Four months later, in order to celebrate such a major achievement The Grand Presentation of the Zaire River Expedition took place at The Royal Albert Hall in London. Over three thousand people attended the presentations, and probably due to the popularity of gorillas I was asked to be one of the eight expedition members to make a presentation. I was listed on the programme to introduce a five-minute extract from the Anglia *Survival* television programme showing Kasimir and his family group and to present a summary of my time with Adrien Deschryver and Lee Lyon at Kahuzi-Biega.

Those of us who had been selected had to appear on stage in full expedition kit, wearing khaki stockings, shorts, shirts, with one arm emblazoned with the Expedition Du Fleuve Zaire badge, and wearing a jungle hat, as if we were all about to disappear into a nearby jungle.

After the 80 minutes of presentations were over, we had to leave the stage and go down into the auditorium of the Albert Hall to mingle with members of the audience, among a comprehensive exhibition of expedition equipment. This included the giant inflatable boats and the Avon Professionals, a mock-up of a 'basher' – a plinth of earth, covered by a ground sheet and a sleeping bag, enveloped by a mosquito net, with a nearby waterproof cape in readiness for a tropical downpour, and some vegetation covering to act as camouflage, together with some rather graphic illustrations of diverse treatments that had been carried out by the medical team at various African communities along the banks of the Zaire River. Just when I was starting to congratulate myself in having managed to present to such a large audience the whole importance of supporting international efforts for the conservation of gorillas, in particular those connected with the conservation of the Mountain gorillas of Zaire, Rwanda and Uganda, a lady came up to me and said, 'Mr Mallinson, I so enjoyed your talk about butterflies.' I could not have been more deflated!

Within twelve months of having been with Adrien Deschryver and the most helpful and friendly Lee Lyon, in Zaire, I received the dreadful news that Lee had been killed while filming a translocation and release of a young elephant into the Kagera National Park in Rwanda. Colin Willock, who played the key creative role in Anglia Television's wildlife series *Survival,* recorded in his book *A Life on The Wild Side:*

A calf weighing about three quarters of a ton came down the ramp from the crate and kept going – straight at Lee Lyon. She had taken every sensible precaution … The elephant kept coming. There would still have been time for Lee to unhitch herself (from her camera battery belt) and escape into the open door of the Kombi. By the time the elephant was only yards away, it was too late … Lee just had time to look up and say 'Adrien' and died. She was buried in Kagera National Park … Adrien Deschryver died a few years later. His heart gave out.

In May 1976, I attended the 26th Annual Conference of Directors of Zoological Gardens of the British Isles and Ireland held at Edinburgh Zoo, under the chairmanship of the zoo's director, Roger Wheater. It was at this meeting that for the first time British and Irish Zoo Directors discussed the establishment of long-term captive breeding programmes for gorillas, orang-utans and chimpanzees. As a result of the meeting I was requested to initially act as the secretary to a panel to look into the long-term breeding of the great anthropoid apes held in this geographical region. Thanks to an enthusiastic response to the questionnaires sent out, a great deal of previously uncollected and correlated data concerning the majority of anthropoid apes held in both zoos and in private hands was accumulated.

As a first step, having recorded 57 individuals of the Western Lowland gorillas represented in twelve different collections, and with my particular focus on gorillas, I contacted John Aspinall, who owned over one third of the gorilla population concerned; he kindly offered the luxurious surroundings of his Clermont Club in Berkeley Square as the venue for the first ever meeting of all owners or custodians of gorillas in the British Isles and Ireland. The chief objective of this meeting, which I chaired, was to explore the common ground the various organisations had between them. In particular, to see how best we could develop a strategy that would benefit the long-term management and breeding of our gorilla population. It was decided that two similar panels should be set up to establish checklists of the numbers of chimpanzees and orang-utans held in zoos in the British Isles and Ireland.

Molly Badham (Director, Twycross Zoo) volunteered to correlate the overall chimpanzee population, while Geoffrey Greed (Director, Bristol Zoo) volunteered to collect the data on orang-utans. This in turn led to the publication of annual studbooks for all three populations of anthropoid apes in the British Isles and Ireland. Dr R.D. Martin (then the Director of the Wellcome Institute of Comparative Physiology at the Zoological Society of London) volunteered to provide the panels with scientific advice, and the meeting at the Clermont Club elected Roger Wheater as the overall chairman of the three anthropoid ape panels. By the end of the meeting it was good to have observed that any previous lack of communication and goodwill between some of the zoo directors had been overcome, and the potential for future co-operation had been pleasantly lubricated. This had been largely achieved by John Aspinall's instruction to one of his henchmen to place some generously-sized flutes of champagne on the table and to top these up frequently.

In October the following year the inaugural meeting of what had been titled the Anthropoid Ape Advisory Panel (AAAP) was held at Chester Zoo. In his opening address, Roger Wheater pointed out that: 'unless those responsible for anthropoid apes in captivity collaborated and coordinated much more closely over the maintenance of adequate groups of animals, a stage might be reached when, in the future, they no longer existed in the various collections concerned. The chief objective of the meeting was, therefore, to examine the situation and to obtain a consensus as to what action was required to ensure that the best possible use was made of existing stocks.' The AAAP recorded a particular landmark when it was given a grant by WWF (UK) to enable it to appoint on a short-term contract the eminent small-population biologist, Dr Georgina Mace, to undertake a genetic and demographic analysis of anthropoid apes, and to make recommendations for their future scientific management.

Because of my direct involvement with gorillas and my work with the AAAP, I was invited to present a paper at the Workshop on Infertility in Male Great Apes held at Atlanta, Georgia, USA in November 1980. My paper was entitled: The Establishment of a Self-Sustaining Breeding Population of Gorillas in Captivity – With Special Reference to the Work of the AAAP of the British Isles and Ireland. I started off my presentation by quoting a part of Dr von Hermes' 1876 description of a gorilla: 'In comparison to a chimpanzee, holds his head higher, producing the impression that he belongs to a better class of society.' Immediately a lady in the front row jumped up and shouted, 'Bravo, bravo' and after my talk an attractive dark-haired lady came up to ask me for the source of such a fine quotation; the lady was Dian Fossey.

In October 1982 I received a letter from Dian Fossey, while she was a visiting professor lecturing at Cornell University, Ithaca, New York. She wrote:

I remain particularly indebted to you for the definition of the gorilla compared to a chimpanzee (von Hermes, quoted by Brehm) – I should never have found it in my own library. I always use it to introduce the obvious difference between the chimpanzee and gorilla, though, I don't dare in front of Jane! [Goodall] My classes nonetheless enjoy it tremendously.

The following year, her outstanding book *Gorillas in the Mist* described her 15 years of scientific study of the endangered Mountain gorilla populations in the Virunga Mountains that straddle the borders of Zaire, Rwanda and Uganda. The book provided the greatest insight into the possible bonding between human and anthropoid ape. The slaughter by poachers of one of her favourite and most habituated gorillas Digit, in 1977, brought the Mountain gorillas' plight to international prominence. Since the mid-1970s, I had exchanged a number of scientific papers about gorillas from the Trust's *Dodo* journal with Dian Fossey, and I was delighted to see that she had made reference to 16 of these publications in the book's bibliography.

I last met Dian Fossey at an international primate meeting in June 1985. The conference Primates, The Road to Self-Sustaining Populations was held at the Zoological Society of San Diego, at which I had been invited to present a paper on The Importance of an Interdisciplinary Approach: Getting the Conservation Act Together. During our discussions, Dian Fossey mentioned that I would be more than welcome to visit her at the Karisoke Veterinary Research Center in Rwanda, an invitation that most regrettably I was unable to take up. For on 27th December, only six months after our San Diego meeting, she followed the fate of her beloved Digit, being brutally murdered, supposedly by poachers, at her base at Karisoke. Her premature death brought to an end the life of one of the best known (and sometimes controversial) figures in primatology. As Ian Redmond was to later record in an obituary (1986) of her:

The research and conservation work that arose, both directly and indirectly, from Dian Fossey's efforts has ensured a future for *Gorilla g. beringei*. If she had never been in the Virungas, there would be few, if any, living there today.

During its 13 years of existence the AAAP provided significant guidelines for the management of anthropoid apes and by the late 1980s more and more zoos were pooling their animal resources, heeding the

advice of the respective studbook holders, and adhering to the scien-
tifically-based management recommendation made by the species coor-
dinators, as appointed by the various national, regional and international
zoo associations. Due to this increased cooperation and coordination
between zoos to maximise the breeding of anthropoid apes, and to
avoid duplication of such efforts, the annual meetings of the AAAP
were discontinued in 1990.

In 1993 Ruth Keesling, the founder of the Dian Fossey Gorilla Fund
(DFGF) in both the US and Europe, invited me to become a member
of the Board of Trustees of DFGF-UK, on which I served for four
years. Also, due to my direct involvement on the Steering Committee
of SSC's Conservation Breeding Specialist Group (CBSG), I was asked
by the group's outstanding and charismatic leader, Dr Ulysses Seal, to
participate in a Population Habitat Viability Assessment (PHVA) workshop meeting for Mountain gorillas at Entebbe, Uganda, in January
1997. The workshop immediately followed a three-day PHVA for chimpanzees that had given me the opportunity to meet a number of prominent field workers. These included Jane Goodall, whose outstanding
book *In the Shadow of Man* stressed the significance of long-term scien-
tifically-based field studies to increase our understanding of the chimpanzees' family life and social hierarchies; particularly in relation to those
of their nearest relative, man.

The result of the planning meeting was a PHVA entitled Can the
Mountain Gorilla Survive?, which took place in Kampala in December,
1997. The JWPT was one of the seven sponsors of this important
workshop, and Dr Ulie Seal appointed me to chair the Governance
Group part of this Viability Assessment. In this I was ably assisted by
Professor John Cooper (Director, Karisoke Veterinary Research Center
at the time of the Rwanda massacres, and a member of JWPT's Scientific
Advisory Committee), and by his wife Margaret (an environmental lawyer,
who had also lectured at the Trust's ITC). During our discussions with
the delegates that had Mountain, Eastern Lowland, or Western Lowland
gorillas in their respective countries, it was clear that little or no communication took place between them. The degree of the 'territorial imper-
ative' and lack of any real cooperation and coordination between those
NGOs involved in the conservation of all gorillas was also most apparent.

Richard Johnston-Scott's excellent book *Jambo – A Gorilla's Story* describes his 15 years of looking after Jambo at Jersey Zoo, his insight into the animals, their psychological make-up, the way they function as a family unit, and how they relate to their carers and to the general public. He describes the eventful August afternoon in 1986, when Jambo demonstrated his exemplary behaviour in protecting a young boy who had fallen into the gorilla enclosure; an event that was captured by a visitor's video camera and subsequently shown on TV around the world. This well demonstrated that gorillas were not the monsters of popular myth. Such a dramatic incident prompted Sir David Attenborough to comment:

> Human beings grow up with the notion of beauty and the beast and that was the notion traded on by films like *King Kong* ... Sadly, logic shows us that the exact opposite actually applies. It is human beings who are the aggressive primates.

Gerald Durrell's epitaph to Jambo was: 'A magnificent individual, courteous and gentle'.

The tremendous progress that the international zoo community has made in establishing a self-sustaining population of gorillas in captivity has been well documented by the International Studbook for Gorillas (2007). By 31st December 2006, the studbook recorded that over 70% of the 874 (397 m; 477 ft) gorillas represented in world zoos had been captive-bred; compare this with the prophecy made just over 90 years ago by W.T. Hornaday: 'A gorilla will never be seen in adult state in zoological gardens.' This overall success in breeding gorillas has had significant additions from the Jersey Zoo, for during a 45–year period the zoo has recorded 14 live births sired by Jambo, and two births sired by the Melbourne Zoo born male Ya Kwanza (who arrived at Jersey in 1993). Since the zoo's first breeding in 1973, Jersey zoo-bred gorillas have been sent on permanent breeding loan to zoos in Australia, Canada, Czech Republic, France, Germany, Switzerland, United Kingdom and the USA; and over 50 descendents of Jersey-bred stock have been now recorded.

After the sudden death of Jambo on 16th September 1992, the *BBC Wildlife Magazine* established The Jambo Award, an annual prize of £100 to a suitable wildlife or conservation charity in honour of the individual animal which, in the view of the readers of *BBC Wildlife*, has done most to make humans more aware of the other animal species with which we share the world. Appropriately, the first award was given to the Digit Fund, that later became the Dian Fossey Gorilla Fund (now The Gorilla Organisation).

Lion tamarins

Perhaps it is in keeping with my enthusiasm for biological diversity that my other great passion within the primate kingdom is almost the other extreme in size; the diminutive Lion tamarins of south-eastern Brazil. It was in December 1519, that the priest Antonio Pigafetta, chronicler of Magellan's voyage around the world, provided the first known reference to the Golden Lion tamarin after observing them in the wild, calling them 'beautiful simian-like cats similar to small lions'. Both the Portuguese and the Spaniards brought marmosets and tamarins back to Europe after their first voyages to South America; and in 1957, the primatologist Ivan Sanderson wrote in his book *The Monkey Kingdom*:

> Being fascinated by their rather uncanny appearance and remarkable intelligence, as well as their endless 'conversation', they became a rage among the aristocracy and enormous prices were sometimes paid for healthy specimens by titled men; who presented them to their wives and daughters and more especially, for some curious sociological reason, to their mistresses who carried the tiny mites in their sleeves or other convenient retreats about their raiment.

It was not until the first half of the 1960s that the doyen of Brazil's primatologists, Dr Adelmar Coimbra-Filho (founder of the Rio de Janeiro Primate Centre – CPRJ/FEEMA), called attention to the severe plight of the Golden Lion tamarin (GLT) in the State of Rio de Janeiro; a species that is one of the most vividly coloured of all mammals, its golden barley-sugar complexioned hairs metallic in appearance and highly iridescent.

In 1970, 65 years after the last reported observation, Coimbra-Filho rediscovered the Black Lion tamarin (BLT) in the State of São Paulo, which until the late 1970s had never been displayed in any zoo collection.

In 1990, the Jersey Zoo was the first to receive on loan from the Brazilian Institute of the Environment and Renewable Resources (IBAMA) and CPRJ/FEEMA two pairs of Black-headed lion tamarin (BHLT) and the first to breed the species outside Brazil.

The Golden-headed Lion tamarin (GHLT) from the State of Bahia had been exhibited at London Zoo in 1869, although by 1972 it had still been in captivity on only three occasions.

A fourth species, the Black-faced Lion tamarin (BFLT) from the small island of Superagui and a few isolated areas on the adjacent mainland of São Paulo state, was first described as recently as 1990. Regrettably, all four members of the genus *Leontopithecus* are threatened, for the remaining area of their limited ranges in the coastal forests of eastern Brazil, the *Mata Atlantica* – a mere two per cent – of their original distribution – is within Brazil's most densely inhabited region, with forest destruction and habitat fragmentation being the chief threats to their survival.

I first visited the Poço das Antas Biological Reserve in the company of Dr Adelmar Coimbra-Filho, Cláudio Valladares-Padua (an ex-ITC Brazilian graduate), and Nick Lindsey (then JWPT's Curator of Mammals) in March 1982. The reserve was home to the main remnant of the wild population of GLTs which, out of an estimated overall wild population of 200 animals, represented the only protected region for as few as 75 individuals. At that time a comprehensive survey of the vegetation of the reserve was being made, prior to the initiation of a reintroduction programme for captive-bred Golden Lions. The subsequent field studies of the status, behavioural ecology, demography and environmental education programme, were the result of two years of negotiations between the Smithsonian National Zoological Park Golden Lion Tamarin Conservation Program (SNZP/GLTCP) and the Brazilian Forestry Development Institute (IBDF), that later became IBAMA and more recently Instituto Chico-Mendes (ICMBio). The ebullient Dr Devra Kleiman (SNZP Research Associate), who ten years previously had published her research recommendations for this species, was responsible for leading this ambitious long-term research programme based initially in the reserve. Its goal was an integrated *in situ* and *ex situ* conservation effort for the species.

During 1983 to 1984 large numbers of GHLTs were being illegally exported from Brazil, via Bolivia and Guyana, and finding their way into the hands of animal dealers and private collections, mainly in Belgium and France. In March 1985 IBAMA formed the International Recovery and Management Committee for the Golden-headed Lion Tamarin (IRMC/GHLT) and requested me to co-chair the committee with Adelmar Coimbra-Filho. Subsequently, in collaboration with IBAMA, the committee was successful in having the majority of the illegally exported Lion tamarins returned to Brazil. In June 1990 JWPT was one of the five sponsors of the first Population Viability Analysis (PVA) Workshop for Lion tamarins, held in Belo Horizonte, Brazil. Ulysses Seal chaired the meeting which reviewed the status of all four Lion tamarin species and set out scientifically based priorities, goals, missions, and action plans for each of the IRMCs, as well as for the management of both zoo and wild populations.

The IRMC for the GLT was chaired by Devra Kleiman; the one for BLT was co-chaired by Faiçal Simon (São Paulo Zoo) and Devra Kleiman; and in addition to my co-chairmanship with Adelmar Coimbra-Filho of the IRMC for GHLT, I was requested to co-chair the committee for the BHLT species with Admiral Ibsen de Gusmão Câmara (President, Brazilian Foundation for the Conservation of Nature – FBCN). Soon after the workshop IBAMA decided that in order to streamline the legislative and administrative aspects of conservation of the four IRMCs, the committees would be recognised by Brazilian law (IBAMA Portaria No. 764), as technical advisers to the government on both the wild and captive populations of the *Leontopithecus* spp. These committees comprised experts in various aspects of Lion tamarin biology, and conservationists including zoo biologists, studbook keepers, curators and administrators, as well as field biologists, protected area managers, educators, and representatives of NGOs active in coordinating conservation efforts for the species.

The recognition by IBAMA of the commitment of the international community to conservation of the genus was reaffirmed in 1991 by the groundbreaking agreement by zoos around the globe to return ownership of captive GLTs to the people of Brazil. By 1993, the committees decided to hold joint annual meeting with IBAMA in Brazil, to discuss progress in research, education, and conservation. In this way the committees were able to look at total populations of the genus *Leonpithecus*, both *in situ* and *ex situ*, and to make appropriate recommendations to

IBAMA. In May 1997 a second PHVA for Lion tamarins was held in Belo Horizonte, with JWPT as one of its major sponsors. In 1999, by acknowledging the significant cooperative and coordinated work of the IRMCs, IBAMA consolidated the committees further by merging them under the new title of the International Committee for the Conservation and Management of the Lion Tamarins (ICCM) – IBAMA Portaria No. 764.

Although I became involved in the conservation work connected with all four Lion tamarin species, my chief interest was the conservation of the GHLTs in their fragmented habitats in the State of Bahia. The Una Biological Reserve is an isolated patch of Atlantic rainforest, originally 5,342 ha (13,200 acres) in size, set aside by IBAMA specifically for the protection of GHLTs. In 1991–2 JWPT, in collaboration with the World Wildlife Fund (WWF-US) and Conservation International (CI) helped raise funds to enable IBAMA, through the Brazilian NGO *Fundação Biodiversitas* to purchase another 673 ha (1,663 acres) of forest, thereby officially increasing the size of the Una Reserve to 6,015 ha (14,863 acres). The tract of forest serves as a 'genetic corridor' between two narrowly connected blocks of the reserve. At this time WWF-US recorded that this forest acquisition represented the 'only example' in Brazil of international cooperation for the purchase of land for a Brazilian protected area. In March 1991, HRH The Duke of Edinburgh (President of WWF), on behalf of WWF-US and JWPT, visited Una to officially present this forest corridor to IBAMA, and a plaque commemorating the occasion was placed on the outside wall of the reserve's headquarters.

In June 1993, an international fundraising effort was coordinated by Lou Ann Dietz (WWF-US), and by the collaboration of the Chicago Rainforest Action Group, through Brookfield Zoo, Chicago, JWPT, WPT-Canada and WWF-US, a further 1,508 ha (3,726 acres) of forest abutting the Una Reserve was purchased. This increased the original size of the reserve by 18% thereby significantly aiding the permanent protection of a viable portion of the Atlantic rainforest. The JWPT published a preliminary international studbook in 1987, and Dr Georgina Mace compiled the first official studbook the following year. The Trust continued to publish the studbook annually until 1993, when it was taken over by the Royal Zoological Society of Antwerp, and the genetic and demographic management of the captive population is now undertaken by Dr Kristin Leus, in association with the GLTs international studbook holder, Dr Jonathan Ballou.

The environmental education programme *Projeto Mico-Leão Baiano* was established in the late 1980s in Southern Bahia by Cristina Alves, a graduate of the Trusts' ITC. It had as its chief objective the conservation of the GHLT and its habitat by developing among the local community an awareness of the importance of conserving both the species and its associated habitat. The Trust's US and Canadian sister organisations, and IBAMA, provided most of the funding for its operation. In May 1994 the Executive Director of WPTI, Dr Mary Pearl, project Director Cristina Alves and I participated at the official opening of the project's Centre for Nature Conservation, to which school children, professionals and the general public had access. The creation of the Centre was made possible thanks to the Executive Committee for Cocoa Planning (CEPLAC), and the State University of Santa Cruz, which had provided an area of 43 ha (106 acres) at its regional headquarters in Itabuna, near Ilhèus, Bahia.

By using the GHLT as a flagship species, JWPT received a grant from J & B Whisky's Care for the Rare fund to support a three-year Environmental Education Programme with the community around the Una Reserve; and in collaboration with other NGOs, JWPT was responsible for the publication of Lion tamarin education posters for both the GHLT and the GLT species, which included an overprint of the artwork/photograph of a conservation message in Portuguese. Since the early 1990s the Trust has supported a number of field research programmes both in the Una Biological Reserve and in unprotected areas bordering the region, as well as having given a number of grants to a series of field research projects connected with the other three species of Lion tamarin.

The Lion Tamarin of Brazil Fund (LTBF) was established by JWPT in 1991, and I asked Gerald Durrell to sign the appeal letter that was sent in 1992 to all holders of the Lion tamarin species outside Brazil, requesting donations to support *in situ* conservation work for the genus. By 1997, the first issue of the ICCM newsletter *Tamarin Tales,* produced by JWPT and edited by Jonathan Ballou (SNZP), recorded that the LTBF had raised over US $60,000. Ten years later, Bengt Holst

191

(Copenhagen Zoo) stated that the fund has now raised over US $1 million, which shows how much world zoos are increasingly supporting conservation projects in their countries of origin for those species they hold in their zoological collections. During my annual visits to Brazil I have been greatly privileged to see all four species of Lion tamarins in the wild state, and to have met so many highly dedicated and professional Brazilian conservationists.

During my last participation at the ICCM for Lion tamarins, at São Paulo Zoo in 2008, I could not have been more delighted to learn that since the Trust's early involvement with the purchase of additional land in the Una Reserve region of Bahia, the protected area now extends to the Atlantic coast. Also, that in 2007, a further 23,404 ha (57,831 acres) of cabucca habitat had been acquired adjoining the reserve, and that a new National Park da Serra das Lontas, consisting of 16,800 ha (41,514 acres), is in the process of being decreed. Similarly, through the collaborative work of the GLT Conservation Programme in the State of Rio de Janeiro, a significantly increased amount of re-forestation, joining up fragmented habitats, has been achieved; and in 2007 a further parcel of land had been purchased to further consolidate the unique fauna and flora of the *Mata Atlantica*. At the 2008 annual meeting of the ICCM success was confirmed; from an estimated wild population of GLTs in 1983 of about 200, there are now more than 1,500 individuals living in an area of approximately 25,000 ha (61,777 acres), over one third of which have captive-bred genes, resulting from successful reintroductions.

The success of the cooperative and coordinated work of the International Committee for the Conservation and Management (ICCM) for Lion Tamarins provides a significant model for other global initiatives by the zoos and conservation bodies. I wholeheartedly agree with the sentiments expressed by Russell Mittermeier in his Foreword to *Lion Tamarins, Biology and Conservation*, in which he wrote:

All in all, I think it is fair to say that the international effort of the past 30 years on behalf of the lion tamarins of Brazil represents one of the great success stories in the global conservation movement. Together with the Muriquis (*Brachyteles* spp) they have long been the flagship species for this critically important 'Hotspot', and without the lion tamarins it is doubtful that this region would have received the attention that it has.

It is undoubtedly a sad reflection on mankind that we have allowed so many species that share the planet with us to hover so close to the brink of extinction. My long-term involvement and enthusiasm for the animal kingdom, in particular with gorillas and Lion tamarins, has provided me with a much greater understanding of the importance of cooperative, multidisciplinary approaches to promote and support biodiversity conservation. I have also come to recognise that without good communication, a degree of sensitivity to the culture of the countries that NGOs work in, and the nurturing of mutual respect in the development of viable partnerships, so many more threatened species will join the irreversible fate of the dodo.

However, as the majority of conservationists are imbued with various levels of enthusiastic optimism, I fully agree with the statement made in 1987 by Michael Soulé:

There are no hopeless cases, only people without hope and expensive cases. That is, given the resources, even a handful of individuals can constitute the basis of a successful effort to salvage a population or a species.

This view of what can be achieved by a few dedicated people has certainly proved to be the case with most of the conservation projects that I have been directly involved with. During my 42 most rewarding years of working for Gerald Durrell's conservation mission and other national and international NGOs, and while learning about the plight of so many species and the pressures exerted upon the world's shrinking biodiversity, I frequently remind myself of just how steep my learning curve has had to be. In particular, I recall the pronouncement made by the Trust's founder on the occasion of my 30th anniversary of working at his zoo. At a meeting in the Trust's ITC Lecture Theatre on 1st May 1989 I was presented with a splendidly mounted and framed photograph of Gerald Durrell and The Princess Royal smiling, with a back view of me talking to her; our Patron, had graciously signed the mount *Anne*. After the presentation, my mentor informed all those members of the zoo staff, and some of the international trainees, present, 'When Jeremy arrived here, he didn't know the difference between a hippopotamus and a hearth-rug.' In spite of a sprinkling of poetic licence he was, of course, almost totally correct.

Chapter Thirteen

GERRY'S DISCIPLES

Through his many books and television programmes, Gerald Durrell acquired a multitude of admirers around the globe, from all walks of life. At the same time he inspired so many people to support conservation projects, not only in their own countries, but throughout the world. He provided people with a greater appreciation of the role of zoos in conservation, education and research, and many came to support his ground-breaking vision for the conservation mission of the Jersey Wildlife Preservation Trust (now the Durrell Wildlife Conservation Trust). Due to the diversity of his disciples and champions – all those who supported the cause – it has been difficult to choose the ones that he himself would have been most likely to select, without leaving out other worthy people. However, all the people I have included in these next two chapters have been known to me personally, and therefore I can vouch for their sincerity in having been either disciples, fans, or long-term supporters of Gerry's visionary conservation ethos.

Perhaps all of us who were involved in the early days of the evolution of Menagerie Manor had come across Gerry through his writings and were untrained amateur naturalists, but we also shared his enthusiasm and passion. Therefore I consider it appropriate to recall in these final chapters some of the accounts either told to me personally, or recorded on television or in radio programmes, by disciples and champions of Gerry's conservation mission. I have included not only examples of the sentiments expressed by some of Jersey Zoo's early team of fledgling staff members, but also the opinions of those who I have considered to have been Gerry's disciples throughout his formative years.

Dr Theodore Stephanides, Gerry's tutor in Corfu during the 1930s, and of *My Family and Other Animals* repute, in which Gerry described him as 'The most remarkable man I ever met; he would extract magic that even Merlin would have envied', and whom he recalled as the most important man in his life, without whom he would have achieved nothing. While Theodore always regarded Gerry as a son.

My first meeting with Theodore was at his flat in London and afterwards during his visit to Jersey, when he signed my first edition copy of Lawrence Durrell's *Prospero's Cell*. His hand-written inscription read:

Reflected Glory:
Of Shakespeare, Milton and the like I may not know the fame; yet rambling on my way through life, I've met with some acclaim. Awed exclamations I have heard and caught admiring looks: 'See there – it's HIM! The Man who's in those thrilling Durrell books!!!' Theodore Stephanides, Les Augrès Manor, 20–5–1968.

My last meeting with Theodore was 15 years later, almost immediately after Gerry and Lee had been to Buckingham Palace to receive his OBE. Gerry had been confronted outside the palace by Eamonn Andrews, the compère of the popular television programme *This is Your Life,* and presented with the programme's famous Red Book. When the recording of the show started in the early afternoon, a number of us Jersey disciples attended, including John Hartley, Catha Weller, Simon Hicks, Shep Mallet and Betty Boizard; followed by a galaxy of friends and admirers, Sir Peter Scott, Lord and Lady Craigton, Dinah Sheridan, Mai Zetterling, Brian Bell (New Zealand), Wahab Owadally and Yousoof Mungroo (Mauritius), and Margo Durrell and her son, the younger Gerry. Larry Durrell was unable to come to London, but provided a recorded interview from his home in Sommières in which he thanked Eamonn Andrews for the chance to salute his brother on the momentous occasion of his having received such a well-earned decoration. He raised a glass of wine as a toast and concluded, 'I hope the animals are dancing in their cages in his zoo.' However, Gerry's most emotional reunions were with his kindergarten teacher, the 87–year-old Miss Squires, and when the programme culminated with his totally unexpected meeting with Theodore.

As Douglas Botting recorded in his biography of Gerry:

> Master and pupil embraced as only two old friends whose friendship went back nearly half a century could, knowing that it might be for the last time – as indeed it was. Then Gerald seized Theo's hand and led him forward towards the camera, raised the old man's hand and lifted it high above his head in a gesture of salutation, triumph and love.

Resulting from the few meetings I had had with the two Durrell brothers, **Lawrence Durrell** and Gerry, when they had been both together, and from talking to others who knew them both quite well, I recognised that in spite of their evident rude banter and verbal sparring, they shared a significant degree of admiration for each other's achievements; thereby each being a disciple of the other. This situation is illustrated by David Hughes, in his portrait of Gerald Durrell *Himself & Other Animals*, when in a conversation with Larry about Gerry, Larry said:

> As a small boy he was impossible. A terrible nuisance. He has recounted the worst of himself as well as the best in that Family book. Oh, it was matchboxes full of scorpions all the time. I didn't dare to sit down anywhere in the house, and of course Mother was there to defend him – the slightest criticism and she would snarl like a bear, and meanwhile there were beetles in the soup … he was intolerable, he needed to be thrashed.

In keeping with such family ridicule, when in 1978 I asked Larry to sign a first edition copy of *My Family and Other Animals* he wrote 'Dammit Jeremy, what would you be doing with such a horrible book?' Whereas his sister had inscribed: 'Dear Jeremy – from a long-suffering family member, Margo x.x.'

Margo Duncan (née Durrell) was quite a frequent visitor to Jersey and since our first meeting during Christmas 1960, I have had the immense pleasure of her company, with other members of the Durrell family, in such diverse places as Frankfurt, Bournemouth, London, Antwerp, Nimes and Memphis. Margo was always brimming over with laughter and fun, and pleasantly flirtatious with menfolk, whom she appeared never to take seriously; but she was undoubtedly greatly proud of her two brothers, in particular her younger one, Gerry.

In Gerry's preface to his sister's book *Whatever Happened to Margo?* he relates:

> From the beginning and every bit as keenly as the Durrell brothers, Margo displayed an appreciation of the comic side of life and an ability to observe the foibles of people and places. Like us, she is sometimes prone to exaggeration and flight of fancy, but I think this is no bad thing when it comes to telling one's story in an entertaining way.

In her book Margo recalls a telephone call in 1947 from their Aunt Patience, a formidable spinster who, among other enquiries about family members, had asked, 'And dear brother Gerald, is he still away, exposing himself to tropical diseases?' But as far as Margo was concerned, she was frequently referred to by Gerry as 'the much-loved Margo', a sentiment that was undoubtedly shared by all who had had the privilege of her company.

David Hughes first met Gerry in 1956 when he was an editor for the publisher Rupert Hart-Davis, and had been given the task of reading the text of Gerry's future book, *Encounters with Animals*. After an office meeting, Gerry asked David if he'd care to join *all* of them for lunch at Bortorelli's in Soho. In David's 1997 published biography of Gerry he recalled, ' "*All*" was crucial. I had learned in two seconds that this man was uniquely inclusive. I had discovered Durrell's gift of drawing others irresistibly into his private orbit. His prompt intimacy had found me a friend for life ... It was clear that Durrell had no vanity (and certainly no conceit), only exuberance. He had a gift of being as interested in my life as his own, and as keen to enrich it – he so distinctly was himself without trying. That defined charisma.'

David remembered a time when, on the terrace at his house in Provence, Gerry expostulated over Larry's absurdity, 'The poor fellow was obsessed with money. His love life was Byzantine.' Hughes went on to recall, 'For a moment Gerry wondered aloud whether the moment had arrived to "press something liquid to the left kidney", but his gaze drifted off into examining the quality of light. This valley in France seemed heavy with ripe fruit. It might have been a Corfiot morning long ago.'

John Hartley joined the Jersey Zoo straight from school in 1961, for Gerald Durrell had been his boyhood hero. Gerry chose John to accompany him on his animal collecting expedition to Sierra Leone in 1965, fondly referring to him as 'Long John' and describing him in the book *Catch Me a Colobus*: 'He is six foot two inches high and immensely thin, so that he looks rather like a Cruickshank caricature, but he was young and a hard worker and he was wildly enthusiastic.' Gerry also described him as looking rather like a shipwrecked giraffe! During John's 42 years of dedication to the Trust's animal conservation work, he served as Curator of Reptiles, Trust Secretary, and Personal Assistant to Gerald Durrell, and after Gerry's death was appointed the Trust's International Programme Director. John acted as the perfect ADC to the Honorary Director, for in spite of a number of ups-and-downs, he always managed to remain cool and collected, and retain the posture of the supreme diplomat.

Beyond John's initial experiences in Sierra Leone, his work took him to many parts of the world. He was responsible for carrying out much background investigation and negotiation for the *Durrell in Russia* series of television programmes, and travelled with Gerry and Lee to locations in the Soviet Union, many never before visited by foreigners, from polar regions in the north to desert in the south, from dense forest in the west to the mountainous east. In his dedication to John in his book *Gerald & Lee Durrell in Russia* Gerry wrote, in his customary affectionate way to one of his disciples: 'For John Hartley – our friend and long-suffering personal assistant, without whose hard work, tact and cheerfulness we would not have achieved so much as we did during our fascinating travels, with great affection.' Perhaps John's major contribution in support of the Trust's conservation mission *Saving Species from Extinction,* was his long-term involvement and coordination of the Trust's support for the conservation initiatives carried out in Mauritius. For here his patience, political networking, and considerable knowledge came to the fore, and in spite of the many obstacles that frequently cropped up, both in Mauritius and on Round Island, he would manage to come up with a viable solution and save the day.

Whenever people approached John and told him that they didn't like to see birds in a captive environment he would say, 'It's a holding operation. We can keep the species in captivity, and keep them going, whilst we address their problems in the wilds and of course in many instances it brings about the possibility of a reintroduction. Today, there are Pink pigeons flying around the forests of Mauritius whose grandparents were born in Jersey. I know, for I caught them – fantastic!'

John recalls how, at breakfast one morning in Mauritius, Gerry said, 'I've often talked about turning the Trust into a sort of miniature university of conservation, and when we see the minister this morning I am going to offer him a scholarship for a young Mauritian to come to Jersey for training.' John immediately responded to the idea with, 'Hang on a minute; we haven't got any facilities, we have nowhere for students to stay, and we haven't any plans'. Gerry replied, 'Your trouble is that you always get bogged down with the minor details of life. I feel sure that you will all be able to solve those problems.'

John's many years of working closely with Gerry allowed him to identify some aspects of the personality of his mentor and hero. Gerry was not a very public man, and his many fund-raising trips and lectures were certainly not his joy in life. His satisfaction was to be with the people who were nearest and dearest to him, and to be surrounded by animals as well. His great pleasures were small dinner parties with close friends. 'I think he was that mixture of great sense of humour, a passionate person, and a wonderful person to be with. Although if he suddenly heard about some awful catastrophe, or the extinction of a species, or whatever, he would take that extremely badly, so moods were often great swings between the highs and lows in life.'

John Mallet, who was to be immediately christened 'Shep' by Gerry, after the English town of Shepton Mallet, arrived with his own menagerie of birds and dogs in 1961. Shep was one of those exceptional animal people who have the equivalent of green fingers when rearing new hatchlings or young mammals; taking equal care of a chick whether it was one of the rarest birds in the world, or one of his favorite Silky bantams. In 1966, Gerry told Shep (Curator of Birds) that he was about to buy a pair of the endangered White Eared pheasants that had been born in Peking Zoo. Shep thought about this for a day or two, then told the Honorary Director that to have only one pair of such a rare species would be risky for obvious reasons, and asked permission to purchase a second pair with his own money. Gerry later recorded that thanks to this remarkably generous gesture it was entirely due to Shep's devotion that in 1969 the zoo had its initial breeding success with this endangered species. Subsequently, a viable captive population of White Eared pheasants has been established in many zoos and private collections.

In January 1968, Shep joined Gerry, Jacquie, Doreen Evans (Secretary) and Peggy Peel (BBC friend) in Mexico, to help Gerry's expedition to secure a group of the diminutive and endangered Volcano rabbit from the pine forests of the Popocateptl region of Mexico. The expedition procured ten rabbits and within six months of their arrival in Jersey the zoo recorded the first captive breeding of this rare species. When I remarked to Shep on the exciting time he must have had in Mexico he replied, somewhat nonchalantly, how he had enjoyed getting to know Gerry and Jacquie properly as friends, but he would have been just as happy to have remained at the zoo caring for his pheasants, waterfowl and Silky bantams. He also repeated Gerry's philosophy on taking animals from their natural habitat, 'I don't want a zoo, let everything be free, but the way things are you have got to try and do something to save animals, so zoos are necessary.' Shep was the Trust's Curator of Birds for a period of 23 years before becoming its Avicultural Adviser in 1987, when David Jeggo took over the role of Curator.

Prior to **Catha Weller**'s coming to Jersey with her husband Sam who had been posted to the Island, she had read only one of Gerry's books *Three Singles to Adventure*, but had fallen in love with the style of his writing. Catha recalled that Gerry and Jacquie were in his office on the Sunday morning when he interviewed her, and perhaps only Gerry would chose to interview people on a Sunday morning. 'You know that I am a clairvoyant. Two years before the interview I described a room to Sam, and it was a very important room which I described in detail. As I walked into the room, it was the room that I had seen. So it was rather extraordinary, and although Gerry didn't say will you start or anything, he need not have bothered because I knew I had the job; or I knew I was going to be back there in some way or another.'

Within a few days of Catha starting her zoo-saving job she assumed that she had been brought in simply to wind the place up. Before coming to Jersey Catha had been in the services during the war, when she had met Sam, and had then gone into advertising in London, but she had never been involved in any fund-raising which she was almost immediately required to do. Jacquie gave her all the fan letters that Gerry had ever received and, with Betty Boizard and Gerry's secretary, Jean Rotherhan, she wrote to all of them to request donations to help form the Trust in 1963. She also had to phone potential big-givers, and one morning Gerry came into her office with some telephone numbers and said, 'Go on.' She replied, 'I don't know what to say, I don't know anything about zoos, and I don't know anything about animals', but he just smiled encouragingly and sat on the edge of the desk and listened to her!

Both Catha and Sam Weller talked about Gerry's great charm (and its being inbuilt in all the Durrells); how he was reluctant to get involved in the cocktail parties that he hated; how he most liked having a handful of people to talk to and then he would be happy. 'Really, Gerry hated going to formal things anywhere, and I remember on several occasions having to ring up at the last minute to say that he wasn't well. I didn't like doing so, I hated it, but I knew that he could never be persuaded to change his mind.' Catha recalled how Gerry would sometimes get very worked up about such social pressures upon him, but if he didn't want to go somewhere, nothing could persuade him otherwise. This applied to his brother too. On one occasion Larry Durrell had been in Jersey and had accepted an invitation, but when Sam and Catha were about to drive him to the luncheon party, he suddenly announced, 'I can't go, I'm not going, I don't feel well enough.' It is the artistic temperament again, isn't it? You hear about this type of attitude all the time with some film star doing much the same sort of thing, backing out of an event at the last moment. A lot of people wanted Gerry as a trophy in order to say, 'We have Gerald Durrell coming.'

I met up with Catha and Sam in 2003, to talk about the early days of the zoo and Trust, and they reiterated the opinion of so many of Gerry's disciples, in how thankful we were that Lee had entered Gerry's life at such a traumatic time for him, and soon proved to be such a benefit to his general well-being. Lee's presence undoubtedly promoted Gerry's zest for living, for he particularly wanted to show her as much of the 'living world' as possible, and it is almost certain that Lee's almost two decades with Gerry extended his life by many years. During my conversation with

Catha and Sam, Sam reflected, 'One will never know, if Gerry and Lee had been together at the time of the Trust's problems in the early 1970s, what would have happened when the Council was trying to trim Gerry's sails. Of course, Jacquie would not have any of this, and more or less influenced him to stay on his own. If he had had somebody perhaps more diplomatic, it might have gone in a different direction.'

While we recognised that Gerry's writing was instrumental to his success in enabling him to pursue his vision, we also acknowledged the important role that **Jacquie Durrell** had played in getting him to write in the first place. His brother Larry had asked, 'Why on earth don't you write a book about these dreadful trips you go on, and make some money for a change?', but Jacquie recalled, 'If I hadn't kicked his butt and forced him to get up and do something, and persistently cajoled him to write something about one of his expeditions, we would still be subsisting on a diet of bread and tea.'

Although I have kept in touch with Jacquie and regard her as a good friend, I had always considered her to be somewhat dispassionate, with that North Country approach to life in calling a spade a spade and when really cross, 'firing from the hip'. However I found a more compassionate side to her when I contacted her after the ambulance took Gerry to hospital, and I told her about the gravity of his condition. The depth of her concern was demonstrated by her immediate response to my communication:

> Dear Jeremy – Thank you so much for telling me about Gerry, what a dreadful business, and I feel for Lee. I would like to see Gerry as and when, for I feel very strongly that it is time to settle our misunderstandings and enter a new phase. If you can explain this to Lee I would be so grateful. Basically I just want to tell Gerry that I remember our time together with affection and gratitude, and at least we both tried to repay the joys we've had from wild places and their inhabitants by the creation of the Zoo/Trust. I'm just sad that we left the meeting for so long. I'm deeply upset by this, Jeremy – one can't share twenty-six years with someone without retaining some warm memories of them and all the things we did together – dreams shared and achieved. Just give him my love and blessings. Jacquie.

Both Catha and Sam visited the 'Mazet' in Provence (which Gerry had bought from his brother Larry) on several occasions. Of such visits Catha said:

> Larry's relationship with Gerry could be sometimes quite stand-offish and vitriolic, and I think that in early years there had been a bit of sibling jealousy and rivalry. Whereas Larry was somewhat of a loner and always very money conscious, Gerry had no idea about money, being over generous at times. However, in latter years they got on very well and Larry thought Lee was superb, and he was happy with what they were doing with his previous home the Mazet.

Catha retired from the Trust in 1974, although she carried on looking after the Durrell personal finances for many further years. Catha died in Jersey in 2005 at the age of 92 – one of the Island's best kept secrets, for even her closest friends thought that she was a least ten years younger! Looking back to the Trust's formative years, all those involved recognise Catha's great contribution, and we have often wondered whether, had Gerry not chosen her to sort out the financial chaos of the zoo in 1962, his dream would have ever reached fruition in the way that it has done.

Betty Renouf (née Boizard), joined the zoo just before her sixteenth birthday and served as Catha's assistant until her retirement. Betty found Catha to be a most jolly person with a heart of gold, wonderful to work with, and with so much to teach. Gerald and Jacquie Durrell treated her with great kindness, which made her feel like part of the family. Betty recalled, 'Mr. D. was always friendly and charming, and delighted in making me blush. He was greatly respected by all staff members.' Betty retired as the Zoo's Accounts Administrator in 2002, after 40 years of dedicated service to the zoo/Trust.

Quentin Bloxam arrived at the zoo straight from school in the autumn of 1965, during my absence in Bolivia. Known to Gerry as 'Q', he was the Trust's Curator of Herpetology by the time he embarked with Gerry, Lee and John Hartley on an animal rescue expedition to Madagascar in 1990. Gerry described him in his book *The Aye-Aye and I* as 'tall, muscular, with a determined-looking face that suggested Bulldog Drummond on the way to rescue his wife Phyllis from the clutches of the unspeakable cad Carl Peterson!'

Quentin was always a dedicated disciple of Gerry and during his 44 years (to date) of working at the Trust, he has travelled widely, particularly undertaking extensive field studies in Madagascar, Majorca and in the Caribbean. In 1995 he was appointed the Zoo's General Curator; in 1997 he became the Trust's Zoo Programme Director, a title that in 2005 was changed to that of Director of Conservation Management. Speaking about Gerry 'Q' recalled:

Gerry had very *very* strong perceived ideas of how he wanted the Trust to develop, and which direction he wanted it to go in. And if you happened to be involved in some situation that he didn't like, and he felt that it shouldn't be developing in that way, he then could be very intolerant, probably justifiably, but I am sure that it was a safety valve for him. But he would never leave things to lie and fester, which would cause resentment ... He would always explain exactly why, and that made it very easy to accept the thunderbolts when they came along.

In connection with such outbursts Gerry once remarked:

I don't suffer fools gladly but I try not to embarrass people, or to be nasty to people, unless they are nasty to me, of course. Then I bring out my sabre. It is probably 'Q' who has received on occasions, probably quite unnecessarily the sharp edge of my tongue, but we are still friends and I have enormous respect for him.

In a recent television interview 'Q' said that Gerry's philosophy originally was what he called 'buying time for species':

We could have animals here, breed them, and then when the situation in the wild had been put right, we could put the animals back. Particularly in the early days, when we had a very diverse collection of unusual animals to work with, which in some cases nobody else had ever had in captivity, and they were invariably the smaller and much more unusual species.

'Q', quite rightly, considered Gerry to be the only person to have the incredible talent of putting humour into both animals and conservation:

> People who read his books just fall about laughing, and all the time this is backed up with a genuine deep abiding love of wildlife, and concern for the conservation of rare and endangered species in a world that he saw, and we still see, deteriorating because we are not looking after our own backyard properly.

'Q' recalled that he had learnt a great deal from Gerry about how best to treat people from different countries and cultures. All of his dealings were based on humour. 'If you can make people laugh and then talk to them sensibly about conservation issues, those people's help and skills are incredibly important. And Gerry had these skills in buckets.'

Richard Johnstone-Scott's encounter with Gerry was shortly after he left school, and used to travel up to London to work on various building sites in Tottenham Court Road:

> I used to read Mr D.'s books and I would be in hysterics, and people would just look at me and think I was mad. His fantastic turn of phrase, the way he wrote was absolutely hilarious. And Mr D. was always a champion of the smaller animals of what he called 'the little brown jobs', and he was my hero.

Richard joined the zoo's mammal section in 1965, and particularly enjoyed working with the anthropoid apes – gorillas, orang-utans and chimpanzees. In 1968 he moved to work in the primate house at London Zoo, and then returned to Jersey for a short period before joining the staff at Howlett's Wild Animal Park in Kent. There for ten years he helped John Aspinall establish an integrated breeding programme for his Lowland gorillas, which soon became the largest population of gorillas outside Africa. Richard returned to Jersey Zoo in 1979, before the official opening of the new gorilla complex, by a great supporter of the Trust and one of its future International Trustees, Jersey's Lieutenant-Governor, General Sir Peter Whitely. In 1981, Richard took a sabbatical and travelled to Rwanda to study the Mountain gorillas in their natural habitat, and since that time he has written extensively about gorillas, including his popular book *Jambo – A Gorilla Story*, and given many talks at international meetings about their husbandry. He has become one of the most knowlegible and respected managers of zoo gorilla populations in the world, and currently serves the Trust as Head of its Mammal Department.

When I asked **Mrs Vi Lort-Phillips** when had she first met Gerry, she told me that it was soon after the zoo had opened and a visitor had just sat on a macaw:

> I used to have a pet macaw, and I was quite devastated that someone could have been so careless as to trip over and squash the poor thing. Gerry was there at the time and was very upset, and I nearly wept with him.

Vi went on to recall how, despite the macaw incident she had thought what a marvellous zoo it was, and she wanted to help. Gerry had heard about Vi's well-respected Jersey garden at La Colline, and her involvement with the International Dendrologists' Society and their subsequent visit to the zoo, so he asked her to form the zoo's first Garden Committee. In those early days her committee had recognised the importance of the grounds of the zoo being properly planned and she, with Lady Guthrie and Major Rollo Hawkins and Ansell, arranged for the garden expert and broadcaster Roy Lancaster to visit the zoo and to help plan the landscaping of the zoological park.

When I showed Vi the photograph of Gerry in Douglas Botting's biography, which had as its caption 'A split-second of the formidable Durrell charm', Vi told me that he could charm a bird off a tree if he wanted to (though not if he was feeing 'offish'):

> I loved him, I really loved him. I don't mean to say that I was in love with him, but he was a great friend and amusing. I never really got through to Jacquie; perhaps she saw me as an intruder … and she probably thought I was rather bossy and interfering, which I probably was! When Lee came on the scene she saved Gerry from himself, and probably gave him another ten years of life.

Vi Lort-Phillips told me how much Gerry had enriched her life, as well as having opened so many people's minds to the importance of conserving the world's fauna. She also referred to her close and warm friendship with Lee.

Vi was the inspirational first Chairman of the Trust's Landscape Committee (1969–1976), and an indefatigable member thereafter. During the years 1975–1986 she served as Director, Vice-President and President of the International Camellia Society. On 24th February 2009, Violet Lort-Phillips celebrated her 100th birthday and, as a consequence, received the congratulatory telegram from Her Majesty The Queen.

Robin Rumboll first heard about Gerry when he was collecting animals in Argentina in the 1950s, when Gerry had stayed at an *estancia* owned by a member of Robin's family. His Aunt Hilda told him about the young British naturalist coming out to collect animals, and the fact that he was particularly interested in endangered species. Robin knew a lot of people who did things with animals (mainly shoot them), and that here was somebody talking about preserving them, which at that time struck a chord with him. His cousin Maurice Rumboll was involved with the conservation of South American animals, so the subject was frequently discussed. In 1965 he ended up in Jersey, when the name Gerald Durrell reappeared in his life, and began the germination of the seed of his subsequent interest in what Gerry was doing.

It was soon after what was sometimes called 'The Palace Revolution' or 'The Palace Coup', when the majority of the Council had resigned over whether they, or Durrell, had the final say in the running of the Trust, that Robin became directly involved. It was the vivacious Lady (Saranne) Calthorpe, chair of the Trust's Fundraising Committee who had personally persuaded him to join her committee. As a chartered accountant, Robin looked after the financial side of things and became the committee's treasurer, and thus met Gerry on a number of social occasions. Not long after 'The Palace Coup' Robin received a call from Catha Weller saying that she needed some help with the account books, so Robin went up to meet Gerry and recalls that:

In the typical Gerry way – you know when he is trying to flatter you – he said: 'I do like you Robin and I think that you are just what we are looking for on a temporary basis whilst we sort things out'. So being so flattered, I must have agreed, and in 1973 I became the Trust's Honorary Treasurer.

Robin's initial acceptance of the duties of Honorary Treasurer, on a temporary basis, continued for 24 years when, in 1997, he took over the role of Trust Chairman from Jurat Geoffrey Hamon. In 2006 he was appointed the President of the Durrell Wildlife Preservation Trust.

Of the early days of his involvement with Gerry and Jacquie, Robin remembered an occasion when the date of the fundraising Dodo Ball clashed with that of Jacquie's birthday, and Gerry had sent his apologies that this time he was unable to attend. Such a decision prompted one of the committee members to write: 'Do you realise that we on the Fundraising Committee are all doing it for you, and you are not prepared to come to our big Ball?' Gerry said to Saranne, who was also trying to persuade him to be present, 'If they are saying that, they are only coming because of me; I thought that they were coming because of the animals!' Robin remembers that Gerry's refusal to attend the Ball caused quite an upset, leading to one committee member resigning. Saranne and Robin tried to pour oil on troubled waters, at the same time recognising, as Robin put it:

If Gerry was in the mood he could be unbelievably charming, and there was no doubt that he appreciated a pretty face, with the girls. And if given the choice between an open shirt at an informal party, and a black tie formal do, he would choose the open shirt every time.

Initially, Gerry had been very much protected by Jacquie, and during this period Robin was not sure whether he got to know the real man, 'Sometimes Gerry used to joke and call me "Mr. Moneybags"; I was the Honorary Treasurer, and as the rules of the Trust say that you've got to have one of these animals as an Honorary Treasurer, I was the best of a bad lot, as it were!' Robin has often mentioned that he was not primarily an animal man, that he couldn't handle reptiles and was not a hands-on person. However after meeting Gerry he had always been totally convinced that his conservation philosophy was right, and that was why he did whatever he could to support him. As the years went by Robin got to know Gerry better, and when he and his wife, Cynthia, stayed with Gerry and Lee at their home in Provence, he found him to be the most relaxed:

> Arriving before lunch we went down into Nimes and to his favourite bar, and sat outside on the pavement having a beer. Then we returned to Mas Michel where Lee would prepare a snack lunch, and this went on all day into the late evening until Gerry would get up and cook stuffed partridges, with pâté de foie gras, which went onto about midnight; just chatting, joking and laughing. During these occasions, we would have some quite serious discussion about the philosophy of the Trust, and during the last years of his life he did share confidences with me. All such very special memories.

Robin reflected that in all probability Gerry used him in many ways to get his own way, but that he always felt that Gerry was an inspired person and that he was always right! If Gerry really wanted something (the purchase of the property Les Noyers as the headquarters of the International Training Centre, for example), the money always seemed to appear, and he concluded, 'Basically, people fell in love with Gerry.'

Simon Hicks was known to Gerry as 'Hurricane Hicks', because of his habit of hurtling from place to place, banging doors as he went. To me, Simon was always the personification of enthusiasm for anything he happened to be engaged in. At the age of 14 Simon came across one of Gerry's books *The Bafut Beagles*, which made him laugh and painted a picture of Africa that appeared so ideal.

> His books were magic. His wonderful description of animals and the way he described people as animals, and animals as people, that were larger than life, just caught my imagination, and you had the feeling what a marvellous person he would be to meet.

Simon had served for four years as a commissioned officer in the British Army, concluding his military career in Cyprus, from where he took the opportunity to travel on various RAF flights to Kenya. Through contacts he ended up spending a night with George Adamson at his Mgwongo Camp in the Meru National Park, Kenya.

> Such a chance encounter with George Adamson, sitting round his camp fire and drinking whisky with him, whilst he puffed at his pipe and talked about conservation, certainly proved to be the most crucial point of my life. For it was on this occasion, at the age of 24, that I decided my future career had to be involved with conservation.

Due to what Simon calls this 'life-changing experience', on his return to England he studied for a Certificate in Field Biology, while working in such jobs as part-time gamekeeper and forester on Exmoor; a Royal Society for the Protection of Birds (RSPB) warden; and field officer of the National Conservation Corps for Volunteers. He came to JWPT in 1975 with a team of volunteers to undertake a pond clearing and bridge building task at Jersey Zoo. After Simon had become the Director of the re-named The British Trust for Conservation Volunteers, Gerry asked him to visit the Trust on the pretext of discussing a future project, but after they had wined and dined well, Gerry took him to one side and asked him, 'What would you say if I were to ask you to join us?'

Simon had been totally unprepared and was flabbergasted at such an unexpected invitation, and was more flattered than anything else. He later recorded:

> As I did not particularly care for zoos, I had to put to one side that my 'hero' had offered me a job as Zoological Co-Coordinator at the Trust, and I had to be quite objective to myself that I wasn't really coming to a typical zoo. For whereas some zoos are ends to themselves, GD's overall conservation philosophy was to put the animal first and everything else will fall into place and, although he was not a practical person, he was the ultimate visionary, who could see problems coming before most people.

Simon served the Trust for 23 years (1976–1998), and for most of this time he was the dedicated, highly popular and professional Trust Secretary. Soon after Simon's appointment as Trust Secretary, Gerald

Durrell remarked, 'He is so full of energy he is like a hive of bees; you can hear him throbbing with energy.' His enthusiasm for the Trust's conservation mission was always compelling and contagious. Apart from being a Durrell Disciple, he was also a great friend of Lee's, about whom he remarked: 'Lee did everything possible that a wife could do to maximise Gerry's life – she was magnificent.' In keeping with Simon's continuing conservation mission he established a UK-registered NGO Conservation Works – Unlocking Opportunities for Conservation, and he is presently living in the Democratic Republic of Congo, with his second wife, Karen Hayes (Extractive Industries Program Director), of the US NGO Pact, 'building capacity worldwide'.

In Mauritius, **Dr Carl Jones** is known as *Docteur Oiseau,* and in David Quammen's book *The Song of the Dodo* is aptly described as 'a tall, sarcastic Welshman with a sheepdog haircut, a weakness for bad jokes, and a manic devotion to native Mauritian wildlife, especially for birds'. During the last 30 years Carl has tirelessly dedicated his life to some of the world's rarest species, in particular the Mauritius kestrel, Pink pigeon and Echo parakeet.

From an early age Carl had been, like so many others, a great lover of Gerry's books and as a consequence, became one of his most zealous disciples. 'GD successfully interpreted animals for the common man,' he said. 'In the same way that an impressionist painter conveys the ambience of a place, his writing brought animal personalities to life.' Gerry was his inspiration and driving force, and Carl saw well beyond captive breeding by recognising the importance of developing meaningful interfaces between captivity and the wild state. After Gerry visited Mauritius with Lee and John Hartley in the early 1980s, the Trust became one of the major financial supporters of Carl's work with the Mauritian Wildlife Foundation, which led to his being appointed the Trust's Conservation Field Department's Programme Director for Mauritius. As an integral part of these conservation projects for both fauna and flora, the Mauritius programme has also been responsible for the restoration of Round Island by utilising world experts, such as the New Zealander Don Merton, in the eradication of alien species, in particular introduced rabbits. To this day, the Trust's long-term involvement in Mauritius with Carl and the Mauritian Wildlife Foundation has represented an exemplary model of what can be achieved with international partnership.

Felicity Bryan of the literary agents Curtis Brown remembers her boss coming into her office and asking whether there were any authors who she would like to take over from a colleague who was leaving, and she had said none, except Gerald Durrell, adding, 'In fact if you don't let me represent Gerald Durrell I will walk out!' In the television programme *The Wildlife of Gerald Durrell*, Felicity told viewers how his writing had captured the imagination of readers of all ages, and how Gerry's 37 popular books had been translated into 31 different languages and were adored by millions worldwide. She talked of the way that Gerry had used his writing as a platform to get his conservation message across, as well as to fund his trips, but as he put it, 'Turning out books is a terrible chore.' Felicity went on to say that reading a book by Gerald Durrell certainly got you close to the animals, but it never got you close to the man himself. 'He celebrated in that he loved entertaining and loved all that, but he also used to get furious and he had a tremendous sort of anger in him, but all for very good reason.'

In connection with such sudden outbursts of anger at someone who had appeared to have a 'couldn't-care-less' attitude toward issues concerning wildlife conservation, Gerry had stated in a television interview:

If you believe in God he should strike you dead for using his world in the way you have, and when I say you, I mean you, and I mean me, and I mean everybody else. It's a most incredible and most beautiful garden, and what have we done, we have trampled through it with our great hob-nailed boots.

Chapter Fourteen

DURRELL'S CHAMPIONS

Gerry's American champions were the 1971 founding spirits behind the establishment of Save Animals from Extinction (SAFE), (later re-named Wildlife Preservation Trust International and now Wildlife Trust) – Dr Tom Lovejoy, Margot Rockefeller and Sophie Danforth, who were later joined by another of their friends, the Washington DC international lawyer Emerson Duncan. The Zoological Society of Philadelphia donated office space to SAFE, and Jody Longnecker was appointed as the administrator in charge of the new charitable organisation.

Tom Lovejoy was a Yale-educated environmentalist and tropical biologist based at the Academy of Sciences of Philadelphia at the time of his first meeting with Gerry, which had taken place in a chance encounter while they were both walking down New York's Fifth Avenue. Like many zoologists and conservationists of his generation, Tom's commitment to conservation had been nurtured in part by reading Gerry's books. It was his immediate friendship with Gerry that had prompted him to help in working out the formula that allowed SAFE to be established, primarily to support the conservation work of the JWPT. Tom not only shared Gerry's conservation ideals, but also had the academic training to support them; and it wasn't long after they met, and got on so well together, that Tom was instrumental in organising a public meeting in Washington's Constitution Hall, where over 3,000 people gathered to listen to Gerry speak about his expeditions and the work of the Jersey Trust.

On Gerry's voyage over the Atlantic on the SS *France,* he was introduced to Margot Rockefeller who happened to be on the liner with her husband Godfrey and their three children. With what has been frequently referred to as 'Durrell's luck', and as Douglas Botting recorded in his biography, '… after much partying in the Rockefellers' suite, by the time the ship was nosing past the Statue of Liberty the Rockefellers were among Gerry's best and closest American friends!'

When **Sophie Danforth** first met Gerry she was already a long-standing member of the Board of the Roger Williams Park Zoo, Providence, Rhode Island, and she had already regarded Gerry as her idol. She had read all his books and was influenced by the ones dealing with his Jersey zoo. At the time of their meeting, she had been struggling to help raise an antiquated Victorian zoo into the new era. Gerry visited Providence to give a lecture, and the deal was that they would split the profits between the Roger Williams Zoo and SAFE. Gerry and Sophie immediately found themselves kindred spirits and Gerry was soon to ask her to become a member of the newly formed SAFE Board of Directors. Sophie recalls: 'We [Tom, Sophie, Margot and Jody] used to meet monthly in Margot's kitchen and most of our records were in shoeboxes. Our main purpose was to raise money and get Gerry's conservation message out.' Sophie remembers how Gerry was well ahead of his time, and a certain American zoo director telling her that Gerry's ideas on breeding endangered animals in captivity, and then reintroducing them back into the wild, were 'just all smoke and mirrors'.

When Sophie visited Jersey soon after they had met she told me how impressed she had been by its spacious grounds, beautiful enclosures and natural habitats.

> We all supported and stayed with Gerry because of his cause, but also because of the man himself. None was ever more witty or fun or amusing; just being with him heightened one's senses and made one feel more alive. At the same time he had a terrific temper and did not suffer fools gladly, but if you were one of his friends there was nothing he would not do for you, and he could be extraordinary compassionate. His love of all living things and his deep concern about the world was legendary.

Tom, Margot and Sophie all continued to serve as Executive Committee Board members of the American Wildlife Trusts (SAFE/WPTI/WT) for many challenging years. Gerry always regarded the three as his closest American friends. Their presence at his and Lee's Memphis wedding in

May 1979 was, with Lee's family, certain to have made him feel very much at home. In November of that year, Gerry, Lee, Tom and I participated at the Third World Conference on Breeding Endangered Species, which was organised jointly by the Zoological Society of San Diego and the Fauna Preservation Society. During this time we dined with Dr Jean Delacour, a member of the WPTI's Scientific Advisory Committee, at the famous Hotel del Coronado, built in 1888 and one of the oldest and largest wooden structures in California. Due to Jean Delacour's encyclopaedic knowledge of birds, particularly pheasants, and Tom's ornithological field studies in Brazil, it was not surprising that most of the conversation around the table was about birds, a subject in which I well recognised my limitations. However, just when I considered I was failing to make much of a contribution, I heard Delacour refer to a Professor Ghigi. On hearing the name I was quick to break my silence by producing what I thought was a real pearl of wisdom and informed my august companions that there was a species of Galliformes called Ghigi's Grey peacock-pheasant, which we bred regularly at Jersey. Whereupon the 89–year-old doyen of the pheasant world somewhat nonchalantly responded, 'Yes, I named the bird after him in 1924, or was it 1925?' I decided that for me, the remainder of the evening would be better spent in garnering ornithological knowledge than in committing any further historical *faux pas*!

Later Tom, Margot and Sophie were appointed Life Trustees (now, Honorary Fellows) of the Durrell Wildlife Conservation, and after Gerry's death in 1995 Tom became the American Trust's Honorary Chairman. Tom serves on many scientific and conservation boards and advisory groups, is the author of numerous articles and books, and is the founder of the US public television series *Nature*. In 1980 Tom was credited with having coined the term 'biological diversity', and in 2000 he gave the respected BBC Reith Lecture on Biodiversity. Since 1989 the Roger Williams Park Zoo and the Rhode Island Zoological Society have provided over 40 annual grants, of US $1,000 each, to conservation projects from the Sophie Danforth Conservation Biology Fund.

During the start of the 1990s **Edward Whitley** visited 26 graduates of the Trust's International Training Centre (ITC), in ten different countries, to see how they were implementing what they had learnt in Jersey. Edward's findings provided the material for his book, *Gerald*

Durrell's Army, which demonstrated how 'Durrell's Army' had marched a long way since the inception of the ITC in 1978. It was due to Edward's admiration of Gerry's conservation vision and the mission of the training centre that he arranged for his family's Whitley Animal Protection Trust to ensure the future of the ITC with a most significant grant of one million pounds.

In Jersey, **Marcus** and **Anne Binney** have been staunch allies and supporters of the Trust for the past 21 years. Since 1991, Anne has acted as chairman of the Trust's Landscape Advisory Committee, whereas Marcus served on the Trust's Council during the 1990s. But most importantly, through their fundraising Domaine des Vaux opera series, held annually at their Jersey home since the mid-1980s, they have raised over £350,000 for the Trust's various conservation projects both in Jersey and worldwide, including support for Livingstone's Fruit bat, Aloatra Gentle lemur, Sumatran orang-utan, Pygmy hog, Echo parakeet, St Lucia parrot and Ploughshare tortoise. One of the many projects that I was directly involved with was the purchase of a corridor of Atlantic rain forest to consolidate the Una Biological Reserve in the State of Bahia, Brazil. This was only made possible by the money raised through the opera performances at their home in 1991. Since such a critical purchase and subsequent presentation of the 'corridor' to Brazil's governmental conservation agency IBAMA, I have been to the Una Reserve on numerous occasions, and during these visits I have reflected upon how the splendid performances of Puccini, and of many others, at the sophisticated venue of Domaine des Vaux generated the funds to enable this tropical region of the *Mata Atlantica,* one of the world's most important biodiversity 'hotspots' to be conserved for posterity.

Gerry had many friends in the international zoo, scientific and conservation community, who were also some of my favourite 'silverbacks'. Among these were Michael Brambell, Janet Kear, Bob Martin, John Knowles, Peter Olney, Roger Wheater, William Conway and Sir Peter Scott. All were advocates of the importance of zoos to play a leading role in 'creative conservation'.

An early and significant supporter of the conservation ethos of Gerry's JWPT was **Dr Michael Brambell**, whom I first met in July 1967, when he was the recently appointed Curator of Mammals at London Zoo. According to Michael, 'Very soon after I joined the zoo, Gerry Durrell

218

had been over to suss out whether the newcomer would be a suitable person for Jeremy to be allowed to meet!' Soon after, we met in London and one result of the meeting was that we arranged for London to send their single male Sumatran orang-utan, Gambar, to Jersey, to pair up with our female Gina. David Attenborough had donated Gambar to London some years earlier, and gave his approval to the move. The important aspect of this arrangement was that it was recorded as a permanent loan, obviating the need for any money to change hands. In those days such animals were assumed to have high financial values, a concept which interfered with maximising their conservation potential. Little did either us recognise at the time that by setting up this arrangement, with the approval of our respective bosses, Gerry Durrell and Colin Rawlins, that we had struck an early, if not the first, blow in the battle to divorce financial value from conservation value. Nowadays, conservation-driven zoos value their animals on their balance sheets at a nominal £1, or its equivalent. Thanks to this loan agreement Gambar and Gina went on to have six young, and several second generation descendents, which all form a part of the international coordinated breeding programme.

In 1972, at the time of the 'Palace Coup' in Jersey (regrettably made much of by the national press), Michael was quick to write to me, saying: 'I think Jersey Zoo is the most exciting new venture in the [conservation] field in this country, and one of the most worthwhile efforts at present going on in zoological collections in the British Isles.'

At the first Conference on Breeding Endangered Species at Jersey in May 1972 (which Gerry, Catha Weller and I had organised) Michael presented the paper on breeding orang-utans, in which he highlighted the importance of being able to transfer animals between zoos in the best interests of the species, without being handicapped by financial ramifications. In July 1976, Gerry and I were able to attend the Second World Conference on Breeding Endangered Species which Michael, with his assistant Sue Mathews, organised at London Zoo, at which such cooperative concepts as a computerised International Species Information System (ISIS) got off the ground. This developed into a global central database, providing animal management information for zoos worldwide.

Gerry asked Michael to serve on our Scientific Advisory Committee, particularly in order for the Trust to be able to take advantage of his zoological and veterinary acumen. However, Michael recalls that his most onerous assignment in this role was to negotiate a fair rate of recompense between the Trust and our local veterinary practice (Nick Blampied & Tony Allchurch) whom he counted as friends! He got the impression that both sides were satisfied with the outcome!

Michael left London Zoo in 1978 to become the Director of Chester Zoo. This made no difference in his relationship with Gerry and the Trust. He recalls the wonderful evening when Gerry and Lee came to Chester to give, in a large and wind-rocked marquee, a joint presentation of their ideals to the membership at Chester. During our 37 years as colleagues, with our wives Odette and Patricia, the four of us have been very close friends. Those of us who know the two of us well will know that Michael was devilishly good at mimicking my voice, even to the extent of taking in some of my closest friends, much to Odette's delight! Throughout this time Michael was always a most valued supporter of Gerry's conservation efforts in Jersey and overseas, and a great admirer of both Gerry and Lee. We were all most fortunate that our ambitions for the future welfare of the animal kingdom enabled our respective career paths to cross in the way that they did.

Professor Janet Kear was undoubtedly Gerry's favourite female scientist, and perhaps such admiration was mutual, for when she was staying with Odette and me in September 2002 she told me, 'Hugging Gerry was perfectly normal, for he was very tactile, very cuddly, very woolly; I mean, he looked as if he was covered in fur.' Janet had been interested in birds for as long as she could remember, and after leaving university in 1959 she secured a job at Peter Scott's Wildfowl Trust at Slimbridge to work on feeding behaviour in geese.

Before Janet met Gerry she had read a number of his books and found him inspirational, but in a quite different way from Peter Scott. In comparing the two, Janet reflected how they were from very different backgrounds, and whereas Gerry was able to joke with people first, and then become serious, Peter was somebody whom you would admire enormously, but who was deadly serious in some respects and not cuddly at all. 'Hugging Gerry seemed perfectly normal. But they were both inspirational lecturers, for they talked very, very well and extremely passionately. I dare say they both talked passionately for they both cared.'

I was also interested to learn from my conversation with Janet about another similarity between Gerry and Peter Scott, that although Peter was a bit of an authoritarian he found it difficult to be beastly to members of staff, and was quite hopeless at sacking people or hauling them over the coals if they needed to be disciplined. Gerry would also leave such tasks for somebody else to do for him. In a similar context I recall that soon after my appointment as his Deputy, Gerry had jokingly told me, 'There is no reason to have a dog, if you have to bark for it!'

Janet was a regular visitor to Jersey. She joined JWPT's Scientific Advisory Committee in 1979, lectured on a number of occasions at the ITC Summer Schools, and in 1995 was elected to the Trust's Council; I also served under her chairmanship of the Zoo Federation's Conservation and Animal Management Committee. For many years Janet was the editor of *IBIS*, the scientific journal of the British Ornithological Union (BOU), and she became its first woman President in its 150 year history. She also edited the Wildfowl & Wetlands Trust's (WWT) journal, *Wildfowl*, and wrote numerous scientific papers on waterfowl and a number of books. Her last work was as editor of the acclaimed *Ducks, Geese and Swans;* it will undoubtedly represent the standard work on Anseriformes for many years to come.

All those who were privileged to have encountered Janet could not fail to be impressed by her integrity, warmth of spirit and friendliness – she was undoubtedly a most endearing person. Such an influence on people was demonstrated when Gerry and Lee first met her husband John (Turner), at the time they had come over from Jersey to give a talk at Chester Zoo. Janet recalled, 'When I introduced John to Gerry, he fixed John with a twinkle in his deep blue eyes and said: "So you're the bastard who has stolen Janet's affection?!"' However, once Janet had told Gerry that one of the Pink-footed geese that John had ringed in Greenland the previous year had recently turned up outside their bedroom window at the WWT Reserve at nearby Martin Mere, in Lancashire – all was forgiven! Janet died on 24th November 2004, and the waterfowl of the world lost one of their most knowledgeable and foremost champions.

Peter Olney had a long-standing friendship with Gerry, dating back to the early 1970s. Peter initially worked for Peter Scott at the Wildfowl Trust, then served The Zoological Society of London as its Curator of

Birds (1969–1991), and then became Director of the Federation of Zoological Gardens of Great Britain and Ireland. He was the editor of the International Zoo Yearbook from 1975–2000, and consultant editor until 2003. In 1989 he asked me to chair the Yearbook's editorial board which I enthusiastically did until 2003.

Peter had told me that he realised early in his curatorial career:

> that Gerry's ideas and his type of zoo were very much the model that we should all be trying to emulate; though I also realised that for many of the older conventional zoos radical changes would inevitably take time and money and might even require a change of governance and a change of ethos. Gerry was without doubt one of the most influential and significant instigators of a change in attitude, not only in the zoo world but also in the public and political perception of zoos.

In the profile of Gerry that Peter wrote for the *Encyclopedia of the World's Zoos* he concluded that:

> Gerry's colourful life illustrates only too well the problems of a basically shy, self-educated man whose passionate advocacy of his own convictions permeated everything he did. The price Durrell paid for this dedication cost him dearly, including his privacy, his first marriage and ultimately his health. He remained however, sensitive, modest, and occasionally unpredictable. As he aged he became a benign patriarch, surrounded by devoted disciples, secure in the knowledge that what he had started would go on.

Peter's happiest memories are of 'Gerry's (and Lee's) unstinting generosity and kindness, with hours of delicious food and wine, passionate discussions about life and people, and always so much humour and laughter'.

I first met **Dr Robert Martin** and his delightful French wife Anne-Elise, at the time of the international conference for the conservation of the fauna and flora of Madagascar, in the island's capital, Tananarive, in October 1970. Bob had previously studied various lemur species in the wild and while on an Oxford University expedition in 1968 he had participated in the documentary *Ghosts at the End of the Earth*, in the

BBC television series *Life About Us*. Bob first met Gerry in Jersey in May 1972 at the time of the First World Conference on Breeding Endangered Species, at which he presented a general paper on lesser primates; after which, Gerry, having immensely enjoyed talking to Bob, asked him to edit the conference proceedings.

In Bob's tribute to Gerry in a special issue of *Biodiversity and Conservation*, he recalled that as a long-standing member of the Trust's Council and of its Scientific Advisory Committee, he had been closely associated with Gerry and with the work of the organisation that he had founded. This had given him the opportunity to witness the progressive expansion and refinement of an institution that is itself unique in many ways. 'Above all', he wrote, 'I greatly value this possibility in my tribute of acknowledging a personal debt to Gerald Durrell for his inspiration and friendship. It is no exaggeration to say that his example and philosophy exerted a major and comprehensive influence on my own interests, teaching and research activities over the past 25 years.'

Bob joined the Trust's Scientific Advisory Committee in 1975 and chaired it for many years, being elected to the Trust's Council in 1978. With Dr Alison Jolly, Bob was a founder of the ITC's Summer School, and served with Lee on a committee called The Durrell Trust for Conservation Biology at the University of Kent. This group had been established by Professor Ian Swingland to give financial support to the Durrell Institute of Conservation and Ecology (DICE), of which Ian was the Institute's founder-director. Bob's extensive research work at ZSL's Wellcome Institute of Comparative Physiology, his academic pursuits at the Department of Anthropology, University College, London, followed by his directorship at the Anthropological Institute at Zurich University, resulted in numerous publications in scientific journals, and eventually to his acclaimed work: *Primate Origins and Evolution, A Phylogenetic Reconstruction*, whose fine animal illustrations were by Anne-Elise. Throughout Bob's time working in Europe he became a regular visitor to Jersey and was an outstanding supporter of the Trust's conservation work and a valuable help to all staff members and ITC students who sought his advice on scientific matters. He became one of Odette's and my best friends within the scientific community. Bob is currently working in America as the A. Watson Armour III Curator of Biological Anthropology at the Field Museum, Chicago.

Professor Ian Swingland became a champion of Gerald Durrell and the conservation mission of the Jersey Wildlife Preservation Trust in the early 1980s. Ian was the Director and founder of the University of Kent's Institute of Conservation and Ecology, and in November 1989, at his instigation, the name was changed to the Durrell Institute of Conservation and Ecology (DICE). At the time of DICE's inception Gerry stated: 'At long last there is an Institute that represents a marriage between ecology and conservation. The science that tells you how the world works. And the science of how it keeps working.' The day following the establishment of DICE Gerry received from the University of Kent a DSc; his third doctorate.

In 1985 Ian became a member of the Trust's Scientific Advisory Committee and in 2005 was elected to serve on the Trust's Council. Throughout this period, through his interdisciplinary approach, innovativeness and entrepreneurial skills, he contributed significantly to various aspects of the Trust's research activities and the promotion of scientific education and awareness on an international basis. After 20 years of direct links with the University the Trust continues with its collaboration with DICE in a number of training courses, both in Jersey and overseas, as well as teaching MSc. and BSc. students for the university.

In a recent letter to DWCT Chairman, Jonathan White, Ian wrote:

Serving on the Board for almost two years has been my very great privilege, alongside my 26–year association and friendship with Gerry and Lee Durrell, and the Trust, and the excellent and committed Directors and staff over this long period ... Personally I have had some very good times with Gerry and Lee, from cooking extraordinary curries and other dishes in Jersey and France ... My experience over the last twenty-six years have been one of the most stimulating and rewarding of my professional life. My colleagues on the Board, and the dedicated staff that supports the Board, are among the most generous and able of any group with whom I have been associated.

Dr John Knowles cannot remember whether it was Gerry's books or news of his groundbreaking Jersey Zoo that first brought Gerry to his attention, but he recalls, 'Whichever order they came in, the fact is that he inspired me to believe that my latent ambition to start a zoo could become a reality. Thankfully it did!' John went on to reflect how Gerry built his zoo on the back of his skills with words, whereas he had to build his (Marwell) with assets acquired in other fields, but with a shared passion. 'Gerry lit a path for me, and at the same time his books gave me much pleasure in the process. Pleasure that grew when, later in life, I got to know him personally and was able to enjoy his wit and kindness at first hand.'

In 1969 John founded the Marwell Zoological Park near Winchester, which he opened to the public in 1972 as a privately owned collection. Later he gave the land, buildings, animals and equipment needed for the operation of a modern Zoological Park over to the registered charity of the Marwell Preservation Trust. In 1998 he retired from his role as Founder and Director of Marwell, a conservation trust that represents one of the world's most successful breeding centres, particularly for big cats and African hoofed animals. In 2000 and 2001 he received honorary degrees from Southampton's two universities – Doctor of Science and Doctor of Business Administration – in recognition of his contribution to the conservation of endangered species and his significant contribution to the local community. It has been both Odette's and my great delight to have shared so many enjoyable times with John and his enchanting wife Margaret at a host of international conferences, and in particular to have gone with them to the Okavango Delta in 1992. This visit gave me the opportunity to visit the Moremi National Park which Robert and June Kay had done so much to promote during my time with them in the early 1960s.

I first met **Professor Roger Wheater** soon after his appointment as Director of Edinburgh Zoo, at a meeting of the Directors of Zoological Societies of Great Britain and Ireland, at Dublin Zoo in 1972. Roger had previously spent 17 years in Africa, and after nine years of service as Uganda National Parks' Chief Warden at Murchison Falls, he was appointed Director of Uganda National Parks prior to the advent of President Idi Amin's brutal regime. Roger recalls reading *The Bafut Beagles* on the banks of the Nile, with hippos grunting in the background. 'On this particular evening such external sounds were masked only by my own chuckles and laughter, for not only was the book highly enter-taining but it also painted a very accurate picture of life in Africa at that time.' Of his first meeting with Gerry he said:

225

He was already expounding in his typically forceful manner his belief that zoos had a huge potential role for captive breeding, research and education. The need to coordinate our zoo activities was already apparent to me, although I suspect that the clarion call of Gerry had helped to give some form to these concerns.

Roger, his charming wife Jeanie, Odette and I have been great friends since our first meeting. Roger held a multiplicity of senior appointments on national, regional and international zoo and conservation bodies. In 1993 he was appointed an Honorary Professor of the Faculty of Veterinary Medicine at Edinburgh University, and in 2004 received a Doctorate from the Open University. After his retirement from Edinburgh Zoo in 1998 he served as Chairman of The National Trust for Scotland.

Roger and I participated in many international conferences, and shared many enjoyable experiences in places as far apart as Poland to South Africa, Singapore to Brazil, and Australia to Denmark. Perhaps the most memorable of these occasions was in January 1990, on our return from having both presented papers at the Sixth National All-India Zoo Directors' meeting at Sakkabaug Zoo, Gujarat, where, with Sally Walker, we had taken the opportunity to visit the Gir Forest to see the remnant wild population of Asiatic lions. We then flew to Oman, where Ralph Daly, Advisor for Conservation of the Environment at the Sultanate of Oman, had commissioned us to carry out some consultancy work, and write a report on His Majesty the Sultan's private Breeding Centre for Endangered Omani Mammals. We had agreed to carry out this commission on the condition that we would be taken to the Yalooni region of Oman, to see the population of Arabian oryx, a species that had been successfully reintroduced to the wild from captive bred stock.

Before this visit I had read Mark Stanley Price's (who was appointed DWCT's Executive Director after my retirement from the Trust in August 2001) excellent account *Animal Re-introductions: the Arabian Oryx in Oman*. Sir Peter Scott's foreword to the book said:

For some years, the Arabian Oryx symbolised man's shameful destruction of the natural world around him. He exterminated from the wild a beautiful and distinctive antelope that had evolved to exploit one of the world's hardest environments. Its ultimate restoration to the deserts of Arabia is now a very real possibility.'

Flying with Ralph Daly in a police helicopter from Muscat, across the vast expanses of Omani desert to Yalooni was, for conservationists as ourselves, one of the most magical, inspirational and rewarding experiences. It was wonderful to witness first-hand a viable wild population of an oryx species whose ancestors had been born in captivity. While visiting another desert region of Oman, in order to see the Arabian tahr and Arabian gazelle, Roger, in spite of the very high temperatures, managed to maintain the highest sartorial standards of an English gentleman abroad, in his smart panama and a silk tie! Gerry considered Roger one of the world's most inspired and forward thinking zoo directors.

When in 1994 I was asked by the editors of the journal *Biodiversity and Conservation* to be a guest editor, with Dr Anna Feistner (at that time, head of JWPT's Research Department), and to select the most appropriate authors for a special issue on the subject of 'Captive breeding and effective conservation', I had no hesitation in writing to those whom I considered to be the two most significant and respected zoo directors in North America – Dr William Conway and Dr George Rabb. Both of these long-serving zoo professionals were advocates of Gerry's conservation mission and of the Trust's international partnership work and they agreed to contribute papers for this special edition of the journal; 'Wild and zoo interactive management and habitat conservation' and 'Coordinating conservation: global networking for species survival' (1995), respectively.

Dr William Conway, known to his friends as Bill, spent 49 years working for the New York Zoological Society/Bronx Zoo where he was the General Director, prior to becoming President of the Society in 1992, which is now known as the Wildlife Conservation Society (WCS). Since the 1960s Conway became a leader in North America in the movement to breed endangered species in zoos and to enhance their educational impact. In 1992 he summed up his vision for zoos in a 'call to action' delivered at a special symposium of the American Association of Zoological Parks and Aquariums (AAZPA) – now the American Zoos and Aquarium Association (AZA). In his address he argued that zoos must get out into the natural world and conserve wildlife where it lives. In recent correspondence that I had with Bill about Gerry, he wrote:

> My direct contacts with Gerald Durrell were few but delightful, even hilarious – and rarely printable. Like Roger [Wheater], I grew to know him through his books. I doubt that I really have enough to say about Gerry to reflect my admiration or do him justice ... but I would be delighted if my comment would serve for it barely scratches the surface of a mountain of admiration for Gerry, but does convey some of my feelings for him, and the delight I took in our contact.

Professor **David Bellamy** was a supporter of Gerry and of the Trust's conservation ethos for some time. He visited Jersey in May 1992, at the time of his opening address at the Sixth World Conference on Breeding Endangered Species: The Role of Zoos in Global Conservation, which was held in the presence of the Trust's patron, The Princess Royal. In 2004 David Bellamy, with Lee Durrell and myself, became patrons of the newly formed Durrell School of Corfu which has its headquarters on the island, and where we have all since participated. In one of his television interviews he related:

> What Gerry did, he got all these animals, these cuddly and wonderful furry things that we should look at and think about, as they are an integral part of the living world of which we all depend, that we all belong. And captive breeding is the only hope for many species in this world. Gerry enthused about things, making people wanting to go and to see these things. He is so understanding [about animals]; he understands [their] society. And he was a part of a family, and he understands that everything he looks at is a part of another family, and he wants people to understand that family life, before he imposes any form of captivity.

John Cleese first visited Jersey Zoo in October 1991 and was shown round the park by Simon Hicks. Such a visit could not have been more appropriately timed, for, when in the late afternoon they entered the Gorilla House, it coincided with N'Pongo giving birth to her eighth offspring Asato, a male. John Cleese was reported to have been so moved by what he saw of the gorilla birth that he later applied for the privilege of adopting the baby, and through Simon's contagious enthusiasm, he soon became an important champion of the Trust's international conservation work. In 1997 he agreed to become a Life Trustee of JWPT. At a later date, when he was in the process of writing the script for his film *Fierce Creatures* (2003), the encounter between Jamie Lee Curtis and an adult male gorilla, which showed the actress's surprise at the degree of compassion that the gorilla showed her, had been very much influenced by John Cleese's own exposure to the comfort of Jambo's gorilla family life in Jersey. His decision to spend two or three days filming *Fierce Creatures* at Jersey Zoo in August 1995, was very much due to his wish to focus upon and support the Trust's global conservation activities. Some time later he was to say in the television programme *A Tribute to Gerald Durrell*:

My own view is that it is enormously important for people to be able to come to zoos and see animals, which must be kept in the best possible condition, to actually see them. Because when I see animals I get a marvellous range of reactions, affection, fascination, respect, amusement. And above all, a lot of the time a sense of wonder, which I don't think we get in our ordinary urban life.

When the actress **Dinah Sheridan** was asked in a magazine interview, if she were a castaway on a desert island who she would choose in the whole world for company, she had no hesitation in choosing Gerry as her companion, although they had never met. When asked why, she said that he would recognise any animal that came out of the bushes, and know what to do with it ... and she knew from his writings that he would be the most amusing and delightful companion. At a later date Gerry and Lee saw Dinah Sheridan in a play; Gerry, ever the romantic, went to her dressing room and, kneeling on one knee, presented her with a bunch of red roses. The mutual admiration society continued from thereon.

In the television programme, *The Wildlife of Gerald Durrell* (2005) **Dr Desmond Morris** said, 'In the early days Gerry was quite angered about the way animals were being kept in a zoo; he wanted them to breed them as I did at London Zoo.' He went on:

One of the reasons I adored Gerry's company was because he was a true hedonist. I am a failed hedonist, I wanted to be a hedonist but I am too much of a workaholic, but Gerry succeeded, he was a born *bon viveur*. He loved his food, loved his drink, perhaps he loved his drink too much. When he sat down with you in a room, you knew that you were going to be entertained, you knew you were going to be more cheerful, more happy, than you were before he came into the room; that was a very special quality that he had. His humour is very important; I don't think people take humour seriously enough, humour is something that oils the wheels of living, it gets you through life, and Gerry and I had very much the same sort of sense of humour. They say people look like their animals, and people often tell me I'm like a chimp, and I always thought of Gerry as being like a great silverback gorilla.

Desmond Morris's general appreciation of Gerry was that he always managed to bring his animals to life and give them personality. More technical zoological writing would be unable to do this but Gerry's way of characterising individuals and giving them names brought them to life, and made them much funnier. That Gerry was such an enjoyable companion and that he managed to put this personality into his books comes off the page, so virtually anyone with a sense of humour and an interest in animals would enjoy his books.

Desmond considered that the obvious benefit of what Gerry was doing at Jersey in breeding captive animals, was that they were safe. He was keeping them secure, and very often they were brought from places where they were no longer safe in the wild. 'I think that if you had to choose, you would rather they were safe in the wild, but of course the wild is very often being chopped down, or destroyed, or polluted, and in those cases a rescue operation has to be mounted.'

When **Sir Peter Scott** came onto the stage for Gerry's *This is Your Life* with Eamonn Andrews, Andrews asked what in his opinion was Gerry's very special achievement. Peter immediately mentioned the breeding of the endangered species that he had at his marvellous zoo in Jersey.

We didn't believe that he would be able to breed half the things that he thought he could but he confounded us all, by breeding them all, or nearly all; and how generations to come will be grateful to him for all of that. This was quite apart from the wonderful books he has written that have conditioned so many people to like animals.

In April 1986 Peter Scott officially opened The Nubel Bird Propagation Centre at the Trust. After he and his wife Philippa were shown round the zoo and saw the many changes that had taken place since their first visit over 20 years before, he wrote to say how exciting it was to see the tremendous progress that had taken place, and to offer his congratulations on the staff's enormously efficient handling of a world project which was achieving so much in practical conservation. In October 1986 I received a letter from Peter saying, 'I have been thinking for some time that it would be nice to have some sort of direct tie between WFT and JWPT.' Enclosed in the envelope was a formal invitation for me to join a new Committee that he was setting up to advise on the development of his Trust for the next ten years.

In recognising the similarities of both JWPT and WFT, with their both having been founded by well-known conservationists, television personalities and authors, Gerry was enthusiastic for me to accept this invitation; for such meetings could well provide some important guidelines and indicators for the future of our Jersey Trust. Therefore, with the permission of the Trust's Board of Management, I participated at three of these 'brain-storming' meetings held at Baden Powell House in London, arranged by the then chairman of the Wildfowl Trust, Sir John Harvey-Jones. Subsequent to these meetings I was elected to serve on the Council of the renamed Wildfowl & Wetlands Trust (WWT), during 1986–1989, and after Peter's untimely death in August 1989, I served two further terms on WWT's Council during the period 1995–2001.

In December 1990, the JWPT was honoured to receive from the Chairman of IUCN's Species Survival Commission, Dr George Rabb, the 1990 Peter Scott Merit Award:

In recognition of the Trust's work in Madagascar, Mauritius, Morocco, Indonesia, Brazil and the Caribbean, as well as the outstanding training programme in Jersey, which had prepared over

240 people from 54 countries for leadership roles in local conservation programmes.

I know how delighted both Peter and Gerry would have been to learn about the recent Accord that has been signed between the Peregrine Fund and the two Trusts, concerning the long-term conservation of the Madagascar pochard in its natural habitat.

In two television interviews **Sir David Attenborough** was recorded as saying:

> Looking after plants, some people have green fingers. I do not know what the equivalent is for people who have extraordinary skill in caring for animals and persuading animals to breed, but whatever that may be the person who has more of it than anyone that I know is Gerald Durrell. I first met him way back in the 1950s; he had been a trainee animal keeper in a zoo but he had not been satisfied with that kind of life, and decided that he would like to collect animals from the wild and keep them himself. He was sitting in South America, Patagonia, when I met him, and he was surrounded by a huge collection of the most extraordinary animals, but he was not happy at handing these over to another zoo; he wanted his own zoo.

Sir David went on to relate how Gerry wanted to look after animals in his own particular way (and how no doubt when he looked back he probably wondered how he had had the nerve); that he had decided to set up his own zoo; how the first modest establishment in Jersey gradually became the headquarters of an institution that has since become world famous and has had a major effect on the cause of conservation – the Jersey Wildlife Preservation Trust. He spoke of the huge popularity of Gerry's books and said:

> The first I read was his *Overloaded Ark* which was hysterically funny … He wrote *My Family and Other Animals* which is about almost another creature altogether, which is the little boy Gerry. But he never wrote about his personal affairs later in life, or about his various relationships with the zoo community; those were undescribed.

While Gerry was recovering in a London hospital from a major operation, I had the honour to showing David Attenborough and his wife around the Jersey Zoo prior to his official opening of our new Jim Scriven Orang-utan Home-Habitat in May 1994. Of this visit, Attenborough later recalled in a 2006 interview:

> I was amazed at the amount of area and space which the animals had, and the number of animals that were actually free. Overall, the impression was a relatively few number of species but that didn't register, because what there were was so good, and living in such natural communities, and interacting with one another instead of just sitting on a bench at the back. It was a marvellous experience ... In the end, his influences through the Training Centre could be his greatest achievement.

It was in 1972 that Gerry had welcomed **HRH The Princess Royal** to the Trust and to show her round the zoo, after which she had graciously agreed to become the Trust's patron. Apart from her frequent visits to Jersey, whenever The Princess Royal travelled to a country where ex-ITC graduates were working she would go out of her way to meet them. The locations were diverse: Madagascar, with those working for the conservation of the endemic Aloatra Gentle lemur; Brazil to meet those involved with the survival of the Lion tamarin; Mauritius to meet graduates working for The Mauritius Wildlife Foundation, and St Lucia to meet graduates working with some of the Caribbean's most endangered species.

'In an introduction by The Princess Royal in an anniversary booklet *'The First Twenty-Five Years – The Jersey Zoo* the Trust's patron stated that The entire year's activities had been directed towards building up a rescue fund to Save Animals From Extinction, the SAFE Fund which will allow "us" to do just that.' The Princess concluded her message with: 'How the work of Gerald Durrell and his team in Jersey was both exciting and pioneering ... Let us just ensure that they can answer any call for help for endangered species wherever it may come from, anywhere in the world.'

During the past 36 years, our patron the Princess visited the Trust on numerous occasions to bring herself up-to-date on progress, as well as officially opening The Gaherty Reptile Breeding Centre in 1976; the

Trust's International Training Centre in 1984; to deposit a 'Time Capsule' beneath the foundations of The Princess Royal Pavilion (PRP) in 1988; and to open The Centre for Conservation Programmes and Research in 1997.

In June 2001, The Princess Royal did me the great honour of attending my farewell retirement luncheon, held at Les Augrès Manor, to which close members of my family, Jersey's Lt-Governor, Air Chief Marshall Sir John Cheshire, Lee Durrell, Robin Rumboll, and some of my closest zoological 'silverbacks' – Michael Brambell, John Knowles, Peter Olney, and Roger Wheater – attended.

Within the contents of the 1988 'Time Capsule' that the Princess planted at the PRP was a letter written and signed by Gerry, which embraced hopes for generations to follow, and ambitions for the future of the natural world:

We hope that there will still be fireflies and glow-worms at nights to guide you, and butterflies in the hedges and forests to greet you. We hope that your dawns will have an orchestra of bird song and that the sound of their wings and the opalescence of their colouring will dazzle you. We hope that there will still be the extraordinary varieties of creatures sharing the land of the planet with you to enchant you and enrich your lives as they have done for us. We hope that you will be grateful for having been born into such a magical world.

Gerald Durrell, 3 December, 1988

Chapter Fifteen

A POIGNANT FAREWELL

Gerry's death gave rise to banner headlines and eulogies in the world's media; among these were: 'TV Naturalist and Author Durrell Dies on 30th January 1995 – Star Whose Love for Animals Delighted Millions' (*Daily Express* 31st January 1995), and 'The Man Who Preferred Animals to People – At least they don't hold cocktail parties' (*Daily Mail* 31st January 1995). Lee and the Trust received hundreds, if not thousands, of letters of condolence from around the world. The letter from John Aspinall was particularly sensitive, poignant, and much appreciated by Lee:

Dear Lee
Forgive the familiarity as we have never met.
   I was saddened to hear of your husband's death. Though we had a great deal in common, both being born in India of colonial families (my grandfather was a civil engineer with the Bengal Nagpur Railway), both auto-didacts, etc., I have no doubt that we would have become good friends if our paths had ever crossed. Like Oscar Wilde, he certainly put his talents into his work and his genius into his life. Genius in both senses, that of capacity and that of spirit. A great man whose apocalyptical vision I share with mounting dread for the fate of the planet. If a dreadful nemesis is in store for our own species I am unconcerned because we deserve whatever thunderbolts the Gods decide to hurl at us. That so remarkable a man should not have been honoured with more than an OBE has either come about from a grave distortion of our own values, or from the possibility that he made it known that he would not accept another honour.

It would be ridiculous to pretend that Jersey can ever be the same without him, but no doubt his guiding spirit will still determine your own actions and all those he influenced so deeply to keep the Trust on track.

To be instrumental in saving so many relatively unknown species such as the Mauritius kestrel and the Pink pigeon and others from extinction will surely be the only monument he would ever have wanted.

I don't have to tell you that he was deeply admired by those who work for my Foundation [The Howletts and Port Lympne Foundation], keepers and management alike.

John

In May 1996, Lee and I visited Howletts and lunched with John Aspinall and his wife, Lady Sarah, and were shown round both his Howletts and Port Lympne Zoos by him. Four years later John Aspinall died, and I was asked by the editor of the *International Zoo News* to write a brief appreciation of him. When I was preparing this, I was fascinated to note the degree of similarity between these two great 'silverbacks', not only their background in India, born within a year of one another and both descendants of railway civil engineers, but also that they had both established their own particular type of zoo, with the object of breeding threatened species in captivity. They had both purchased a gorilla with their own money. Their extensive personal libraries covered the same topics – big game shooting in Africa, the travels of explorers in South America, tales of Shikaris in India, and the fiction of Rudyard Kipling, Oscar Wilde, Rider Haggard and Conan Doyle.

To put into some type of perspective how the early 'zoo establishment' regarded such inspirational interlopers Brian Masters wrote in his biography, *The Passion of John Aspinall,* how Sir Solly Zuckerman (later Lord Zuckerman, one time Secretary of The Zoological Society of London) had the feeling that Aspinall should not be taken seriously or be encouraged, and how Zuckerman thought of him as a dilettante. Similarly, Gerald Durrell was never in any doubt that Lord Zuckerman viewed him in the same light. Fortunately, 'The old order changeth, yielding place to new', for both John Aspinall and Gerry were soon to prove by their actions, through their passion and inspirational vision, what could be achieved.

In David Hughes' delightful book, which is a tribute to Gerry and his zoo, he wrote, 'He had created a country house where creatures in need were the guests. No snobbery was involved or class distinction. His method was to make nature pause, to impose a moratorium on freedom for animals privileged by their rarity.'

Within six months of Gerry's death a Memorial Celebration of his life took place at the Natural History Museum in London on 28th June 1995. Over a thousand Trust members and devotees took part in the celebration which was held in the presence of The Princess Royal. In a subsequent television tribute to the Trust's founder, the Trust's patron stated that she considered Gerald Durrell's perhaps greatest contribution to conservation was his ability to get people who had never thought about it to take an interest in wildlife, and she remarked:

I think his ability to write, and to transfer his enthusiasm for wild life onto the printed page for people who had never stopped to think about it before, was quite an astonishing talent in awakening people's interest in a way that had never been done before.

In the early autumn of 1996 Lee introduced me to Douglas Botting, the person chosen to write the biography of my mentor. We gradually remembered that we had had a chance encounter 21 years previously, over breakfast at the Hotel Amazonas in Manaus, Brazil. I had just arrived from Bolivia after my failed search for Colonel Fawcett's mitla, whereas Douglas was about to set sail with his wife and two companions, on a weatherbeaten motorised sailing boat called (in Brazilian Portuguese) *The Good Jesus of Sailors*, on a 2,400 km (1,500 miles) journey to the upper reaches of the Amazon to Iquitos and beyond. Douglas told me that he had dug out his mosquito-spotted Amazon diary and that part of his entry for 27th October 1965 recorded:

… but the most interesting encounter was first thing at the hotel with a young Englishman who is wandering through the Amazon region alone on a recce mission on behalf of a cause known as animal conservation. Nice, bright, committed chap. I hope he'll survive the trip – but I don't suppose he will.'

After having read his diary entry, Douglas wrote to tell me how fortunate it was that his pessimism had proved unfounded!

To conclude such a varied collection of diverse viewpoints about my august mentor, with regard to his writings, his character, his vision, and overall contribution to the conservation of the world's threatened wildlife, I will say this. I fully appreciate how very fortunate I had been to have returned from Africa to my home in Jersey when I did, and therefore to have been in the right place, at the right time, when Gerry had just founded his Jersey Zoo. As a consequence, and without question, I can only consider myself to be the luckiest person I know. In spite of my somewhat hybrid background, for Gerry to have considered that I was an appropriate ingredient to help him nurture the development of his Jersey Wildlife Preservation Trust is a great honour. Throughout my 42 years of benefiting so much from 'The Touch of Durrell', and working at his creation, in spite of some of the mistakes that I am sure I made, he always provided me with his unswerving support, a generous amount of friendship, and a considerable degree of deep affection. Perhaps the most treasured accolade that I received during my time with him was when he asked me to be the 'best man' at his wedding to Lee – a person I soon became a disciple of too.

So, all in all, I was able to spend my time and earn my living directly involved with the animals I so cherished. My career enabled me to travel to many different parts of the world, which, in turn, well satisfied an always youthful spirit of adventure. It provided me with the opportunity to meet a wonderful diversity of dedicated people, and to undertake many stimulating and varied tasks that I so much enjoyed. Such good fortune in my working life fully accords with Sir Nöel Coward's dictum that 'Work is so Much More Fun than Fun!'

Three days before Gerry's death in Jersey, and our last spell of laughter together, he asked, 'Tell me, Jeremy, just how long have you been with me for?' and I replied, 'For just over half of your 70 years, Gerry.' Whereupon he was quick to respond, with the customary humorous twinkle in his deep blue eyes, 'I'm so pleased that I only took you on a temporary basis!' I responded to this by saying how I had always thrived in an atmosphere of uncertainty, and how I had so immensely enjoyed, thanks very much to him, a career embracing numerous uncharted challenges that had subsequently led to many significant successes.

Gerry's legacy to 'mother earth' will undoubtedly continue to bear fruit, particularly through the reading of his books that will be certain to recruit many more Durrell disciples and champions. This, in turn, will be sure to lead to an increased appreciation of the need to conserve the world's shrinking wildlife and wild places, as well as providing a greater awareness of the significance of the diverse conservation work of the Trust that he began in Jersey 50 years ago.

A little over a month after his death, Gerry's ashes were laid to rest beneath a small Jersey-pink granite slab in the eastern corner of the forecourt of Les Augrès Manor. The stone was inscribed with words written almost 90 years before by an early American prophet of the conservation movement, William Beebe, and chosen by Lee:

The beauty and genius of a work of art may be reconceived, though its first material expression be destroyed; a vanishing harmony may yet again inspire the composer; but when the last individual of a race of living things breathes no more, another heaven and another earth must pass before such a one can be again. *William Beebe, 1906*

Postscript

'A DREAM TO SUPPORT'

The future role of the Durrell Wildlife Conservation Trust

So, where to now? After 50 years of hands-on, pioneering conservation this is **the** question for the Durrell Wildlife Conservation Trust to answer. Sadly, we do not lack for opportunity, as any quick trawl through the media so graphically informs. Clearly biodiversity is in deep and deepening trouble, with extinction rates for all species – from the iconic to our own favourite 'little brown jobs' – reaching devastating levels.

For a small and charitably funded organisation, even one that tackles so well above its weight as the Trust does, the key challenge is where to focus and how to make the greatest impact. In considering the future, we can turn to the past and our rich legacy to guide us, as well as to the enduring vision and philosophy of our founder, Gerald Durrell, more relevant today than ever. But will this be enough? I do not think so. To our passion and commitment, our knowledge and techniques we must add the harder edges of prioritisation, targeted efforts, greater scientific rigour and a pragmatic 'conservation triage'. In short, our efforts and resources need to produce more output and accomplishments and must not be dissipated. Heroic endeavours yes – that's what the Trust does and we are proud to take on challenges other institutions shy away from – but we must avoid truly lost causes. Tragically, we will have to turn away from some fights, those that even we believe cannot be won. In doing so, however, we will ensure we win others and hopefully, in time, the war for conservation.

Looking to the future, the Trust will, and must, build on our niche legacy of 'hands-on' conservation and pioneering developments. Over

241

the years the Trust has assembled an effective conservation toolbox. Our tools – tried and tested – include breeding programmes, *in-situ* and *ex-situ*, habitat restoration, invasive species remediation, translocations, reintroductions and more. Now is the time for vital new tools to be added, beginning with a 'targeting and radar' tool. We need to pick our fights with care, and the TopSpots methodology, developed by Professor John E Fa, which identifies the most precious areas of high endemicity, is how we will do this. But, with over 200 TopSpots further prioritisation is needed, requiring a 'conservation triage' where, just as in hospitals, the focus on those species and habitats that can be saved.

Our future also includes building greater 'in-country' capacity working with governments, industry, farmers and communities, to establish sustainable 'local' projects. In turn, this creates greater demand for training and education, a perfect call to arms for our International Training Centre to expand in capacity and capability. To date our mini-university has trained almost 2,500 students from 122 countries, helping to develop future conservation leaders. As important to the courses run in Jersey, are those taken 'on the road', for example an Island species restoration course recently delivered to 25 Pacific Rim students in Guam. Exactly the right model for our future.

Finally, what of the role of our Jersey headquarters? More than just our spiritual home, the Jersey HQ will prosper as a centre of conservation excellence. Here we will continue to develop our conservation knowledge and techniques – as the recent addition of a DNA sequencer to determine the genetic health of animal populations demonstrates; here we will continue to lead in the knowledge of animal husbandry and breeding techniques; here our International Training Centre will continue to develop the best of the best; here we will demonstrate to our visitors the vital need for conservation, winning their hearts and their minds; and here we will be an enduring 'ark' for those animals that most need our help.

To our mission of 'saving species from extinction' it is time to add a clear vision for the future, a vision that sees the Durrell Wildlife Conservation Trust each year and every year, fighting to redress the balance between animal kind and human kind. We will not be dismayed by setbacks and, celebrating our successes, we commit ourselves to achieving a thriving and sustainable natural world.

As it always has been, the Trust will continue as a conservation beacon, a beacon of hope and a beacon lighting the way forward.

Paul Masterton
Chief Executive Officer
Durrell Wildlife Conservation Trust

For further information write to:
Durrell Wildlife Conservation Trust
Les Augrès Manor, La Profonde Rue,
Trinity, Jersey JE3 5BP
Website: www.durrell.org
Email: info@durrell.org

BIBLIOGRAPHY

Anderson, C.J. (1855). *Lake N'Gami*. London: Hurst and Blackett.

Anderson, C.J. (1861). *The Okavango River*. London: Hurst and Blackett.

Anne, The Princess (1984). A Message. In *The First Twenty-Five Years – The Jersey Zoo*. p.5. Jersey: A Jersey Evening Post Souvenir Publication.

Baker, S.W. (1866). *The Albert Nyanza*. London: Macmillan.

Bates, H.W. (1864). *The Naturalist on the River Amazons*. London: John Murray.

Beebe, C.W. (1906). *The Bird its Form and Function*. New York: Henry Holt and Company.

Blyton, E. (1944). *Tales from the Bible*. London: Methuen & Co.

Botting, D. (1999). *Gerald Durrell – The Authorised Biography*. London: HarperCollins.

Brehm, A.E. (1896). *Life of Animals*. Chicago/London: University of Chicago Press.

Bull, P. (1969). *Bear with Me*. London: Cassell.

Burton, R.F. (1880). *The Lake Regions of Central Africa*. London: Longmans.

Chaillu, du P. (1861). *Explorations & Adventures in Equatorial Africa*. London: John Murray.

Coward, N. (1944). *Middle East Diary*. London: Heinemann.

Coward, N. (1953). *The Noël Coward Song Book*. London: Michael Joseph.

Darwin, C. (1859). *On The Origin of Species*. London: John Murray.

Delacour, J. (1953). *The Pheasants of the World*. London: Country Life.

Durrell, G. (1953). *The Overloaded Ark*. London: Rupert Hart-Davis.

Durrell, G. (1954). *Three Singles to Adventure*. London: Rupert Hart-Davis.

Durrell, G. (1954). *The Bafut Beagles*. London: Rupert Hart-Davis.

Durrell, G. (1956). *My Family and Other Animals*. London: Rupert Hart-Davis.

Durrell, G. (1958). *Encounters with Animals*. London: Rupert Hart-Davis.

Durrell, G. (1960). *A Zoo in my Luggage*. London: Rupert Hart-Davis.

Durrell, G. (1961). *The Whispering Land*. London: Rupert Hart-Davis.

Durrell, G. (1961). *Island Zoo*. London: Collins.

Durrell, G. (1961). *Look at Zoos*. London: Hamish Hamilton.

Durrell, G. (1964). *Menagerie Manor*. London: Rupert Hart-Davis.

Durrell, G. (1966). *Two in the Bush*. London: Collins.

Durrell, G. (1972). *Catch Me a Colobus*. London: Collins.

Durrell, G. (1975). Foreword. In *Breeding Endangered Species in Captivity*, ed. R.D.Martin vii-xii. London: Academic Press.

Durrell, G. (1992). *The Aye-Aye and I*. London: HarperCollins.

Durrell, G. & L. (1986). *Gerald and Lee Durrell in Russia*. London: Macdonald.

Durrell, L. (1945). *Prospero's Cell*. London: Faber & Faber.

Durrell, L. (1960). *Clea*. London: Faber & Faber.

Durrell, L. (1961). *Sappho*. London: Faber & Faber.

Durrell, L. (1962). *The Alexandria Quartet*. London: Faber & Faber.

Durrell, M. (1995). *Whatever Happened to Margo?* London: André Deutsch.

Fawcett, B. (1953). *Exploration Fawcett*. London: Hutchinson.

Fisher, C. (ed). (2002). *A Passion for Natural History: the Life and Legacy of the 13th Earl of Derby*. Liverpool: Liverpool Museums and Art Galleries on Merseyside.

Fleming, P. (1933). *Brazilian Adventure*. London: Jonathan Cape.

Fossey, D. (1983). *Gorillas in the Mist*. London: Hodder & Stoughton.

Goodall, J. van Lawick (1971). *In the Shadow of Man*. London: Collins.

Hachisuka, M. (1953). *The Dodo and Kindred Birds, Or, The Extinct Birds of the Mascarene Islands*. London: H.F. & G. Witherby.

Hill, O.W.C. (1960). *Primates, Comparative Anatomy and Taxonomy IV*. Edinburgh: The University Press.

Hill, O.W.C. (1966). *Primates, Comparative Anatomy and Taxonomy VI*. Edinburgh: The University Press.

Hodgson, B.H. (1847). On a new form of hog kind *Suidae. Journal, Asiatic Society of Bengal* XVI: 423–428.

Hornaday, W.T. (1915). Gorillas past and present. *Bulletin of the New York Zoological Society* 18: 1181–1185.

Hughes, D. (1997). *Himself & Other Animals – A Portrait of Gerald Durrell*. London: Hutchinson.

I.U.C.N. (1964). *Zoos and Conservation*. Supplementary Paper No. 3 pp. 48. London: IUCN/ICBP/IUDZG.

Jackson, C.E. (1999). *Dictionary of Bird Artists of the World*. Woodbridge: Antique Collectors' Club.

Johnson, P, Bond, C. & Bannister, A. (1977). *Okavango, Sea of Land, Land of Water*. Cape Town & Johannesburg: C. Strunk Publishers.

Johnstone-Scott, R. (1995). *Jambo, A Gorilla's Story*. London: Michael O'Mara Books Limited.

Kay, J. (1962). *Okavango*. London: Hutchinson & Co.

Kay, J. (1964). *Wild Eden*. London: Hutchinson & Co.

Kear, J. (ed) (2004). *Ducks, Geese and Swans,* 2 vols. Oxford: Oxford University Press.

Knight, C.W.R. (1943). *All British Eagle*. London: Hodder & Stoughton.

Lydekker, R. (1893–94). *The Royal Natural History*, 6 vols. London: Frederick Warne & Co.

Maberly, A.C.T. (1959). *Animals of Rhodesia*. Cape Town: Howard Timmins.

Mallinson, J.J.C. (1971). The pigmy hog *(Sus salvanius). Journal, Bombay Natural History Society*, 68(2): 424–433.

Mallinson, J.J.C. (1971). A note on the hispid hare *(Caprolagus hispidus). Journal, Bombay Natural History Society*, 68(2): 443–444.

Mallinson, J.J.C. (1989). *Travels in Search of Endangered Species*. London: David & Charles.

Mallinson, J.J.C. (1999). *'Durrelliania'*. Jersey: Bigwoods Premie Printers.

Martin, R.D. (1990). *Primate Origins and Evolution*. London: Chapman & Hall.

Martin, R.D. (1995). Tribute, Gerald Durrell 1925–1995. *Biodiversity and Conservation*, 4: 531–534.

Masters, B. (1988). *The Passion of John Aspinall*. London: Jonathan Cape.

Mittermeier, R. (2002). Foreword. In Kleiman, D.G. & Ryland, A.B. *Lion Tamarins Biology and Conservation*. Washington: Smithsonian Institution Press.

Olney, P.J.S. (2001). Gerald Durrell 1925–1995. In *Encylopedia of the World's Zoos*, ed. C.E. Bell, 1 A-F: 380–383. Chicago & London: Fitzroy Dearborn Publishers.

Quammen, D. (1996). *The Song of the Dodo*. London: Hutchinson.

Ransome, A. (1930). *Swallows & Amazons*. London: Jonathan Cape.

Roberts, A. (1940). *The Birds of South Africa*. Johannesburg: The Central News Agency.

Roberts, J. (1963). *My Congo Adventure*. London: Jarrolds.

Sanderson, I.T. (1957). *The Monkey Kingdom*. London: Hamish Hamilton.

Schaller, G.B. (1964). *The Year of the Gorilla*. Chicago: The University of Chicago Press

Smeeton, B. (1961). *Winter Shoes in Springtime*. London: Rupert Hart-Davis.

Smeeton, M. (1959). *Once is Enough*. London: Rupert Hart-Davis.

Smeeton, M. (1961). *A Taste of the Hills*. London: Rupert Hart-Davis.

Snailman, R. (1976). *A Giant Among Rivers*. London: Hutchinson.

Soulé. M.E. (ed) (1987). *Viable Populations for Conservation*. Cambridge: Cambridge Universty Press.

Speke, J.H. (1863). *Journal of the Discovery of the Source of the Nile*. Edinburgh/London: Blackwood & Sons.

Stanley, H.M. (1890). *In Darkest Africa*, 2 vols. London: Samson Low & Co.

Stanley-Price, M.S. (1989). *Animal Re-introductions: the Arabian Oryx in Oman*. Cambridge: Cambridge University Press.

Waller, H. (ed) (1874). *The Last Jounals of David Livingstone in Central Africa from 1855 to his Death*. London: John Murray.

Warin, R. & A. (1985). *Portrait of a Zoo*. Bristol: Redcliffe Press.

Waterton, C. (1878). *Wanderings in South America*. London: Macmillan & Co.

Wheater, R.J. (1994). Foreword. In *Creative Conservation, Interactive Management of Wild and Captive Animals*, ed, P.J.S. Olney, G.M. Mace & A.T.C. Feistner, xxv-xxix. London: Chapman & Hall.

White, G. (1789). *The Natural History and Antiquities of Selbourne*. T.C. Howard: Paster Noster Row Press.

Whitley, E. (1992). *Gerald Durrell's Army*. London: John Murray.

Willock, C. (2001). *A Life on the Wild Side*. Berkshire: World Pheasant Association.

Yealland, J. J. (1958). *Cage Birds in Colour*. London: H.F. & G. Witherby.

INDEX

249

C25 19